The Visual Poetics of Raymond Carver

The Visual Poetics of Raymond Carver

AYALA AMIR

LEXINGTON BOOKS
A division of
ROWMAN & LITTLEFIELD PUBLISHERS, INC.
Lanham • Boulder • New York • Toronto • Plymouth, UK

Published by Lexington Books
A division of Rowman & Littlefield Publishers, Inc.
A wholly owned subsidiary of The Rowman & Littlefield Publishing Group, Inc.
4501 Forbes Boulevard, Suite 200, Lanham, Maryland 20706
http://www.lexingtonbooks.com

Estover Road, Plymouth PL6 7PY, United Kingdom

Copyright © 2010 by Lexington Books
First paperback edition 2012

Excerpts from *What We Talk About When We Talk About Love* by Raymond Carver copyright © 1974, 1976, 1978, 1980, 1981. Used by permission of Alfred A. Knopf, a division of Random House, Inc. Excerpts from *Cathedral* by Raymond Carver copyright © 1981, 1982, 1983. Used by permission of Alfred A. Knopf, a division of Random House, Inc. Excerpts from *Fires* copyright © 1983, 1984 by the Estate of Raymond Carver. Excerpts from *Where I'm Calling From* copyright © 1986, 1987, 1988 by Raymond Carver.

Cover Photography: "Phonebooth" by Tirtza Even copyright © 2010

All rights reserved. No part of this book may be reproduced in any form or by any electronic or mechanical means, including information storage and retrieval systems, without written permission from the publisher, except by a reviewer who may quote passages in a review.

British Library Cataloguing in Publication Information Available

The hardback edition of this book was previously cataloged by the Library of Congress as follows:

Library of Congress Cataloging-in-Publication Data
Amir, Ayala, 1963-
  The visual poetics of Raymond Carver / Ayala Amir.
    p. cm.
  Includes bibliographical references and index.
  1. Carver, Raymond, 1938-1988—Criticism and interpretation. I. Title.
  PS3553.A7894Z53 2010
  813'.54—dc22   2010010238

ISBN: 978-0-7391-3921-9 (cloth : alk. paper)
ISBN: 978-0-7391-3922-6 (pbk. : alk. paper)
ISBN: 978-0-7391-3923-3 (electronic)

∞™ The paper used in this publication meets the minimum requirements of American National Standard for Information Sciences—Permanence of Paper for Printed Library Materials, ANSI/NISO Z39.48-1992.

Printed in the United States of America

Contents

Key Abbreviations	vii
Acknowledgments	ix
Introduction	xi

PART I: MOVEMENT

1	"I Don't Do Motion Shots"—Representation of Movement	3
2	"Does That Have a Hidden Meaning?"—Dialogue	21

PART II: THE EYE OF THE CAMERA

3	"Whoever Was Using This Bed"—Voice	47
4	"Why Do I Notice That?"—Vision	69

PART III: SEEING AND MEANING

5	Raymond Carver's "Man in a Case"—Frame and Character	105
6	Singularity or Doubleness—*Effet de réel* or Symbol?—Toward Conclusion	145

Conclusion	175
References	179
Index	189
About the Author	197

Works by Raymond Carver

KEY ABBREVIATIONS

V	"View Finder"
WYPB	*Will You Please Be Quiet, Please?*
WWTA	*What We Talk about When We Talk about Love*
Cathedral	*Cathedral*
WICF	*Where I'm Calling From: Stories*
Fires	*Fires: Essays, Poem, Stories*
AOU	*All of Us: The Collected Poems*
CIYN	*Call If You Need Me: The Uncollected Fiction and Other Prose*
CS	*Collected Stories*

Acknowledgments

My first encounter with Raymond Carver's stories took place in 1989, through the Hebrew translation of *Cathedral*. A long time passed from that day until I began to write about Carver. However, I am still grateful to the translator of that slim volume—Moshe Ron—who eventually introduced a very enthusiastic Israeli audience to all of Carver's short fiction. Professor Ron also read an early version of this study and helped me greatly with his keen remarks.

Baruch Hochman accompanied this project from the very beginning. I cannot thank him enough for the time and effort he invested in it, and for his insightful comments and suggestions. Shimon Sandbank tirelessly read early drafts and chapters and has been a constant source of encouragement and inspiration. John Landau, in reading groups and conversations, stimulated ideas and enriched my thoughts. My good friends and colleagues, Shachar Bram and Tirtza Even, introduced me to new and exciting perspectives on the topics discussed here. Special thanks go to Sara Friedman for her generosity in sharing her knowledge and acute sense of style. Aloma Halter, Eva Weiss, Naomi Michlin, and Batnadiv HaKarmi-Weinberg helped in editing the manuscript and preparing it for publication. Thanks to *The Raymond Carver Review* and its editor, Robert Miltner, who published an abridged version of the first chapter in the opening issue. Finally, I would like to thank my students at the Hebrew University of Jerusalem. My first ideas and thoughts originated from their fresh and original responses to Carver's stories.

The book is dedicated to my dear parents, Michal and Tsion Amir, for their unconditional love and support, and to Yizhar.

Introduction

In his article "Raymond Carver: A Still, Small Voice," Jay McInerney describes how Raymond Carver taught literature and creative writing at Syracuse University in the early eighties. According to McInerney, Carver was not a born teacher, to say the least: He had no definite method, he preferred listening to lecturing, he avoided criticizing his students, and he mumbled when he spoke. His demeanor suggested that he was not at all comfortable with such a position of authority.

Among his classes, Carver taught the course "Form and Theory of the Short Story"—a title he inherited from the graduate English catalogue. His students were young writers, and together they read stories by authors Carver admired: Flannery O'Connor, Maupassant, and Chekhov. By discussing writing that moved him, Carver overcame his nervousness. One semester, an earnest PhD candidate with a tendency toward theory took Carver's class. After a few weeks of free-ranging and impressionist reading, the young theorist protested: "This class is called 'Form and Theory of the Short Story,' but all we do is sit around and talk about the books. Where's the form and the theory?"

"Ray looked distressed," McInerney recalls. "He nodded and pulled extra hard on his cigarette. 'Well, that's a good question,' he said. After a long pause he said, 'I guess I'd say that the point here is that we read good books and discuss them. . . . And then you *form* your own *theory*.' Then he smiled."[1]

This moving anecdote adds to the composite portrait of Raymond Carver which has accrued through the many stories and memories collected after his death. The portrait depicts a modest and unpretentious man driven by his intuition and heart rather than by changing fashion. He declared more than once that his main principle was "no tricks." His literary essays declare his preference for life over art, for the concrete and clear over the abstract and sophisticated, and for content over technique. "Life, always life," he writes in the end of one of these essays.[2] His friends and teachers remember him as a passionate listener and consumer of anecdotes and juicy stories, as a man with little interest in philosophy, theoretical abstractions, and all sorts of "isms."[3]

A similar attitude toward theory and abstraction also characterizes many of the critical responses to Carver's work. Critics often describe his writing as humanistic. They view Carver as leading the return to life and to "good old realism," a trend that came as a backlash to experimental, self-conscious literature. Carver himself nurtured this image in his essays and interviews. It also seems that the significant interest in his biography stems from a feeling that Carver wrote about what he had known and experienced directly. Kim Herzinger, in his essay on minimalism, characterizes the work of Carver and his followers as avoiding irony, communicating with the reader "at eye level" and meaning what it says.[4] Many of the papers on his work are thematic by nature. They speak of Carver's "world," of his sensitivity to the plight of blue-collar people, of the way he exposes the dark side of the American dream, and of the moral demand made by his stories—a demand for empathy and communication.[5] Internet sites devoted to Raymond Carver are full of readers' responses declaring that they like him because he writes about life, real people, and real feelings.

In a sense, Carver's work encourages such a response. Any theoretical model seems inadequate when trying to apply it to stories that demand that we read them as real life rather than as case studies of abstract structures. The characters strike us as real people rather than carriers of ideas or "nodes in the verbal design."[6] They arouse the reader to identification and sympathy, and so to resist cold textual analysis. Some might conclude that Carver's work, with its seemingly unsophisticated use of language and plot, offers no insights into the nature of literature. Such readers would argue that it is neither rich nor interesting enough to stimulate a discussion of fundamental literary issues.

Things are not so simple, however, as indicated by a reminiscence of the writer Richard Ford, who was one of Carver's closest friends. Ford recalls his first encounter with the man and his work in a public reading of Carver's story, "What Is It?" (The title was later changed to "Are These Actual Miles?") Interestingly enough, Ford also begins by noting Carver's "still small voice":

> His voice was typically hushed, seemingly unpracticed, halting almost to the point of being annoying. But the effect of voice and story upon the listener was of actual life being unscrolled in a form so distilled, so intense, so *chosen*, so affecting in its urgencies as to leave you breathless and limp when he was finished. . . .
>
> One learned from the story, many things: Life was this way—yes, we already know that. But *this* life, *these* otherwise unnoticeable people's suitability for literary expression seemed new. One also felt that a consequence for the story was seemingly to intensify life, even dig-

nify it, and to locate in it shadowed corners and niches that needed revealing so that we readers could practice life better ourselves. And yet the story itself, in its spare, self-conscious intensity, was such a *made* thing, not *like* life at all, it was a piece of nearly abstract artistic construction calculated to produce almost giddy pleasure. . . . The story was definitely *about* something, and you could follow it easily—it was about what two people did in adversity which changed their lives. But here was no ponderous naturalism. Nothing extra. There were barely the rudiments of realism. This was highly stylized, artistic writing with life, not art, as its subject. And to be exposed to it was to be bowled over (Ford's emphases).[7]

Ford describes writing that intensifies life and dignifies it, one that has a direct influence on our own lives, a story that is "about something." Yet this story is also a made thing, possessing a self-conscious intensity, not like life at all. It is abstract, constructed, and artistic. Ford's observations, which reveal his own poetic vision, render very precisely the mixed feelings generated by Carver's work. He formulates the tensions that will reappear in some of the critical responses that did not settle for the "real life stories" label. It is a tension between raw life and a self-conscious, calculated, highly stylized art; between morally involving the reader ("practice life better") and delighting him in an aesthetic "giddy pleasure"; between something that is concrete and particular ("actual life . . . this life") and at the same time constructed, distilled, and intensified. Ford keeps referring to the artistic form of the stories. Moreover, he speaks of substance that has been transformed into form—of life that has been condensed and abstracted.

Indeed, while Carver's penetrating stories seem at first glance to be slices of life, torn from reality and put into words very simply, even casually, the failure of his many epigones has shown that precise transcriptions alone cannot compare to the master's highly stylized stories. He truly carves from life something completely different from actual life. We are clearly dealing with a writer who is well aware of his medium and constantly exploring its boundaries, thus implicitly taking a stance toward it. As Ford observes, Carver does so by choosing realms of experience and character that we did not know were suitable for literary expression, and by creating realistic writing that has "barely the rudiments of realism" (at least in one of its definitions).

While Ford insists that the subject of the story he heard, calculated and artistic as it was, was *life* and not *art*, others hold a more extreme view of Carver's work. Randolph Runyon sees his seemingly "extrospective" (i.e., reality-oriented) stories as actually *intro*spective, meta-fictional stories that weave together another story about their own links and relations.[8] Even more extreme is Marc Chénetier, who almost discards the thematic aspect of Carver's work in favor of what he terms his "rhetoric." For him, the events in the stories are mere "excuses," and their creator is a typical postmodern writer, writing circular, self-concerned stories.[9] Carver's realism is similarly challenged by some critics. Although he does not break any law of reality or probability (expect perhaps in his late story "Blackbird Pie"), some think that the dreamlike quality of his stories yields an untraditional realism. The unconventional relationship between fiction and reality in Carver's stories brings to light—in Claudine Verley's words—"the affinity between realism and the uncanny."[10]

Readers' judgment of Carver's work reveals a polarity similar to that displayed by the more analytical responses noted above. Carver lived to see his work become praised and popular to the point of being imitated, yet also the target of harsh criticism. He won the label (much disliked by him) of "minimalist." Those who criticize him contend that "less is less," that his spare style is merely an uninspired technique and that his sentiments are not authentic. Some consider his popularity to be an indication that he appeals to the lowest common denominator, namely to readers who avoid reading challenges. Such opponents explain that Carver deals with issues like alienation, loneliness, and romantic crisis, which are suitable for young readers who happen to dictate trends and fashions.[11]

This research was born from an encounter I witnessed as a teacher between Carver and a young audience such as the one slandered above. Armed with the preconception that Carver writes real life stories in simple language and easy style, I used his stories to illustrate some issues of narratology. These issues included the rhythm of the scene technique, the covertness of the narrator, the inner point of view, and external characterization that does not penetrate the character's mind—a cluster of traits typical of the poetics Carver inherited from Hemingway. These aspects of Carver's writing attracted many labels: Behaviorism, Minimalism, Hyperrealism, and Lean Literature. I soon learned, however, that Carver's work did not serve me as I expected it to do. Year after year I used his stories as an example of fiction that uses the eye-of-the-camera technique, which strives to neutralize any meditating consciousness and to represent reality "as it is." Yet year after year my students insisted that these are "consciousness stories." They had a hard time ascribing to his stories the usual oppositions of inside-outside and showing-telling (mimesis-diegesis). For them, these were not neutral pieces, documenting outer reality and actions. They argued that Carver's stories were marked by subjectivity, that they referred to inner reality not only through symbols or suggestion, but also in a deep and fundamental manner that involved the reader and the reading experience. This apparent contradiction—between the allegedly objective, external, and reality-oriented nature of his work and the subjective, internal, and consciousness-oriented sense it can generate—struck me as the reason for their great interest in Carver. Moreover, their responses echoed my feelings, and in a sense released me from my rigid categorizations and preconceptions.

Other tensions arose during our shared reading of his work. It appeared, for example, that Carver's hyperrealism cracks the mimetic illusion: that the manner in which the time of the text follows the time of the story in lockstep reveals gaps inherent in the scene technique. We discovered that the covert, impersonal narrator is always present, as it were, by its striking absence, and that the random facts of external reality relate in a very elusive way to structures of meaning and symbolism. It seemed that Carver, who brought this poetics to its extreme in his 1981 collection *What We Talk about When We Talk about Love*, had pushed his tools past their breaking point, which then defined a new trajectory for his work. The teaching experience revealed to me the deception in the façade of Carver's stories, where what you see is not what you get. This deception may be held responsible for the polarity of readers' and critics' responses—both emotional and analytical—to Carver. For me, it opened up an opportunity to reexamine what I perceived as the definition of his poetics.

It is worth noting Carver's place in the history of American literature, which may partly account for the complexity of his work. Carver, whose stories were published in the seventies and eighties, revived Hemingway's poetics while absorbing other influences, such as the rugged realism of Sherwood Anderson. He was also influenced by modernist American poetry—especially that of William Carlos Williams—which, in some of its manifestations, strives to purge language of the contamination of metaphor in order to reach for the thing itself.[12] At the beginning of his writing career, however, he experimented with writing like Faulkner, who focused intensely on the mirroring of reality in personal and collective memory (e.g., in Carver's story "Furious Seasons").[13] Faulkner's writing overflows with metaphors and verbal embellishments, following a wholly different poetics from the one Carver chose in the end. Moreover, the trend he led—of returning to reality (and its surface) and to life-oriented (rather than self-oriented) literature—may be viewed as an example of a common dynamic in the history of literature, in which waves of behaviorist, "hyperactive" literature reactively follow waves of self-centered, consciousness-oriented literature, and vice versa.[14] It seems that Carver's work both recalls an earlier poetics and responds to later poetics—those of the wave of self-conscious literature from the sixties and seventies. He was not simply reacting to this style; he even admired some of its practitioners, such as Donald Barthelme.[15]

Is it correct then to discard the labeling of Carver's writing as "real life stories" that use the eye-of-the-camera technique? Not necessarily, because the conception of the eye of the camera itself has been challenged and problematized. The approaches that photography used to imply have now been questioned, including adherence to external reality, representing the world as it is, presenting a neutral vision unmediated by consciousness, and capturing a moment isolated in time. In fact, as Martin Jay has suggested, photography played a crucial role in challenging the very possibility of an objective or innocent vision of reality.[16] As a result, rather than dismissing this visual metaphor, I propose a reexamination of its two poles, photography itself as well as its application to Carver's texts, and an expansion of the interaction between them.

Furthermore, it is important to remember that Carver not only followed in the tradition of Hemingway's behaviorist writing, but also adhered to the genre of the short story, which Carver revived and refined. I will therefore combine the eye-of-the-camera metaphor with another metaphor, common in literary discourse—that of the short story as a picture, an analogy that goes back to Edgar Allan Poe's critical writing.[17] The similarity between a picture and a short story lies in the tendency of many short stories to focus on a present state rather than to unfold a chain of events that extends over a long period of time. It is common to discuss short stories in terms of stasis and of spatiality, attributed (justly or unjustly) mostly to pictures. The genre is therefore perceived as one that challenges, as it were, motion and time dependency, which are more "natural" to literature. The metaphor of the picture has been also used to describe the experience of reading short stories. It has been suggested that the brevity of the short story and its typical focus on a single dramatic event freezes in the mind of the reader an image that, for him, embodies the story as a whole. Sometimes this image appears explicitly in the story itself.

The attributes implicit in the metaphors of the eye of the camera and of the picture—visibility, spatiality, and stasis—remain foreign to literature. Any discussion of them takes pains to emphasize their metaphorical nature. However, both analytic and intuitive readers attribute these qualities to Carver, using visual art metaphors to describe his work, drawing analogies from photography and styles of painting like hyperrealism and photorealism. Carver's preference for the visual and palpable over the abstract and conceptual draws him even closer to Hemingway in terms of the emotional point of departure. For both writers, this choice is motivated by feelings of disappointment and dissolution. Some see Carver as a product of, and a spokesman for, the generation disillusioned by the trauma of the Vietnam War. His writing certainly reflects his recognition of the limits of the American dream.[18] Like Hemingway, a member of the "lost generation" produced by the first World War, Carver replaces failing ideas with a concrete and palpable world. He avoids fake feelings by employing emotional restraint, and eschews verbal bravado while prizing both actions and silence. While the dominance of silence in Carver's world is commonly seen in the lacunae and remarks like "what's to say?" within his dialogues, it is also evident in his very suspicion toward words themselves, as expressed by his choice of lean poetics. The work's spareness and self-reduction seem to constitute an effort to eliminate the barrier between the reader and the world of things, imitating pure vision, where one verbalizes only that which is necessary. In that sense,

Carver's writing confronts itself, questioning the very medium it chose.[19] His writing therefore demands an exploration of its relationships to other media. It is worth noting that the puzzled reactions to his poetics—its negative reception by critics who question its entitlement to the category of literature, who refer to it as "post-literate literature,"[20] who wonder where the artist is in such poor and laconic rendering of random and incomprehensible facts—all may be compared, with the necessary reservations, to the reception of photography, toiling hard and long to gain the status of art among those who regarded it as banal, flat, and cliché-ridden. I will refer to these issues in chapters 4 and 6.

Stasis or the freezing of motion is another quality that stretches the boundaries of literary expression, connecting it to other media that are not as time-dependent as literature. Carver spoke of his stories, on different occasions, in terms of visual images or snapshots freezing a moment.[21] There is more than one factor in Carver's writing that generates the impression of stasis. The first is the structure of the story. Unlike stories based on an unexpected development or turn in the plot, Carver's work rarely included such revelatory surprises or a punch line. While he frequently declared his fondness for the traditional structure of a story, such an affinity can hardly be discerned in his own stories. There *is* a story, but only in its most basic definition—a report of events. Seldom are our other expectations of a story fulfilled: No conflict reaches a climax and there is no resolution or closure at the end.[22] Summarizing the plot would hardly fill one line, and would often sound vapid. Regarding Carver's story, "What's in Alaska?" one critic justly stated that the notation of the events is so slight you can hardly call it a story at all.[23] While some of his stories are comparatively traditional and have a more familiar, dramatic structure, the typical Carverian story describes an everyday state of affairs where motion is "stationary," to use Blanchot's insight, rather than composed of a series of developments with attendant ups and downs.[24] This structure, which gives the *impression* of stasis, embodies the condition of his characters, who often find themselves facing dead-end lives without real choices. Stasis often characterizes their posture as well. Loyal to the visibility of his world, Carver tends to describe his characters through their gestures rather than their thoughts. They often stand, frozen in a contemplative melancholy that led critics to compare them to Edward Hopper's painted figures and George Segal's sculptures.[25] Here too there is a similarity between the negative reaction to Carver's stasis (discussed in chapter 5) and the reception of photography, which has long been accused of making its subjects frozen and rigid, thus foreshadowing the final rigor mortis of death.[26]

However, as mentioned earlier, photography has advanced beyond the uncomplicated connotations it used to convey: adherence to visible reality unmediated by consciousness, stasis, flatness, and randomness. These attributes have undergone *ongoing questioning*. The visual metaphors associated with Carver's work—the eye of the camera, the snapshot, and the glimpse—can therefore be used as a key to uncover the tensions that also structure his aesthetics, tensions that are indicated by the responses to his work. My purpose in focusing on the "photographic" qualities of Carver's stories is to explore the dynamics of seeing and unseeing, movement and stasis, as structuring principles *and* as themes. I argue that Carver's stories encourage an open and multifaceted conception of vision and movement, which contributes to the dual impression of his work as both extrospective and introspective, both focusing on outer reality and immersed in subjectivity. In the course of the study it will be shown how this argument pertains to the form of the text and the reading process as well as to the text's themes, events, and characters.

Indeed, the essential and deep connection between the content and themes of Carver's world and the issues of representation implied by his poetics should be noted here. My simple assumption is that form is content. By "form," I mean both the genre and the poetical choices exhibited by the text—showing instead of telling, having a covert (rather than an overt) narrator, choosing scene instead of summary, etc. I argue that the recurrent themes (or "obsessions," to use Carver's term)[27] of the stories—the intertwining of closeness and alienation, the inability to achieve intimacy, and communication failures—are reflected in and made palpable by the form and "technical" aspects of the story, as well as in the reader-text dialogue.

The process of reading the text and endowing it with meaning thus simulates the events in the fictional world. While reading the text and deciphering it, the reader undergoes processes that are analogous to those of Carver's characters who are struggling to establish a connection with the world and other people. Should we then call these stories meta-fictional? Allegories of reading? I would not rule out this possibility, as long as we maintain their tight connection to life. Carver does refer directly to meta-literary issues in his stories about writers, artists, and photographers. However, he contributes to the reflexive inquiry into narrativity and textuality by skillfully revealing the very point where experience and poetics are two sides of the same coin. The aesthetics he chose form an integral part of his characters' existential issues. The people in Carver's stories convey his literary conception by their everyday struggle to cope with themselves and others. "I was trying to make a connection," says one of his characters (in "Viewfinder," *WWTA*, 13), implicitly including the character's effort to make a connection between events in his life, his attempt to communicate with another person, and, in addition, the reader's work in meaningfully linking various components of the text. In that way, the reader's stance vis-à-vis the represented world is parallel to that of the character, who is trying to comprehend his or her experience and communicate with his or her surroundings.

Indeed, communication plays a key role in Carver's world, as he has often admitted. "Art is a linking between people. Art is not self-expression, it is communication," he declared on several occasions.[28] Clearly, reading is a very particular form of communication, and the issues of communication presented in the story cannot be projected directly onto the process of reader-text "communication." Therefore I use the word "communication" in its broader sense, referring to any kind of link or contact that builds a conduit between separate beings. Note that this sense is broad enough to include both the concept of movement, which implies continuity, and that of vision, which creates various relationships between the viewer and object as well as among objects.[29] This notion of communication will also include the communication between characters as well as between reader and text. Moving between these different aspects of communication will allow me to illustrate instances in which the blockage of one channel of contact opens up another. It will also enable me to show how fragmentation and randomness, which seemingly interfere with building connections, may actually yield new opportunities for movement and communication. This line of thought is inspired by Gilles Deleuze's conception of movement and vision, discussed mainly in chapter 5.

Before addressing the structure and theoretical framework of this study, some clarifications are in order. Regarding the reader-text relationship, it is important to note the growing awareness in recent years of the cultural and historical context of the reader. This approach may result in a significant expansion of a text's scope of meanings, making it more fluid. No doubt it hinders the construction of an ideal, uniform, "reasonable" reader. When I discuss the reader in this study, I am referring to a composite reader based on my own reading experience combined with others I have encountered through the years. Besides encompassing the range of possible interpretations, my "reader" refers to a *dynamics* of reading prompted by Carver's texts—a dynamics that often generates diverse interpretations. The idea that the reader "fills in gaps" (elaborated by Iser, Ingarden, Perry-Sternberg, and implied in Auerbach's reading of the Bible) works well with Carver's spare texts, which give away so little and hide more than they disclose. I will offer here a reading of some of Carver's stories but do not suggest singular ways of closing the gaps in his work. Furthermore, in the sixth and final chapter, I attempt to show how these texts succeed by opening up a space that compels and accommodates the subjectivity of any reader.

While it is important to clarify who the reader is, it is just as important to establish who Carver is. This issue of identity is especially significant in Carver's case for two reasons. One is the importance of the personal-biographical dimension of Carver's work. In many stories he used materials from his own life, and they tell of a man similar to him in many ways. Carver is not unique in that sense. As people familiar with him and the events have noted, this fact does not make his stories any less fictional or artistic. Even a story like "Intimacy," no doubt inspired by Carver's relationship with his first wife, Maryann, "wasn't about Maryann," as he made clear.[30] Nevertheless, Carver's life story has become an integral part of the discussions of his work. This is partly due to the fact that his biography has the key ingredients needed to concoct a myth: birth into a low class, struggle and sacrifice for his art, substance abuse, near death, rebounding to brief fame, and premature death, perhaps a price for past transgressions. Carver's death at the age of fifty, just as he achieved success, left behind friends and family members who were eager to document his life with oral and written memories. All of this, no doubt, contributed to the attention given to the man behind the work. And as the people who were close to him (tactfully) commented, Carver himself, to an extent, nurtured his mythic status as a "working-class hero."[31] This mixture of circumstances makes it very difficult to avoid "intentional fallacy," to detach Carver the person from Carver the writer, to ignore his biography and draw no analogies from his life to his fiction.

The issue of Carver's identity also demands attention because of his special relationship with his editor, Gordon Lish. Carver owes Lish much of his fame, as well as what might be considered the *differentia specifica* of his work. The scope of Lish's involvement was first revealed when Carver published some longer versions of previously published stories, but became more apparent after his death, when his heavily edited manuscripts were discovered. A slightly sensational *New York Times* article, published in August 1998, revealed that Lish's massive cuts and edits, which caused major changes of plots and endings, contributed a great deal to the sparse, suggestive, and enigmatic nature of Carver's stories.[32] The recent publication of *Beginners*, the manuscript version of "What We Talk about When We Talk about Love" (in *Collected Stories*, The Library of America, 2009) confirmed the extent of Lish's influence on Carver's style.

Hence, parallel to the diffusion of Carver's private life into his work, his work itself was invaded by outside influences. Both cases involve a question of boundaries—those that define the work as an autonomous text and those that define it as a product of one uniform or homogenous consciousness. The first case questions the boundary between the real and the fictional. The second challenges the boundaries of the corpus itself, raising the question of whether the object of this study can simply be called Carver's stories. In fact, in these special circumstances lurks a very current debate. On the one hand, in the spirit of our time, we may dismiss the urgency of such concerns by saying that this corpus is as valid and uniform as any other, that such boundaries have always been arbitrary, being a product of the interests and viewpoints of those who set them. Therefore, the discovery that some of Carver's work does not "belong" to him is merely a concrete and proven manifestation of the argument that any seemingly unified subject is in fact invaded by outside influences and affected by external mechanisms. Still, the excitement that followed the discovery of Lish's role in the creation of the stories, as well as the intensity with which the connection between the man and his work had been discussed, cannot be ignored. They prove that even in our time, there is an interest in unity and a will to discover the unique essence of a work or a corpus, define its boundaries, and divine its source.

It may thus be stated, in the complex spirit of our time, that the name "Carver," reappearing so many times in the course of this book, probably has no connection to the man who lived and died between the years 1938 and 1988, or to the kernel of personality that generated the unique stories left to us. What I found out, however, was that the intimate encounter with another consciousness, which belongs to the experience of reading literature as such, and was particularly intense in this case, made me feel closeness and familiarity with this imagined creator of the stories. This study is a result of my dwelling upon texts which in their totality embodied for me the consciousness of a writer. As any consciousness opening up to another—regardless of the circumstances—it was accessible at times and elusive at others, surprising in its contradictions and irregularities, integrated from many sources, yet still crystallized in a uniform image. All the texts connected to the name "Carver"—revised or original, fictional, essayistic, and autobiographical—had a part in forming my conception of the man and his work. As a result of this subjective encounter, aware as I am of its delusions and limitations, I chose to refer to Carver's work as a single entity, and to see its discrepancies and contradictions as its ever-changing shades. While I do note the differences between the texts revised by Lish and those published posthumously—which presumably express Carver's aesthetic preferences—I do not privilege the latter as more authentic. As a rule, I have quoted from the standard collections of Carver's stories, as published during his lifetime and right after his death. These are the stories that established his status as a major short-story artist and have influenced a whole school of writing. I also refer to Carver's nonfictional texts and to facts from his life in order to make my arguments more concrete, though not necessarily to give them empiric validity.

Critics note some chronological developments in Carver's stories, in terms of both style and content. The style was more elaborate in his later stories, compared to the laconic earlier ones. In respect to content, the later work displays a tendency toward openness and contact between self and other. Some recognize in his corpus a circular pattern of return to the features of his first stories.[33] Despite these critical responses, and while taking into account Lish's part in determining the character of Carver's early prose, I chose not to read his stories chronologically. I use different stories, from different times, to construct each chapter's argument. Some I dwell upon, and others I mention briefly. In several I examine Carver's poetics, while in others I focus on thematic aspects and the characters' experience. These aspects are also discussed in a comparative reading of texts by Carver's favorite writers (Hemingway, in chapter 2; Flaubert, in chapter 4; and Chekhov, in chapter 5).

The theoretical framework of this study is exposed gradually and more space is given to theoretical texts as the study proceeds. However, Carver's preference for text over theory guided me in my attempt to tailor the theory to fit the stories and not the other way around. I do use Carver's work as a springboard to a theoretical discussion (especially in Part III). Nevertheless, it is the stories that cast light onto the theory and they remain my point of departure, dictating the direction of my discussion and determining my choice of relevant thinkers.

This approach requires a flexible and somewhat eclectic use of theory, which draws upon different schools and methods. My point of departure is narrative study, or narratology, and its treatment of the representations of time and space in fiction. However, my focus on the eye-of-the-camera metaphor as a narrative strategy led me to the discourse of photography and cinema and to thinkers who explored the relationship between literature and visual art. Expanding the framework in this manner allowed me to treat Carver's oeuvre as a case study for discussing the visual dimension of fiction in the broader context of representation and subjectivity in literature as opposed to other media. Among the thinkers and ideas I discuss in detail are Gilles Deleuze's reflections on cinema (chapter 5), Robbe-Grillet's conception of description in literature and cinema (chapter 3), and Roland Barthes's seminal work on photography (chapter 6). I also refer to Lacan, whose discussion of vision in his later writing is inspired by a sixteenth-century painting. A special place is given to literary thinkers who focus on literature but have expanded their approach to accommodate broader interests. These critics include Elaine Scarry, who uses findings from cognitive psychology to explain the formation of mental images in the mind of the reader; and Ann Banfield, whose linguistic analysis of the language of fiction has led her to explore the contact points between literature and photography.

The growing interest of literary scholars in the visual or image-forming aspect of literature is part of what W. J. T. Mitchell has termed the "pictorial turn," namely the increasing interest of thinkers from different fields in the question of vision, indicating a search for a new visual paradigm for our time.[34] There are several reasons for, and manifestations of, this "turn," including post-structural preoccupation with the issue of representation; psychoanalytic development of the concepts of vision and gaze, especially in the writing of Lacan (such as in "The Mirror Stage" and the later *Four Fundamental Concepts of Psychoanalysis*). Also to be considered are the feminist exploration of the representation of women in the visual arts, mainly in the cinema; and postcolonial concern with the image of the Other, as reflected in the concept of vision and in the "scopic regime" of the dominating culture. In any event, the growing interest in vision and related topics has affected literary discourse and softened the rigid boundaries defining each medium. Lessing's traditional division, assigning time to literature and space to painting, no longer reigns in literary discourse. There is a growing awareness of aspects of temporality in our processing of objects of visual art, as well as the role of spatial and visual experience in the reader response to texts (as discussed in Ellen Esrock's *The Reader's Eye*, for example).[35] This new approach is certainly connected to the development of modern thought, in which definitions of time and space have been challenged, with each dimension now encroaching upon the other.

Another theoretician who has opened up the borders between different media, thereby promoting a more flexible understanding of fields, is Mieke Bal. Bal's work was originally in narratology and semiotics, from which she arrived (via the study of point of view, or "focalization," in fiction) at the points of contact between literature and the visual arts. In her introduction to the 1988 issue of *Style*, she named the field "visual poetics," which she regards as an expansion of semiotics. In discussing the goals of this new field of study, Bal defines some possible linkages between word and image, underscores the importance of visual experience, and suggests using its concepts—such as perspective, composition, and color—in discussing literature. She concludes by stating that while nobody denies the essential differences between these arts, cooperative research could benefit literature as well as visual art.[36] In Bal's subsequent studies of narrativity in painting (in her 1991 book on Rembrandt) and visuality in literature (in her 1997 book on Proust), she puts into practice her notion of visual poetics, revealing its potential for rereading literary texts and articulating what she would later call "a genuinely visual moment in literature."[37] To Bal's position, which aptly expresses my own, I have added an emphasis on the metaphorical aspects of the visual approach as applied to the study of literature, and I will refer to the question of interdisciplinarity itself in the course of my discussion.

Although this study does practice visual poetics on Carver's works, the topics covered in each of the chapters still overlap—however loosely—with more traditional issues of literary and narrative study: duration, dialogue, narration, description, literary frames, character, and meaning. In fact, one of the purposes of this study is to reflect upon these issues in the context of visual approaches.

The book is divided into three sections, each one consisting of two chapters. Each part is structured around a binary opposition that the two chapters explore from different angles. These binarisms are movement and stasis, inside and outside, and opened and closed.

Part I—"Movement"—deals with the tension between movement and stasis in Carver's description of movement and action and—in a metaphorical sense—in his dialogues. Chapter 1 explores how movement is manifested in Carver's stories. It questions the assumption of linearity and continuity suggested by the use of the *scene* technique. It connects this camera-like mode of representation to the existential condition of Carver's characters. Chapter 2 expands the discussion of movement and continuity to their metaphoric representation in Carverian dialogues, exploring issues of communication and miscommunication. It examines the dynamics of Carverian dialogue, which vacillates between identity and difference, and between idiosyncrasies and cliché.

Part II—"The Eye of the Camera"—examines the fluid borders between subject and object both in the telling of the story and in describing its space. Chapter 3 characterizes Carver's typical narrator as absent and impersonal, a quality which suggests, as it were, the eye of a camera. Embodying what Ann Banfield calls *unoccupied perspective*, the narrator is presented as devoid of subjectivity and consciousness while at the same time embodying the most personal experience—that of the possibility of one's own absence. The narrator thus incarnates the condition of Carver's characters, who are facing states of detachment and crisis. Chapter 4 is the backbone of this study, as it builds on previous issues under discussion, connecting them to the major topic being researched—vision in, and visibility of, the fictional world. It characterizes Carver's modes of describing and verbalizing a visible reality through different ways of looking: the direct look, the sidelong look, the glimpse, and the eyes shut. Theories of description and vision, including those of Robbe-Grillet and Lacan, are analyzed to show how the limitations and delusions inherent in a seemingly direct and objective mode of description reveal the subjective presence of a consciousness.

Part III—"Seeing and Meaning"—provides a new approach to the portrait of the Carverian character, and relates it to the dynamics of meaning production and the use of descriptive detail. The first part of chapter 5 discusses the relationships between character and space—both actual and textual—in Carver's stories. It examines the different senses implied by the term *frame* in literature, comparing it to frames in the visual arts, especially in photography and cinema. In the second part of the chapter I describe Carver's typical character, enclosed in a case-like space, as that of a viewer in an *optic situation*, as defined by Deleuze. This *optic situation* creates a unique relationship between vision, action, and time, and much like Carver's frames, blurs the distinctions between stasis and movement, inside and outside, and opened and closed. The chapter includes a reading of Deleuze's research on cinema, linking it not only to Carver but also to the formalist concept of defamiliarization and to the role of stasis and vision in modernist literature. Chapter 6 begins with a discussion of the father-son relationship in Carver's work and life. The relationship incarnates the polarities of identity and difference and of singularity and doubleness, which are central to Carver's work both thematically and structurally. The duality of this relationship is distilled by examining Carver's use of descriptive details in light of Ronald Barthes's work on photography and literature. Both meaningful and devoid of meaning, the superfluous, "visible" detail in Carver's work is shown to be the means by which literature breaks through the boundaries of fiction and taps into the most personal experience of the reader.

Notes

1. Jay McInerney, "Raymond Carver: A Still, Small Voice," *New York Times Book Review*, 6 August 1989. http://query.nytimes.com/gst/fullpage.html?res=950DE6DD1530F935A3575BC0A96F948260&sec=&spon=&pagewanted=2 (accessed January 30, 2008).

2. Carver's literary essays were republished in Raymond Carver, *Call if You Need Me: The Uncollected Fiction and Other Prose*, ed. William L. Stull (New York: Vintage Books, 2001). His life-oriented approach is evident mostly in "All My Relations" (pp. 208–18) and the end of "On Where I'm Calling From" (p. 202).

3. Carver's intellectual and literary tendencies are also described by Richard Cortez Day and by Maryann Carver in Sam Halpert, *Raymond Carver: An Oral Biography* (Iowa City: University of Iowa Press, 1995).

4. Kim A. Herzinger, "Introduction: On the New Fiction," *Mississippi Review* 40–41 (1985): 7–22.

5. William Kittredge addresses the moral aspect of Carver's work in Halpert, 152. William Stull discerns in Carver's later work a tendency toward Christian grace and brotherhood. See William L. Stull, "Beyond Hopelessville: Another Side of Raymond Carver," *Philological Quarterly* 64:1 (1985): 1–15. See also Marc A. R. Facknitz, "'The Calm,' 'A Small, Good Thing' and 'Cathedral': Raymond Carver and the Rediscovery of Human Worth," *Studies in Short Fiction* 23:3 (1986): 287–96. For a recent study analyzing the milieu of the blue-collar people as Carver's chronotope, see G. P. Lainsbury, *The Carver Chronotope: Inside the Life-world of Raymond Carver's Fiction* (New York: Routledge, 2004).

6. This semiotic approach to characters in literature is described in Shlomith Rimmon-Kenan, *Narrative Fiction* (London and New York: Routledge, 2002), 33.

7. Richard Ford, "Good Raymond," *The New Yorker*, 5 October 1998, 74 (30): 72.

8. Randolph Paul Runyon, *Reading Raymond Carver* (Syracuse: Syracuse University Press, 1992), 4.

9. Marc Chénetier, "Living On/Off the 'Reserve': Performance, Interrogation, and Negativity in the Works of Raymond Carver," in *Critical Angles: European Views of Contemporary American Literature*, ed. Marc Chénetier (Carbondale: Southern Illinois University Press, 1986), 164–90. Other critics think that Carver's work is as self-conscious and calculated as the postmodern stories of the sixties and the seventies. See Thomas LeClair, "Fiction Chronicle—June 1981," *Contemporary Literature* 23:1 (1982): 87; Alain Arias-Misson, "Absent Talkers," *Partisan Review* 49:4 (1982): 625–28; and Arthur M. Saltzman, *Understanding Raymond Carver* (Columbia: University of South Carolina Press, 1988), 1–19. For an argument against the view of Carver as a postmodern writer, see Arthur F. Bethea, *Technique and Sensibility in the Fiction and Poetry of Raymond Carver* (New York: Routledge, 2001).

10. Claudine Verley, "'Errand,' or Raymond Carver's Realism in a Champagne Cork," *Journal of the Short Story in English* 46 (2006). http://jsse.revues.org/index502

.html (accessed January 27, 2010). In this intriguing essay Verley shows how Carver's "Errand" lays bare the challenge to realism that is latent in his entire work. On Carver's untraditional realism, see also Lori Chamberlain, "Magicking the Real: Paradoxes of Postmodern Writing," in *Postmodern Fiction: A Bio-Bibliographical Guide*, ed. Larry McCaffery (New York: Greenwood Press, 1986), 13–14; and the editor's introduction to the book (pp. xvii–xviii).

11. On Carver's reception, see Kirk Nesset, *The Stories of Raymond Carver: A Critical Study* (Athens: Ohio University Press, 1995), 1–8. Bill Mullen, "A Subtle Spectacle: Televisual Culture in the Short Stories of Raymond Carver," *Critique* 39:2 (1998): 99–102.

12. A. O. Scott notes Carver's preference for the lucid, charged language of the modernist poets (Pound, Williams, Stevens, O'Hara, and Lowell), who preferred "things" over ideas. See A. O. Scott, "Looking for Raymond Carver," *The New York Review of Books*, 12 August 1999, 54–59. Carver describes his first encounter with modernist poetry in his essay "Some Prose on Poetry," in *All of Us: The Collected Poems* (New York: Vintage Books, 1996), 265–67.

13. See Halpert, 145.

14. This pattern in the history of literature is described in Dorrit Cohn, *Transparent Minds: Narrative Modes for Presenting Consciousness in Fiction* (Princeton: Princeton University Press: 1978), 9.

15. Regarding Carver's relationship with the wave of self-conscious literature, see Runyon, 3–6; Chénetier's "Living On/Off, " 189–90; and Saltzman, 10–11. In his interviews and essays, Carver repeated that he had nothing against experimental literature and declared his admiration for Barthelme. See his 1983 interview in Marshall Bruce Gentry and William Stull, eds., *Conversations with Raymond Carver* (Jackson and London: University Press of Mississippi, 1990), 58. However, Carver expresses his reservations about literature that is too self-absorbed (ibid., 210).

16. Martin Jay, "Photo-unrealism: The Contribution of the Camera to the Crisis of Ocularcentrism," in *Vision and Textuality*, ed. Stephen Melville and Bill Readings (Durham, NC: Duke University Press, 1995), 344–60; and *Downcast Eyes: The Denigration of Vision in Twentieth-Century French Thought* (Berkeley: University of California Press, 1994), 124–47.

17. Edgar Allan Poe, "Nathaniel Hawthorne's *Twice-Told Tales*," in vol. 11 of *The Complete Works of Edgar Allan Poe*, ed. James Harrison (New York: George D. Sproul, 1902), 108. For an elaboration on Poe's concept of the short story as a picture, see Jean Pickering, "Time and the Short Story," in *Re-Reading the Short Story*, ed. Stephen Melville and Bill Readings (London: Macmillan Press, 1989), 48; and Valérie Shaw, *The Short Story* (London: Longman, 1985), 9–10, and throughout the text. This line of thought is also manifested in Jane M. Rabb, ed., *Short Story and Photography 1880s–1980s: A Critical Anthology* (Albuquerque: University of New Mexico Press, 1998). Regarding the synchronic nature of short stories in Russian Formalism, see Fredric Jameson, *The Prison House of Language* (Princeton: Princeton University Press, 1972), 74.

18. See, for example, John Barth, "A Few Words about Minimalism," *New York Times Book Review*, 28 December 1986, 1–2. Among other witty names, Barth calls minimalist writing "Post-Vietnamese literature." See also Douglas Unger's comment

in Halpert, 122. Carver's disillusionment with the American dream is expressed mostly in his autobiographical essay "Fires," in *Fires: Essays, Poems, Stories* (New York: Vintage Books, 1989), 28–39.

19. On Carver's preference for silence and sensory experience over words, see Scott, 59. For Christof Decker, Carver's visual and sensory experience forms an alternative channel of communication. See Christof Decker, "Faces in the Mirror: Raymond Carver and the Intricacies of Looking," *Amerikastudien* 49:1 (2004), 35–49. On Carver's preference for vision over hearing and sound, see Graham Clarke, "Investing the Glimpse: Raymond Carver and the Syntax of Silence," in *The New American Writing: Essays on American Literature Since 1970*, ed. Graham Clarke (London and New York: St. Martin's Press, 1990), 118–20. Similarly, McSweeney recently used the glimpse metaphor to describe stories by Carver and other short story writers. See Kerry McSweeney, *The Realist Short Story of the Powerful Glimpse: Chekhov to Carver* (Columbia: University of South Carolina Press, 2007).

20. Saltzman, 5. Examples of this negative attitude toward minimalism and toward Carver can be found in Bill Madison, "Less Is Less: The Dwindling of American Short Story," *Harper's*, April 1986, 64–69; and in John Biguenet, "Notes of a Disaffected Reader: The Origins of Minimalism," *Mississippi Review* 40–41 (1985): 40–45. These issues are further discussed in chapter 5. The negative response to photography goes back to Baudelaire. See Charles Baudelaire, "The Modern Public and Photography" (1862), in *Classic Essays on Photography*, ed. Alan Trachtenberg (New Haven: Leete's Island Books, 1980), 83–90. Regarding the reception of photography as flat and cliché-ridden, see also Mieke Bal, *The Mottled Screen: Reading Proust Visually*, trans. Anna-Louise Milne (Stanford: Stanford University Press, 1997), 3. See also Susan Sontag, *On Photography* (New York: Farrar, Straus & Giroux, 1973).

21. Gentry and Stull, 106, 156, and 222–23.

22. In many interviews, Carver expresses his fondness for traditional structures of stories. Two of his interviewers comment, however, that his own stories lack the traditional structure of a plot that develops, reaches a climax, and then has a resolution. Instead, Carver's stories are characterized by a static quality and often have an open ending (I discuss this oxymoron in chapter 5). Carver admits that maybe he prefers the classic structure because of its absence in his own works, and that his characters' condition does not lend itself to the "solutions" implied by the classic model (Gentry and Stull, 111).

23. Martin Scofield, "Negative Pastoral: The Art of Raymond Carver's Stories," *The Cambridge Quarterly* 22:3 (1994): 243–62.

24. Maurice Blanchot, "Everyday Speech," *Yale French Studies* 73 (1987): 15. On Carver's introducing the "everyday" to American literature, see Marc Chénetier, "Cultural Tradition and the Present II: The Everyday and Mass Culture," in *Beyond Suspicion: New American Fiction Since 1960*, trans. Elizabeth A. Houlding (Philadelphia: University of Pennsylvania Press, 1996), 219–27.

25. On the resemblance of Carver's work to visual arts generally and to Edward Hopper's and George Segal's works in particular, see Clarke, especially pp. 117–18. On the resemblance of minimalist literature in general and Carver's writing in particular to hyperrealism in painting, see Ann-Marie Karlsson, "The Hyperrealistic Short Story: A Postmodern Twilight Zone," in *Criticism in the Twilight Zone: Postmodern Perspectives on*

Literature and Politics, ed. Danuta Zadworna-Fjellestad and Lennart Björk (Stockholm: Almqvist & Wiksell International, 1990), 144–53. William Stull compares some of Carver's stories and characters to situations and figures in paintings by Hopper, Hanson, Goings, Bechtle, and de Andrea (pp. 4–5). Saltzman relates Carver's work to hyperrealism and paintings by Richard Estes (p. 13).

26. See Jay, "Photo-Unrealism," 349. Jay, *Downcast Eyes*, 133–35.
27. Gentry and Stull, 198.
28. See, for example, Gentry and Stull, 58.
29. This broader sense of the term "communication" is used by Gilles Deleuze when he discusses movement. See Gilles Deleuze, *Cinema 1: The Movement-Image*, trans. Hugh Tomlinson and Barbara Habberjam (Minneapolis: University of Minnesota Press, 1986). Deleuze uses this concept throughout the whole book, especially when discussing issues of frame (pp. 17–18).
30. See Richard Ford's testimony (in Halpert, 160), where he insists on the self-sustenance of Carver's stories. The same approach is also evident in Tobias Wolff's testimony (ibid., 156–57).
31. See for example in Halpert, 75, 158.
32. D. T. Max, "The Carver Chronicles," *The New York Times*, 9 August 1998, http://www.nytimes.com/1998/08/09/magazine/the-carver-chronicles.html?pagewanted=1 (accessed January 29, 2010). For recent discussions of Lish's editing, which followed Tess Gallagher's intention to publish Carver's original drafts, see Charles McGrath, "Whose Words: I, ~~Editor~~ Author," *New York Times*, 28 October 2007. http://www.nytimes.com/2007/10/28/weekinreview/28mcgrath.html?_r=2&emc=eta1&oref=slogin&oref=slogin (accessed January 30, 2008). See also "Rough Crossings: The Cutting of Raymond Carver," *The New Yorker*, 24 December 2007. http://www.newyorker.com/reporting/2007/12/24/071224fa_fact (accessed January 30, 2008). This article also introduced some of Carver's letters to Lish, the original draft of "What We Talk about When We Talk about Love" (originally titled "Beginners") and Lish's edit.
33. On the development in Carver's writing, see Adam Meyer's review and general thesis in *Raymond Carver* (New York: Twayne Publishers, 1995).
34. W. J. T. Mitchell, "The Pictorial Turn," in *Picture Theory: Essays in Verbal and Visual Representation*, ed. W. J. T. Mitchell (Chicago: University of Chicago Press, 1995), 11–13. On the reasons for the "visual turn," see Martin Jay, "Vision in Context: Reflections and Refractions," in *Vision in Context: Historical and Contemporary Perspectives on Sight*, ed. Teresa Brennan and Martin Jay (New York: Routledge, 1996), 3–12. The term "scopic regime" was coined by the cinema theoretician Christian Metz.
35. Ellen Esrock, *The Reader's Eye: Visual Imaging as Reader Response* (Baltimore: Johns Hopkins University Press, 1994). Esrock believes that for many years the visual response to literature was suppressed by the adherence to plot and was considered inferior. She offers an overview of visual approaches to literature in phenomenology, psychoanalysis, and other disciplines.
36. Mieke Bal, "Introduction: Visual Poetics," *Style* 22:2 (1988): 177–78. Some very convincing arguments in favor of the use of spatial-visual metaphors in literature are presented by W. J. T. Mitchell, who sees them as reflecting the essence of literary experience. See W. J. T. Mitchell, "Spatial Form in Literature: Towards a General Theory,"

Critical Inquiry 6:3 (1980): 539–67. In his other works, Mitchell discusses the concept of image, especially in *Iconology: Image, Text, Ideology* (Chicago: University of Chicago Press, 1986). Another figure worth mentioning is Wendy Steiner, who, in the introduction to her book, relates the comparisons between the arts to fundamental issues of the modern era. See Wendy Steiner, *The Colors of Rhetoric* (Chicago: University of Chicago Press, 1982), xi–xiv.

37. Mieke Bal, "Poetics, Today," *Poetics Today* 21:3 (2000):479.

Part I
MOVEMENT

CHAPTER 1

"I Don't Do Motion Shots"
REPRESENTATION OF MOVEMENT

Viewfinder

Raymond Carver's story "Viewfinder" is a first-person narrative told by a lonely man who has shut himself up in his house after his wife and children have left him. He describes his encounter with a handless photographer, who offers him a picture of his house. The two engage in a mysterious conversation; it seems that the photographer, an occasional visitor, keenly grasps his host's mental and existential condition, even though the host has not explicitly shared it with him or with the reader. The encounter culminates in a series of photographs taken at the request of the narrator. The scenes in which the photography takes place make explicit a theme of representation central to the story, while its implications have an even broader reach.

The shooting session in "Viewfinder" begins after the photographer has guessed that the narrator's family "cleared right out" (*WWTA*, 14), implying that he, too, has suffered from some type of family breakup. "They're what gave me this" (13), he says, gesturing to the hooks he has in lieu of hands. "I sympathize," he adds while thanking the narrator for his hospitality. His host replies, "Show me, show me how much" (14), and then asks the photographer to shoot him and his house. "It won't work," says the photographer, "they are not coming back" (ibid.). However, the two step outside nonetheless; the photographer adjusts the shutter, and the shoot begins:

> We moved around the house. Systematic. Sometimes I'd look sideways. Sometimes I'd look straight ahead. "Good," he'd say. "That's good," he'd say, until we circled the house and were back in the front again. "That's twenty. That's enough." (ibid.)

Much like other actions described in the story, this act seems whimsical and without reason. We can only guess its meaning. Perhaps the narrator wishes to see himself from the outside, to look at himself through the eyes of the photographer and the camera, thus telling his story and that of the abandoned house in pictures rather than in words, knowing that either way, "they" are not coming back.

However, the psychological motivation behind the host's curious behavior is less important in this context than the manner in which the series of photographs is executed. The photographer works "systematically," step by step. He creates a sequence of pictures in which the background is adjacent segments of a house. Were the pictures to be placed side by side, they would create only a partial and false sense of continuity: the arrangement would appear fragmented, lack inherent flow, and depend on the eye and the imagination of the viewer to set the photographs in motion. The sequence is based on adjacent, immobilized images of the pictures' subject—the host. It conveys the gestures that comprise movement, but not movement itself, which appears to be more than the sum of its parts. It seems that not all the segments of time and space have been detected, and that even if the interspaces were further reduced, movement itself would still elude the spectator. The subject's positioning has cut off actual movement, just as the click of the camera has cut off represented movement.

Viewing such photos may be compared to scanning pictures on a roll of film, for which only accelerated, successive viewing creates the illusion of movement. It is also comparable to the movement of the eye along the contact sheets of the chronophotographer Edward Muybridge, who used several cameras in alternating split-second intervals, thus creating sequences that registered previously invisible details in the body movements of people and animals. Naturally, this comparison is only partial: In "Viewfinder" the movement seems not to take place in front of the camera at all, as it does in the celluloid roll and in Muybridge's pictures, and the intervals between clicks are much longer than the split seconds intervals of those movement sequences. However, the similarity is still striking: "Viewfinder" suggests the will to represent movement, but ends up arresting it, while Muybridge's photographic process fractures continuous movement, no matter how "systematic" it seems. Paradoxically, these two photographic series exploring movement demonstrate precisely the impossibility of fully representing it. The proximity of time-points and space-positions actually underscores the elusiveness of the passage between them.

There are other types of photography in "Viewfinder," however. The narrator, after being photographed in various positions with the house as a background, asks the photographer to take his picture while he stands on the roof. There he finds a few rocks and asks the photographer to shoot him while he throws them:

> "Ready?" I called, and got a rock, and I waited until he had me in his viewfinder.
> "Okay!" he called.
> I laid back my arm and I hollered, "Now!" I threw that son of a bitch as far as I could throw it.
> "I don't know," I heard him shout. "I don't do motion shots."
> "Again!" I screamed, and took up another rock. (15)

This is the end of the story, which photograph-like freezes the throwing gesture. Two options of photographic representation are thus offered. One is a series of successive photographs of the subject, which obtains its movement from the moving eye of a potential spectator, a series based on the "motion picture(s)" principle. The other possibility is the "motion shot," the stone-throwing photograph. This photograph seems to express a resistance to representing movement in a series of successive static positions, and a will to contain it in a single shot, independent of the moving eye or of the rolling of film. However, the possibility of such a photograph is questioned: "I don't do motion shots," says the photographer. His concern is understandable—he does not want the picture to be blurred, but I believe that this statement reflects a broader issue in Carver's work.

To further understand the implications of this statement, it is important to note that "Viewfinder," like many of Carver's stories, is written in the *scene* mode, namely a duration technique in which there appears to be a one-to-one correspondence between the time of the story (or fabula) and the time of the text (or sujet).[1] The scene mode manifests a literary ideology, that of "showing" or mimesis, which embodies a wish to, as it were, place the reader inside the occurrences of the story and minimize narratorial mediation as much as possible. Carver thus continues the Hemingway tradition, which strives to imitate the eye of the camera by accompanying the events "as is," without editing or selection. Moments follow each other successively and visible space is described accurately. However, the scene mode, as simple as it sounds, intrinsically negates itself. As implied by Mieke Bal's discussion of narrative duration, the scene technique's very effort to cling to story time—a task that can never be fully accomplished—exposes the impossibility of representing continuity and the unavoidable breakdown of rhythm.[2] My analogy is probably clear by now: The photographer and the narrator, circling the house together at the same pace, symbolically express the aspiration for a correspondence between text and story, representation and "reality." However, the series of pictures underscores the break in sequence inherent in the very act of representation. The possibility of tracking movement is but an illusion; continuity is false and delusive. This also holds true in the series of "motion pictures," and in the use of the scene mode. The scene mode, which allegedly represents continuity, might actually break the illusion of succession, supported by the linearity of the text. By taking the clinging-to-story-time to its extreme, it exposes the omissions—however minute—that any representation of movement and time entails.

Sequence breaking is thus inherent in the very act of representation. The story hints at this meta-poetically with the comment "I don't do motion shots," and in other ways as well— which become especially apparent if we compare two versions of the story. "Viewfinder," like other stories by Carver, has more than one version. The first version was published in 1978, and is nearly identical to the manuscript version in *Beginners*, republished in 2009. Among the many differences between the two versions is the addition of the phrase "I don't do motion shots" in the latter version. The disparities, no doubt, were motivated by Gordon Lish's editing of the story before it was published in the collection *What We Talk about When We Talk about Love*. As mentioned in the introduction, Lish's role in shaping the nature or quality of Carver's earlier stories has been recently acknowledged. It seems that Lish changed the texts radically, reducing and thinning them out, adapting them thereby to the somewhat notorious label "minimalism" or "lean prose." The commonly held view is that these changes were more in accord with Lish's brand of experimental poetics than they were consistent with Carver's "natural" style, as revealed in his later stories. The recently published stories and letters from Carver to his editor support this view.[3] In fact, even in Carver's lifetime the republication of some expanded and altered versions of early works seems to reflect his liberation from Lish and a return to what he "truly" intended his stories to be. Despite all this, I believe that the declaration, "I don't do motion shots," added to the final *WWTA* version, is compatible with other changes made in this particular story, thus making it (inter alia) a meta-literary statement.

Indeed, the final version, whose final statement questions the very possibility of representing motion, contains more segmented sequences than the first version (1978). This is mostly manifested in the syntax and layout of the text. The final version is cut into more pieces. Sentences that were previously located within paragraphs now receive their own lines. The sentence, "I wanted to see how he would hold a cap" is detached from the following paragraph, which originally supplied it with background and an explanation: "I knew how he used the camera" (*V*, 50).[4] A few paragraphs later, in the first version, the phrase "I took the photograph from him" is followed by the details of what the narrator sees in the picture ("There was the little rectangle of lawn, the driveway, carport."). The description in the final version is *not* connected to the photograph, and the text uses the neuter "a" instead of the definite "the," thus showing no familiarity with the objects. It seems that the house now stands alone, detached from its representation or suggestion of its presence in the act of looking at the photograph. The emotional reaction to the photograph ("Why would I want a photograph/picture of this tragedy?") also appears in a separate line in the final version, detached from its description. These are but a few examples of the alterations the story has undergone. In addition to this process of fragmentation, many sentences have been shortened and prepositions have been omitted. Again, as much as these changes reflect Lish's hand (revealed by other stories he edited), I believe that they carried out in practice the possibilities of the text, unearthing a deep current in the story, which was reflexively phrased in the ending of the final version. Listening to recordings of Carver reading his stories, one can hardly ignore the staccato rhythm with which he read, so different from the soft, mumbling flow of his everyday talk.[5] It is this rhythm that the final version of "Viewfinder" enhances and punctuates.

The abridged final version also has increased fragmentation in the flow of meaning. Information gaps widen. The wife and kids, mentioned in the first version, are only "they" in the final. The work habits of the photographer have been omitted, as well as some emotional expression ("It still hurts," says the photographer in the original version. "You were right on the target," says the host when his guest sees through his plight [*V*, 51–52]). The parallelism between the sense of loss and its incarnation (the loss of limbs) and the analogy between the two characters is explicit in the early version: "You feel like she cut the ground right out from under you! Took your legs in the process" (*V*, 52). This symbolic layer of the story is merely implied in the final version, requiring the reader to decipher it. The fragmentation of movement corresponds to the fragmentation of meaning both when reader response is needed and in the dialogue, which is especially curious in this story. The exchange of words seems to indicate both deep familiarity and total estrangement, revealing an inexplicable emotional link between people who otherwise seem to talk past each other (qualities I will elaborate on in the next chapter).

It is important to note that despite the changes made to the final version, the text still clings to the time-space frame of the events in the "front" of the story. With the exception of one comment—the narrator notes that he discerned the photographer before he knocked on his door, thus deviating slightly from the present time—the abridged version does not skip over substantial chunks of time or move to other locations. The key difference between these versions is that in the final version, various kinds of fragmentation have been introduced. The changes in the 1981 version do not have a direct impact on the scene technique. However, they underscore the discontinuity lurking in the text, and challenge the illusion of succession that the scene technique strives to create.

In Muybridge's photos, the spectator perceives the fragmentation of movement because he looks at the successive acts almost simultaneously, that is, side by side, rather than one after the other (unlike a motion picture, where each picture rapidly replaces the previous one).[6] When reading a text, illusions of continuity and movement are created by the linearity of the reading process, which produces the "one after the other" sense of the represented actions while automatically filling in the inevitable gaps between them. It seems though that the final version of "Viewfinder" deliberately attempts to hinder the reader's work of connecting and stitching together the sequence of events, scattering bumps, as it were, in the text in order to hamper the passage (or movement) between its parts. The reading process thus illustrates the difficulty in representing continuous movement. It emphasizes the gaps that *scene* representation usually treats as a necessary evil, and either tries to cover up, or distract the reader's mind from them.

Fractioning of Movement

At this point, I would like to expand beyond "Viewfinder" in order to examine what I would call the "fractioning of movement" in various aspects of Carver's work and in other stories. I define the "fractioning of movement" as the representation of movement or action that emphasizes the inevitable segmenting of continuity inherent in the very act of representation, thus making movement a mere juxtaposition of gestures that seem to be connected and to follow each other, but in fact are separated from each other by brief intervals. This process is noticeable mostly in the way Carver describes body movement by tracking the minute details of physical action. A good example is "Errand," in which Carver elaborates on a marginal episode in the death scene of Anton Chekhov, as described in Henry Troyat's biography of the Russian writer. Carver does not quote Troyat verbatim. However, one can hardly fail to notice where Troyat ends and Carver begins. Only Carver would describe Chekhov's doctor pouring champagne into a glass or measuring the pulse of a dying man without missing one gesture, revealing him to be a kind of literary Muybridge.

To use Roland Barthes's terminology, Carver's poetics shows preference for *catalysts* (i.e., events that expand, pad, and delay the main action) over *kernels* (i.e., events that advance the plot). Carver's domain is the everyday, comprised of routine actions rendered deliberately, dwelling upon each of their components. In "Preservation" Sandy's body movements, while throwing stale food into the garbage can, include the lifting of its lid. In "Careful," Lloyd, who rises from the sofa, does not forget to pick up a dirty glass on his way to the kitchen. Lingering over secondary acts, while making the action palpable, also serves to distract the reader from its immediate purpose and role in the story. Furthermore Carver manages, in different ways, to siphon momentum from body movement, to crumble it into merely adjacent gestures, and in the process, to defamiliarize it radically. Thus "Little Things" (the former "Popular Mechanics")—a story about a couple literally grappling over their baby—draws much of its terrifying power from an accurate description of actions detached from their purpose or their emotional content, focusing instead on the limbs and motions involved: "The kitchen window gave no light. In the near-dark he worked on her fisted fingers with one hand and with the other hand he gripped the screaming baby up under an arm near the shoulder" (*WICF*, 153). The description of an emotion-filled action that is reduced to its basic elements both enhances and hinders the reader's vision, as if he too were wrapped in the darkness of the room.[7] The scrupulous detailing of simultaneous motions, reported one after the other, delays the reader's grasp of the overall situation. The tangle of limbs (the husband's hands, the wife's fisted fingers, the arm and shoulder of the infant) is blurred by the absence of possessive adjectives ("an arm" or "one hand").

Sometimes, when action is fractioned into its basic elements, one gesture—typical, but unnecessary—sticks out, like the gesture of putting a hand behind the back while drinking, in "The Train": "The old man got up from the bench and moved over to the drinking fountain. He put one hand behind his back, turned the knob and bent over to drink" (*Cathedral*, 152). Again, it seems that the description is meant to induce visualization, but at the same time, the minor gesture underscores the mechanical aspect of physical action. This is even more conspicuous in "Neighbors": "Bill and Jim shook hands beside the car. Harriet and Arlene held each other by the elbows and kissed lightly on the lips" (*WICF*, 86). The minor gesture of holding each other's elbows hollows out the ritual of parting, emphasizing the element of mimicry in the "neighbors" relationship. This minor, perfunctory action is displayed center stage, as it were, in the theater of decorum. It is remarkable for being insignificant and unintentional, and thus defamiliarizes the act as a whole. The eye-of-the-camera technique works here by focusing in on a marginal, nonrepresentative movement that seems to be captured accidentally, an effect that has played a major role in the way that photography has influenced the development of the concept of vision.[8]

At other times Carver tears a single gesture from the causal chain of events. A fist hitting a head introduces the main familiar-strange event in "Careful": "The day she came, he was on the sofa, in his pajamas, hitting his fist against the right side of his head. Just before he could hit himself again, he heard voices downstairs on the landing" (*WICF*, 266). The meaning of this gesture becomes clear in the next paragraph: "He'd awakened that morning and found out that his ear had stopped up with wax." However, the comic—as well as the emotional and symbolic—effect of a man hitting his head with his fist had already had its emotional influence on the reader.[9]

In "Cathedral," a hand moves, detached from its owner—a description that contributes to the comic tone coloring the suspicion of a host toward an unwelcome guest: "The blind man let go of his suitcase and up came his hand"

(*WICF*, 361). It is not only the outsider (in the story and outside of it) who feels the detachment of gesture from its performer. The characters may feel it as well. In "Are These Actual Miles?" a tormented husband, waiting for his wife to come back from "selling the car," becomes an observer of his own actions: "He looks at his hand. It makes a fist as he watched" (*WICF*, 134).

Despite the above examples of the variety of effects of the description of movement (palpability, visibility, mechanical impact, disruption of vision, hindering of perception, defamiliarization), it is still possible to discern a common pattern: body movement is fragmented into micro-movements. While adjacent in text, space, and time, these movements have been loosened from their performer or purpose. Paradoxically, meticulously tracking the details of movement disrupts its reception by inserting gaps, freezing it and fractioning it.

Sometimes actual gaps are inserted into the description of one movement in the form of other descriptions. This is the case with an intense motion, bursting with contradictory feelings, as described in "Where I'm Calling From." J. P. puts his hand on a door handle during a visit by his wife, who suggests that they will eat out, thus exposing him unintentionally to the seduction of drinking. In the meantime the motion of the hand is fragmented and interwoven into the text design, intermittently emerging and disappearing into it due to the shifting gaze of the narrator and the separation between what he sees and what he hears:

> "Come on now, Roxy," J. P. says. *He has his hand on the doorknob.*
> "He told me he learned everything he knew from you," I say.
> "Well, that much is sure true," she says. She laughs again. But it's like she's thinking about something else. *J. P. turns the doorknob. Roxy lays her hand over his.* "Joe, can't we go into town for lunch? Can't I take you someplace?"
> J. P. clears his throat. He says, "It hasn't been a week yet."
> *He takes his hand off the doorknob and brings his fingers to his chin.* "I think they'd like it if I didn't leave the place for a little while yet. . . ."
> J. P. looks down. *He's still holding the knob*, even though the door is open. *He turns the knob back and forth.* (*WICF*, 294, my emphases)

It is important to note that, in accordance with the general character of Carver's work, the fractioning of movement does not verge on radical disruption of narrative conventions, as for example in an extreme lengthening of the duration of the text. While the texts show an interest in slow motion ("silent movements of men languorous and heavy with meaning," ["Will You Please Be Quiet, Please?" *WYPB*, 244]), the general impression is still of a realistic, scenic report of events. In most cases there is a plausible motivation behind the unconventional perspective, like an emotional issue or the drunkenness of the observer. However, Mieke Bal's concept of the slowing of "text time" relative to "story time" indeed applies somewhat to Carver's stories.[10] Slowdown, she says, combines with the difficulties of seeing, when perception breaks down. It is not the kiss (that Proust describes), but the "nuances of perception that accompany it." In fact, vision is modified in a sort of magnifying glass, since slowdown splits "the vision into multiple elements" and "an entire drama of vision inserts itself between fabula and story." Let me emphasize again that Carver's slowdown does not interrupt the reader's understanding of what he "sees." In that sense Carver's work is different from the *nouveau roman* texts, in which the texture of events and objects is distorted as if through a powerful magnifying glass, losing entirely its familiar look in the process. However, the splitting and dispersion of visible action (as a result of the lingering of the gaze) and the delay and disruption of the perception of action are easily discernible in his stories. Dwelling on the details of action dispossesses the moving person of his body parts, detaching movement from its purpose and context. Most of all, movement itself is confiscated from its observer, no longer available as an uninterrupted flow, thus underscoring the very effort it takes to see. In "Signals," an entire silent scene is captured through the corner of the eye, its description segmented by a rhythmic insertion of verbs indicating vision, "When Wayne looked back, he *saw* Aldo take Caroline's waiting hand, *saw* Aldo draw his heels smartly, *saw* Aldo kiss her wrist" (*WYPB*, 226, my emphases). The rhythmic scattering of verbs pertaining to vision in the above sequence illustrates how the gaze frames segments of action that are adjacent in time and space, while interrupting the sequence of their presentation. In "Where I'm Calling From," the seeing verbs indicate the shifting of the gaze of the narrator between the husband and the wife:

> *I see* this woman stop the car and set the brake. *I see* J. P. open the door. *I watch* her get out, and *I see* them hug each other. *I look* away. Then *I look* back. (*WICF*, 293, my emphases)

Whereas "Viewfinder" presents us with the difficulty in representing movement, here the difficulty lies in the process of perception. Verbs indicating vision—to see, to watch, and to look—seem to underscore the presence of the observer, the clinging of his gaze, and the continuity of perception. However, these verbs are also located in the elusive passages between situations, thus constituting a persistent effort to bridge them. The observer has an unhindered view of the situation, and the description is of figures in motion. Yet, perception and representation entail the omission of connecting links and the disruption of movement. Much like "Viewfinder," where the click of the camera cuts the continuity of movement, these last examples offer an observer who produces a series of snapshot descriptions that are adjacent but not interconnected. It is no accident, of course, that these shorts in perception happen while looking at a husband and a wife whose connection is itself questioned—the inability to connect projects itself upon the observer's experience.

"Feathers"—Before and After

My movement between the representation of motion and of perception in general is not as unintentional as it might seem. It is in accordance with my belief that the doubt of the very possibility of "doing motion shots" expands beyond the meta-literary scope and issues of representation. It seems to reflect the mental condition of Carver's characters. They are often somewhat paralyzed when facing a movement or a change in their life or surroundings. This is apparent most of all when a character tries to put a finger on the moment when the actual rupture occurred. I therefore think that the poetic principles discussed here are connected to a basic existential experience, which is embodied in Carver's special use of *scene*, as well as in other representation modes. I will describe this experience by examining the story "Feathers" from the collection *Cathedral*. "Feathers" is a very different story from "Viewfinder." It is much fuller and does not adhere to the scene mode as the earlier stories do. However, a network of symbols and motives makes this story a thematic complement to the poetic issues raised by "Viewfinder."

Jack, the first-person narrator of "Feathers," and his wife, Fran, visit his coworker and friend, Bud. During dinner the couple is introduced to Bud's wife, Olla, their baby, Harold, and their unusual pet—a noisy peacock named Joey (possibly a tribute to a fan of peacocks, Flannery O'Connor, and to her story "The Displaced Person"). The visit breeds all kinds of peculiar and amusing events, and the initial suspicion makes room for closeness. However, unlike "Cathedral," which is similar in its concept of a visit, this story ends with a bleak epilogue. This ending reveals that there are no more visits between the couples and that the friendship does not continue. The evening further marks a turning point in the life of Jack and Fran. It made them parents to a child who, according to his father, "has a conniving streak in him" (*WICF*, 355), a child who causes a deterioration in their relationship.

Underlying Jack's story is an indirect effort to reconstruct this turning point that changed his life. At the time, Jack felt the uniqueness of the encounter and in a burst of euphoria, he promised himself never to forget it. Although he admits that fulfilling his wish to remember the evening had turned out to be "bad luck" (*WICF*, 354), he refuses to see it as the beginning of the change for the worse:

> Later, after things changed for us, and the kid had come along, all of that, Fran would look back on that evening at Bud's place as the beginning of the change. But she's wrong. The change came later—and

when it came, it was like something that happened to other people, not something that could have happened to us. (*WICF*, 354)

Even so, Jack does recognize a connection between the evening and the change: Bud and Olla's baby moved Fran, who until then did not care for children. That night she slept with Jack and asked him "to fill her with his seed" (345). As a result a child was born who, like most of the children in Carver's work, created a separation between the parents. Nevertheless, Jack not only refuses to identify this event as the cause of the change in his life from good to bad, but he also has a hard time connecting the change to himself: It seems that the change had occurred to "other people." No specific event, nothing coming from his wife or from himself, could explain the chasm gaping between past and present, between the long-haired Fran (a "big tall drink of water" [333]), and present-day Fran ("She cut her hair a long time ago. She's gotten fat on me, too" [355]). She now sits beside him during evenings of silence, which replaced the evenings of closeness and dreams for the future. Jack has difficulty containing these two opposite situations within himself, and the passage of time between them eludes him: "Hell, where's the time gone since?" (332). Instead he clings to his memories, and the story ends with a nostalgic tone. Indeed, to prove that he is wallowing in the past, the memories are told as if he forgot the retrospective distance and has no hindsight during narration. Thus, for example, Jack says that he does not believe that his wife will actualize her threat to cut her hair ("she knows I'm crazy about it" [334]), although by the end of the story, prior to the time of narration, she has already done it.

In fact, the theme of an elusive transition between what precedes the change and what follows it is suggested in the description of the evening itself. Similar to other stories by Carver, "Feathers" is teeming with unusual accessories: objects and characters of bizarre and amusing flavors, mentioned in a hint of condescension to Bud and Olla's plebeian tastes. Among them are a swan-shaped ashtray that billows smoke and a plaster cast of teeth that sits on the television near a vase of flowers ("the horror-show teeth on top of the TV" [342]). We learn that the frightful teeth serve as a reminder of the debt Olla owes her husband for financing her orthodontic treatment.[11] They were "the most crooked, jaggedy teeth in the world," (341) comments Jack, and Bud gets up and puts the cast teeth near his wife's (now) straight teeth: "Bud had gone to the TV and picked up the teeth. He walked over to Olla and held them up against Olla's cheek. 'Before and after,' Bud said" (343). The use of the phrase "before and after" is an interesting example of Carver's flirting with popular culture, ever present in his work, and not only in the silent television flickering in the background of his stories. The expression obviously alludes to the ads promising a radical change for the better if one would only use a specific product. The "before" picture presents an undesirable situation (fat figure, long nose, pimples), while the "after" picture depicts an ideal state of affairs (toned body, perfect nose, smooth skin). The two pictures are side by side, and the time elapsing between them is referred to only in words (and is surprisingly short). The proximity of the opposite images and their simultaneous presentation supports the implied message that the change happened in a miraculous leap forward, a sprint through time. "The orthodontist who fixed Olla's teeth must have been a whiz," says Fran, in that spirit (342).

Jack's feeling that he cannot bridge the gap between sweet memories and the bitter present is a dark reversal of the media's mirage. The time elapsing between the "before" state of happiness and the "after" state of discontent is absent in the story, as well as in Jack's mind. Accordingly, the text skips over chronological time, a device that is atypical for Carver who prefers, as we have seen, a minute tracking of successive events. Here he chooses instead to place side-by-side two situations that did not follow each other, and let the textual omission represent a mental omission. Whereas the preceding examples indicate the characters' failure to face the elusive transition between situations and capture movement and the change it entails, here the gaze is averted from the moment of transformation ("the change happened much later"). However, this crucial difference coexists with a basic similarity. The text does suggest the possibility that the crisis began at Bud and Olla's (while denying it), and it places side-by-side the "before" and "after" situations. It this way it highlights the elusiveness of movement and the difficulty in locating the breaking point and transformation, making it one of the story's main themes. Widening the gap between opposite situations highlights the impossibility of linking them together or verbalizing the passage between them.

In fact, the evening itself presents us with an ungraspable relationship between opposites, especially between beauty and ugliness. One opposition was already mentioned, that is, between the crooked and straight teeth. The main attractions of the evening—the baby and the peacock—present another. The peacock was purchased for one hundred dollars, because as a child Olla had seen a picture of a peacock in a magazine and experienced it as "the most beautiful thing" (347). As for the baby, "calling him ugly does it credit" (349). However, the baby and the peacock are also presented as analogous, with several similarities: their shrill voices, their shared role in bringing the two couples together, and the way their viewers run out of words when they see them: "We both knew it was a peacock, sure, but we didn't say the word out loud" (336)—and of the baby: "'Ah!' said Fran. No words would come out of my mouth" (348–49). In fact, the very opposition between the baby and the peacock is ambiguous. None of the adjectives that Jack uses to describe the peacock suggest beauty. The detail that marks it, for example, is its gray legs, of all features. The baby, on the other hand, is "no Clark Gable," but as his father says: "Give him time. With any luck, you know, he'll grow up to look like his old man" (349). Indeed, it seems that the key to understand the sliding between polarities and their crumbling into each other is to add the context of time and change. As much as the sight of the baby horrifies Jack, he also admits:

> It *was* an ugly baby. But for all I know, I guess it didn't matter that much to Bud and Olla. Or if it did, maybe they simply thought, so okay if it's ugly. It's our baby. And this is just a stage. Pretty soon there'll be another stage. There is this stage and then there is the next stage. Things will be okay in the long run, once all the stages have been gone through. They might have thought something like that. (*WICF*, 353, Carver's emphasis)

Understanding the present state as "just a stage" is different from expecting a miraculous stage-skipping transformation, as much as it is different from being caught in a crisis, which caused an unbridgeable gap between past and present. Attributing this understanding to Bud and Olla and not to the narrator is meaningful. Although put into words by Jack, this insight does not describe *his* experience of time and change. He simultaneously faces the crooked teeth and the straight teeth, the disturbing cast and the vase of flowers, the swan and the smoking cigarette, the baby and the peacock. In his mind the "before" and "after" of his marriage collide with each other: intimacy and silence, the beautiful Fran and the unappealing Fran. It is the passage between them that he failed to comprehend—the moment of change which eludes him.

In a sense, Jack's reaction is typical of many of Carver's characters who experience the gap between the happiness of "before" and the crisis of "after" without being able to identify the moment of change. As if facing a reversed miracle, they cannot contain in their mind more than an ungraspable chasm between opposite situations. Indeed, "Feathers" is not the only Carver story that expresses bewilderment in the face of inexplicable change, the feeling that it was something that had happened to other people. In stories in which the minds of the characters are penetrated or verbalized, they often wonder, in different ways, at the transformation that has taken place in their lives or emotions or in the personality of a beloved or close character (e.g., in "Fever," "Menudo," and "Intimacy"). The wife in "Intimacy," wondering about the existence and loss of intimacy, locates the change at a certain time—the fourth decade of her husband's life. In "Will You Please Be Quiet, Please?" a man in crisis expresses the will to face the moment that shifted his life into a different direction. In "Why Don't You Dance?" the "before and after" juxtaposition consists of an analogy between a young couple launching its life together and a lonely man who went through a divorce or breakup.

Another version of facing change but failing to locate or define its source is found in stories where the changeover is felt while it's happening, but the character finds it hard to link it with the specific event which is its cause. In "Sixty

Acres" one specific event (Lee's confrontation with a gang of boys invading his property) is experienced, while it is happening, as a crucial break and a failure. Yet the protagonist comments: "Nothing had happened" (*WYPB*, 72). This lack of correlation between the minor event and its impact on the character's life is also found in "Whoever Was Using This Bed," in which a harassing telephone call and a talk at the break of dawn make the narrator feel like he crossed an invisible border to a strange place, but he does not know how he got there. In "The Hair" a small, disturbing event shakes the very foundation of the protagonist's life. In this story, as William Stull says, one can see how Carver, inspired by Chekhov, prefers what "becomes" over what is "happening."[12] Carver, much like the photographers of the fifties, shifts the focus of his short stories from the "decisive moment" to the "non-events" of life, which paradoxically turn out to be decisive. Similarly, Marc Chénetier says that Carver's stories deal with pure change, not with the events, but with what lies between them.[13]

Thus there are many ways to approach the crisis, and many literary means to express it. Sometimes the two sides are juxtaposed with an abyss gaping between them; sometimes the gaze is focused on what precedes the change or what follows it. In other cases, the gaze is fixed on the very heart of the change, but without fathoming its meaning. In any event, the change is always painfully felt, but remains ungraspable. We can conclude then by the saying—along with Gilles Deleuze's interpretation of Bergson—that when movement and change are experienced only through the adjacent and immobile stances of "before" and "after," they are in fact happening "behind one's back," and are thereby inaccessible to whoever experiences them.[14]

Conclusion

Muybridge's photographs created a revolution in painting. They revealed movements that were incompatible with the era's concept of motion, and a difference of opinion erupted as to the right way to paint it. For example, his famous pictures of a galloping horse revealed that the horse lingers in the air with his legs bent, not stretched, as they appear to be. Suddenly a fissure erupted between the visible and the real. The minute tracking, step by step, of the stages of action, seemed to sabotage the impression of movement. The snapshot, says Thierry de Duve, attempts to illustrate the sign and verb "the horse gallop," but in the process "steals the life outside and returns it as death." The series leaves us with images deprived of movement. All that is left is a name, a shape, and a stasis. "This is why it appears as abrupt, aggressive, and artificial, however convinced we might be of its realistic accuracy."[15] As a result, says de Duve, the effect of a snapshot is that of the "real unreality," an effect that was attributed also to photorealism (in painting) and to hyperrealism (in painting *and* literature). De Duve explains that representing movement through a series of successive gestures exposes the artificiality of separating events. It thus challenges the very concept of "event," revealing that events are fundamentally changed when isolated from a sequence. Leo Charney adds that movement photographs represent the invisible and hidden in the forces of life and the basic inability to represent such forces. Here too, the closer the events are to each other, the more conspicuous this is.[16]

Based on this principle, Carver's use of the series-of-snapshots technique succeeds in challenging the illusion of continuity despite the linearity of the text. He achieves this by meticulously tracking actions, a technique that parallels his characters' obsessive need to perceive (in one character's words) "the tiny makings of the catastrophe that thereafter set their lives on different course,"[17] and to locate the moment of change. Both levels—the poetic and the psychological—are marked by an awareness that one cannot bridge the gap between "before" and "after," an awareness sometimes accompanied by a contradictory feeling that the "after" was in fact already present in the "before."

In this way, the problem of representing movement, expressed allegorically in "Viewfinder," is closely bound up with the experience of the characters who suddenly feel deprived of any sense of continuity, a feeling that shakes their sense of reality. Their experiences are reproduced, as I have been trying to show, by the reader who experiences the text as both continuous and fragmented. However, the connection between Carver's use of the aesthetics of mimesis (or "showing") and its connection to his portrayal of characters in crisis, reaches beyond the representation of movement and his use of the *scene* technique. This connection is manifested in his choice of narrator, the way that space is perceived and represented, in characterization, the tension between seeing and acting, and in the way the text involves the reader in the search for continuity and meaning. All of these issues will be discussed in later chapters. Furthermore, the disconnect between events corresponds to communication failures, which dictate the nature of Carver's dialogues. Talks and talking people in Carver's world will be discussed in the next chapter, where I will be returning—through the question of representing speech—to the effect of the "real unreality," as it is manifested in a fictional text.

In reading and analyzing "Viewfinder," I referred solely to the first of the two series of shots—that in which the photographer follows the man encircling his house. I avoided the other possibility—or impossibility—that ends the story: the photograph which encloses movement and at the same time expresses it. The photographer declares that he doesn't do motion shots. But is it really impossible to photograph the man throwing a rock or the flying stone? Is the series of snapshots the only option of "motion pictures"? Doubting that, I will maintain in the background of my discussion the other possibility and let it gain its proper place as this study proceeds.

Notes

1. For a summary of the *scene* mode and its characteristics, see Gérard Genette, *Narrative Discourse*, trans. Jane E. Lewin (Ithaca: Cornell University Press, 1980), 86–112.

2. Mieke Bal, *Narratology: Introduction to the Theory of Narrative* (Toronto: University of Toronto Press, 1997), 106.

3. For a discussion of the nature of the changes Lish made, see Scott, 54–59. See also Stull and Carroll's note on *Beginners* in Carver's *Collected Stories* (New York: Library of America, 2009), 990–98, which includes Carver's "anguished letter" to Lish, asking him not to publish the book in its edited version.

4. The first version of "Viewfinder" ("View Finder") has been published in the *Iowa Review* 9:1 (1978): 50–52 (cf. *Beginners*, in *CS*, 757–60). The story was initially entitled "Hooks" (according to Rabb, 249) and "The Mill" (see *CS*, 999).

5. The American Audio Prose Library issued recordings of Carver reading his stories in 1983. These recordings include three stories ("A Serious Talk," "Fat," and "Nobody Said Anything") and an interview with Kay Bonetti.

6. Deleuze (in *Cinema* 1, 5) elaborates on the contribution of Muybridge's motion pictures to the cinema's concept of movement.

7. Tom Stoppard calls Hemingway's prose "atomic" in "Reflections on Ernest Hemingway," in *Ernest Hemingway: The Writer in Context*, ed. James Nagel (Madison: University of Wisconsin Press, 1984), 19–27.

8. This is the "sidelong glance" aesthetic, which I discuss further in chapter 4. Alan Spiegel talks of this photographic effect and finds it in the prose of Joyce and Hemingway. See Alan Spiegel, *Fiction and the Camera Eye: Visual Consciousness in Film and the Modern Novel* (Charlottesville: University Press of Virginia, 1978), 93–101.

9. Runyon noticed this gesture is detached from any reason or purpose, and therefore links it to episodes from previous stories (165).

10. Ball, *Narratology*, 108. Ball defines here three elements: text, fabula, and story; "story" refers to the way the elements of the fabula are organized in a specific text (as "aspects").

11. Apparently, the autobiographic source of this story is the mold of crooked teeth belonging to Tess Gallagher, Carver's second wife. See Bob Adelman, *Carver Country: The World of Raymond Carver* (New York: Arcade Publishing, 1990), 114.

12. William L. Stull, "Raymond Carver Remembered: Three Early Stories," *Studies in Short Fiction* 25:4 (1988): 468.

13. Chénetier, "Living On/Off," 168. Regarding Carver's interest in the theme of change, see also Gentry and Stull, 166.

14. Deleuze, *Cinema* 1, 3.

15. Thierry de Duve, "Time Exposure and Snapshot: The Photograph as Paradox," *October* 5 (1978): 113–25. The discussion about Muybridge and the citation is on page 116. De Duve describes two ways of classifying photography: the snapshot, which refers to an event but does not convey the flow of things, thus representing the elusiveness of the referent; and the slow time-exposure, which creates an autonomic picture, detached from the event of the unfinished past. De Duve's interpretation of the snapshot is com-

parable to Barthes's description of the photo as standing for an unaccomplished past, a gesture cut in the middle. I will refer to these ideas in chapter 6. When writing about the "unreality of the real," de Duve quotes Barthes's earlier work on photography, "Rhetoric of the Image." On "the real as unreal" effect in literature and its reasons, see also: Christine Brooke-Rose, *The Rhetoric of the Unreal: Studies in Narrative and Structure, Especially of the Fantastic* (Cambridge: Cambridge University Press, 1981), 291–310. On the "real as unreal" in superrealist painting, see: Christine Lindey, *Superrealist Painting and Sculpture* (New York: William Morrow and Company, 1980).

16. Leo Charney, "In a Moment: Film and the Philosophy of Modernity," in *Cinema and the Invention of Modern Life*, ed. Leo Charney and Vanessa R. Schwartz (Berkeley: University of California Press, 1995), 289–90. Charney points out the paradoxes in modernist approaches to representing movement (referring mainly to Walter Benjamin) and their relationship to the cinematic experience.

17. "Were there other men, he wondered drunkenly, who could look at one event in their lives and perceive in it the tiny makings of the catastrophe that thereafter set their lives on a different course?" in "Will You Please Be Quiet, Please?" (*WYPB*, 243).

CHAPTER 2

"Does That Have a Hidden Meaning?"
DIALOGUE

Subterranean Movements

In an amusing simile, Nathalie Sarraute compares dialogues in behaviorist novels to "the heavily circled little clouds that issue from the mouths of the figures in comic supplement drawings."[1] Those writers sensed, Sarraute argues, that the purpose of dialogues in literature is to convey the subterranean movements underlying our existence—the indefinable vibrations, which she considers the hidden source of our life. However, while the behaviorists acknowledge the power of everyday talks and the way they "permit the reader to sense movements underneath them that are more numerous, sharper and more secret than he can discover underneath actions," their methods were wrong.[2] First, Sarraute specifies, the words "he said" or "she said," which intersperse these dialogues, do not allow the reader to experience the flow of subterranean movements, "whose unceasing play constitutes the invisible woof of all human relationships and the very substance of our lives."[3] Secondly, those writers who aspire to re-create a lifelike dialogue use the model of the theatrical dialogue, even though they lack the means to convey nonverbal information. Resorting to the conventions of theatrical dialogue places the novel in a position of inferiority. Instead, she maintains, literature has to shape its own unique dialogue that will make the most of its unique qualities. A writer who succeeded in this task, according to Sarraute, is the English writer Ivy Compton-Burnett. Her dialogues are located "somewhere on the fluctuating frontier that separates conversation from sub-conversation." In the effort to contain sub-conversation—namely the psychic, preverbal subterranean movements stimulated by the contact with another person—and to resist their "constant pressure," "the conversations stiffens, becomes stilted, it adopts a cautious, slackened pace."[4]

In *her* novels, Sarraute found ways to represent the tension between conversation and sub-conversation. However, the methods used by Compton-Burnett and Sarraute to capture the subterranean movements created by "this terrible desire to establish contact" will not be discussed here. I use Sarraute's observations mostly as a frame of reference for an examination of the representation of conversation that she denounces, namely, the dialogue of the behaviorist tradition which Carver continues in many ways.[5]

Which of the elements raised in Sarraute's discussion are worth considering? First, there is the element of movement. For Sarraute, the subterranean movement pertains to her fluid concept of character, a "substance as anonymous as blood, magma without name or contours," which is embodied in invisible, slight vibrations, rather than in discrete actions of the kind the behaviorists describe.[6] In her book *Tropisms* she likens this slight movement to the reaction of plants to light. Subterranean movement is therefore an idiomatic, rich concept, which encapsulates her unique philosophy of life, personality, and relationship. Let me borrow, however, Sarraute's evocative image in a partial, somehow parasitic, manner. I believe that the idea of an underlying movement, especially one that stems from "this terrible desire to establish contact," is also helpful when considering Carver's conversations, even at the expense of slightly veering away from Sarraute's original meaning. By metaphorically extending the approach in the first chapter, this chapter will be devoted to the issues of movement and continuity in a conversation, as manifest in Carver's dialogues.

Another issue raise by Sarraute is the question of the qualities that distinguish—or should distinguish—dialogues in literature in comparison with dialogues in other media. When criticizing behaviorist writing, she compares their lifelike dialogue to the intense dialogue of the theater, loaded with hidden meanings, which in literature seems artificial and mechanical. This observation raises some questions: What is the relationship between these two types of dialogues that literature turns to—theatrical dialogue and the dialogue in "life"? What kind of meanings is each of them imbued with? What is the interaction between the verbal and the nonverbal, the overt and the covert, in each of these two types? And how do they differ from dialogues in literature? Against this theoretical backdrop these questions will be addressed by a reading of a dialogue by Ernest Hemingway—clearly a behaviorist writer and an important influence on Carver, especially on his treatment of dialogue.

"Hills Like White Elephants"

It is no accident that "Hills Like White Elephants" has become a favorite item for editors of anthologies, since in this story Hemingway takes to extreme the qualities that have made him an icon for writers, and the story is a perfect model of his "tip of the iceberg" technique. Confined to the present, the story opens in medias res without informing the reader at any stage about the circumstances of the story. A man and a woman wait for a train in a remote station somewhere in Spain. The hilly landscape reminds the woman of "white elephants." From their conversation, one guesses that the young woman is pregnant with the child of the American man who wants her to have an abortion, and that to please him and to repair their relationship, she will proceed with it.

Typically of Hemingway, the dialogue draws most of its power from what is left unspoken. The words "pregnancy" or "abortion" are never mentioned, the man merely talks of an "operation," and the conversation revolves around "it." This ellipsis, although probable in a conversation between two intimate people who are talking about a sore subject, also achieves a strong literary effect. It is consistent with other omissions more essential to Hemingway's technique: The story avoids any exposition or an overt display of emotions, either as expressed by the characters or explained by the narrator.[7] This is precisely the technique Sarraute describes in her criticism of behaviorist writing where the author locates himself "at a point as remote from himself as from the reader"; where the author lets the events narrate themselves, leaves the reader to himself, and allow characters "to live lives of their own."[8] This technique is driven by the belief that "showing" the situation engendering the emotions is far more effective than their explicit expression. It is needless to say that events narrating themselves or a reader who is "left to himself" and the whole "showing" or mimesis approach—extended here to the realm of hearing—are merely a metaphor, when it comes to a literary world mediated by language. However, the question still stands: how does Hemingway succeed so well in creating the effect of nonverbal material within a media constructed solely of words? How does he formulate the unformulated to achieve this effect on the reader? One way is to approach the issue in question indirectly ("operation" in lieu of "abortion"). The following dialogue is another way by which the unformulated finds expression:

> "And we could have all this," she said. "And we could have everything and every day we make it more impossible."
> "What did you say?"
> "I say we could have everything."
> "We can have everything."
> "No, we can't."
> "We can have the whole world."
> "No, we can't. It isn't ours any more."
> "It's ours."
> "No, it isn't. And once they take it away, you never get it back."
> "But they haven't taken it away."
> "We'll wait and see." (374)[9]

When the young woman talks of "everything" that has been taken away, by way of an *expansion* she refers to the particular loss she is about to experience. Another technique is implied in the name of the story and in her remark of "hills like white elephants":

> "They look like white elephants," she said.
> "I've never seen one," the man drank his beer.
> "No, you wouldn't have."
> "I might have," the man said. "Just because you say I wouldn't have doesn't prove anything." (371)

By referring to the hills, the girl frames the contours of the unsaid by its adjacent presences. Besides the *indirect expression* ("operation") and the *expansion* ("everything"), what takes place here is a *deviation* from the emotional hub of the story, which paradoxically helps to highlight it. Moreover, the dialogue now enters a zone located between the characters and the reader, who is invited to symbolically link the "elephants hills" with the same thing happening in the young girl's body, which she refers to, perhaps unconsciously, despite her lover's denial.

These two typical dialogues illustrate another matter which Sarraute's concept of sub-conversation covers: The conversation encompasses feelings, which though not verbalized, remains present in the conversation through elusive elements such as intensity and tone. These feelings are expressed, for instance, in neutral phrases such as "What did you say?" which reveals the man's distraction and impatience, even as he keeps declaring his love for the girl. They are also present in the repetition of certain words ("No, we can't"), through which the girl's misery—denied by the end of the story ("I feel fine")—strives to express itself. Hemingway's dialogues often look hollow, when in fact this emptying of any information seems to give room to the emotional content of the conversation. Similarly, in Hemingway's "The Killers," it is the aggressive rhythm, rather than the content of the ridiculously void dialogues, that gradually fuels the story's sense of menace and tension.

Hemingway's dialogues support Sarraute's comparison of behaviorist dialogues to theatrical dialogue, which is "denser, tauter, more compact and of higher tension." Lacking an external narrator to supply exposition (as in fiction) or rich visual images (as in cinema), theatrical dialogue is compelled to set up its own context; it "must be self-sufficient," since "everything rests on it."[10] This demand has also been analyzed by Eric Rohmer, in an essay comparing dialogue in the cinema to dialogues in literature and theater. Informed by Aristotle's poetics (through the prism of French classicism), Rohmer tracks a tension in every dialogue, a tension between the "necessary," defined as "everything in the text that is indispensable to the clarity of the intrigue"—and "verisimilitude."[11] In theater, due to its limitations, the demands of the necessary are stronger. Applying this observation to Hemingway, we could say that by giving up the novel's privilege of an external, overt narrator (thus banning the reader from the characters' background and consciousness), he willingly restricts himself to the theater's limitations. He is thus subjected to "the necessary" at the expense of verisimilitude. He therefore must employ the theater's means of compensation: As in a play, Hemingway's dialogue has to create its own context and to find indirect ways of allowing it to unfold. Unlike a play, it has no actor to convey the tone and the emotional layers of conversation and therefore has to use additional words to express it. Amidst all these demands and limitations, the element of verisimilitude in the dialogue dwindles. This is partly because, as Rohmer clarifies, verisimilitude is the element most susceptible to going out of fashion. However, the main reason that verisimilitude wanes is that this dialogue, like the theatrical dialogue and unlike dialogues in life, is committed mostly to "the necessary" and to a hidden context, unknown to the outsider spectator or listener.[12] The feeling that Hemingway's dialogues are imbued with additional meanings stems precisely from this commitment. Hemingway might have "an ear for dialogue," as Carver remarks, "but no one ever talked in real life like they do in Hemingway's fiction. At least not until after they've *read* Hemingway."[13]

As if he had in mind Hemingway's white hills, Larry McCaffery compares watching Carver's characters interact, to "spending an evening with two close friends who you know have had a big fight just before you arrived" when "even the most ordinary gestures and exchanges have transformed meanings, hidden tension, emotional depths."[14] Indeed, the sense of a charged dialogue, conveying unspoken tension and menace and pointing at an underlying void, was attributed both to Carver and Hemingway. Carver acknowledged, on several occasions, Hemingway's influence and saw his "Cat in the Rain"—another story about a failed relationship between a man and a woman—as a model story.[15] The dominance of dialogue, the use of direct discourse, and the repeated "he said" and "she said" are the most noticeable qualities of Carver's stories. In some he devoutly adheres to Hemingway's scenic technique, as for instance in "Signals," where the casual conversation between a couple in a restaurant seethes with undercurrents of hostility and anger. Still, throughout his career, Carver developed his own distinctive mold of dialogue, which is considered innovative. In this chapter I would like to examine Carver's dialogue in view of the questions raised during the discussion of Sarraute and Hemingway: How does the exchange of words convey that subterranean movement stimulated by the contact with another person? How does a conversation build its context, and what is the nature of this context? What is a conversation loaded with? And what distinguishes Carver's dialogue from dialogues in life and in other media?

"Alaska"—Echoing

The "serious talk" in the story by this title never happens, but conversations do take place in Carver's world: talks between family members filled with accusations ("A Serious Talk," "Gazebo," "One More Thing"), talks between strangers at a chance meeting ("Fat," "Viewfinder," "Collectors," "Are You a Doctor?"). There are also parlor talks between friends and acquaintances, where the conversation is the focus of the story ("What We Talk about When We Talk about Love" or "What's In Alaska?"). Naturally, different circumstances breed different kinds of conversation. In Carver, however, they are unexpectedly similar in the way that they represent an overlooked, autistic dialogue, which is transmitted along two separate channels.[16] Paradoxically, talks between strangers show occasional flickers of inexplicable, deep understanding, while talks between couples are often stiff and polite, or the speakers talk past each other. This may lead to the conclusion that a spouse is often a stranger and a stranger might be more understanding than a spouse. However, beyond this painful (somewhat banal) realization, it points to the dynamics of conversation as such. It indicates the dialogue's movement, or oscillation, between the poles of familiarity and strangeness, which are not always dependent on whether the speakers are, in fact, familiar, or unfamiliar, with each other.

The point of departure when analyzing this dynamic will be "What's In Alaska?". It was published in Carver's first, 1976, collection, *Will You Please Be Quiet, Please?* (the title and first story allude to a phrase from "Hills Like White Elephants"). The eccentricity of the conversation in this story is realistically motivated: Helen buys her husband, Carl, a water pipe for smoking marijuana, and they invite a couple of their friends to celebrate the purchase. The story is told from Jack's point of view. Jack and his wife are considering moving to Alaska. The get-together teems with hidden feelings of jealousy and anxiety (it is implied that Mary, Jack's wife, is having an illicit affair with Carl); the story's achievement is not in the indirect way the conversation builds the realistic context, but in its authenticity. Carver succeeds in creating a convincing mimesis of an "out-of-synch" exchange, affected by the drug which causes shorts in thought and speech.[17] However, the effect of the drug (or alcohol in other stories) merely takes to an extreme or emphasizes the dynamics of conversation as such. In that sense, it is similar to the factors of strangeness and familiarity which embody contradicting forces in any conversation.

In "What's In Alaska?" Carver, no doubt, was oblivious of Sarraute's idea of the right way to treat dialogue in fiction. The conversation sounds like a direct transcription of a talk which has been neither filtered nor processed. Boxer and Philips rightly link this quality to the voyeuristic disposition of Carver's first collection, where the narrator stands aloof from the characters, eavesdrops, as it were, on their conversation, and reports it verbatim:[18]

Helen laughed. "I was just thinking about Alaska, and I remember them finding a prehistoric man in a block of ice. Something reminded me."
"That wasn't in Alaska," Carl said.
"Maybe it wasn't, but it reminded me of it," Helen said.
"What about Alaska, you guys?" Carl said.
"There's nothing in Alaska," Jack said.
"He's on a bummer," Mary said.
"What'll you guys do in Alaska?" Carl said.
"There's nothing to do in Alaska," Jack said. (*WICF*, 80)

And later, when Cindy the cat brings a mouse into the house:

"What about the mouse?" Mary said.
"What the hell," Carl said. "Cindy's got to learn to hunt if we're going to Alaska."
"Alaska?" Helen said. "What's all this about Alaska?"
"Don't ask me," Carl said. (81)

An ideal conversation might be likened to an improvisation, where the speakers share a theme, and while elaborating on it, illuminate different aspects of it. This conversation, on the other hand, is more like an echoing, where a fragment of speech is being repeated again and again. Like the water pipe, the word "Alaska" passes between the interlocutors but remains an unopened subject. As other locations referred to in Carver's stories (San Francisco, Portland), Alaska is but an empty label with few characteristics (hunting, ice), while the speech "verges on the incantatory," being devoid of any information.[19] The focus is on the very articulation of the word, not on its content, and it seems that by just sharing the word, the participants also share an imaginative common destiny (suddenly Carl and Helen are also "going to Alaska"). The word's circulation between the speakers creates circles or loops in the exchange of words, in keeping with the situation of a get-together which is also potentially circular (supposing that a dialogue between two people is linear).[20] The conversation, a fraction of which was quoted here, keeps returning to its starting point, while the word itself, crude and trapped in itself, is unable to extend and reach an external referent. Hence the impression of a void in the conversation, which Jack's response to the question "What's in Alaska?" conveys well: "There's nothing in Alaska."

The story abounds with similar loops, where a word or a phrase is scattered between speakers who echo each other, while leaving untouched the real subject of conversation. The following piece of conversation certainly does not inform the reader about "what's funny":

"What's so funny?" he said, grinning. "I could hear you laughing."
"We were laughing at Helen," Mary said.

> "Helen was just laughing," Jack said.
> "She's funny," Carl said. (73)

These loops have simpler versions, when only two speakers echo each other:

> "Did we have coats? I don't think we had coats."
> "What? I don't think we had coats." (83)

Or within the words of one speaker: "No, I only opened one. I think I only opened one. I don't remember opening more than one" (76). The echoing effect reappears in all of Carver's collections (in stories such as "Night School," "Signals," "After the Denim," "Preservation"). A mechanical repetition hampers the progression of talk, while disconnecting the word from its meaning. Much like Hemingway's dialogues, this conversation prevents words from fulfilling their referential task. There is, however, a substantial difference: While Hemingway does not verbalize the unsaid, his dialogues as a whole evoke, by different techniques, past events and emotions. The words work indirectly in reconstructing the fictional context from which the dialogue has been torn. Due to their commitment to this context, Hemingway's dialogues—like theatrical dialogue, subjected to the demands of "the necessary"—are "dense, taut, compact and at higher tension." In Carver's dialogue, on the other hand, when the speakers echo each other, the words lose any connection to their context, and it seems that any time they are repeated, emotions drain from them.

My use here of "context" has the sense Jakobson used in his definition of referential function, namely as external (though fictional) reality.[21] Context, however, may be also understood as textual context, namely the words and sentences which surround the word. In that sense, "Alaska" is situated every time in a different context; but does the change in context breed new meaning, as Carver's titles—torn from a particular context in the text—often do? In fact, here the word works in the opposite direction: It is not the context which grants it meaning. Rather, the word itself, which remains opaque in any context, works on its surroundings. By its repetition, it casts a net, as it were, over the conversation, revealing its inner structure of repetition, circularity, and fragmentation. Through this word the dialogue comes to represent the inner currents that underlie the conversation, rather than its circumstances (love, jealousy, or smoking marijuana), which, unlike the circumstances of Hemingway's story, remain unclear through the end. While the dialogue in "Hills Like White Elephants" is the "tip of the iceberg," suggesting a hidden world of emotions and memories, Carver's dialogues—especially in his conversation stories—are like the recording of a seismograph, measuring the vibrations in the substratum of conversation.[22] The dialogue expresses Carver's deep interest in communication as such. As Arias-Misson observes, his "stories are not simply the texture of talk but *about* talk."[23]

The substratum of conversation brings us back to Sarraute's sub-conversation and its subterranean movement, though in a different sense than Sarraute has given it and in a metaphoric use. Applying movement to dialogue in general, and to Carver's "What's in Alaska?" in particular, might be done on two levels: the first pertains to the dialogue's integration in the movement of the story and the chain of events. Every dialogue is part of the story's sequence of events, and as pure *scene* it even supports their linearity. However, in Carver's dialogues, with their effect of circularity and their obsessive return to the conversation's starting point, the linearity and progression of the story is obscured by the impression of stasis in the conversation. The second level, on which movement applies to conversation, pertains to the dialogue being an external symptom of a potential of the continuity of meaning between speakers. This continuity is dependent on a passage between different stances in the conversation, namely the concepts that each of the speakers has of the subject matter. Bridging these positions establishes contact, and therefore "movement" in the dialogue. The word's etymology suggests this process: the particle "dia" is "what traverses, crosses, circulates (cf. dialysis, diachrony, dialect)."[24]

How can we describe the movement of dialogue in "What's in Alaska?"? Is there any continuum of meaning between speakers who echo each other? What kind of passage transpires here? When a word is mechanically repeated, passed on as is between the speakers, there is no exchange in the exchange of words, and no input from the participants is brought to the verbal encounter. Hence it is impossible to discern different positions in the conversation, between whom the dialogue moves. No continuum, based both on similarity and difference, is created in the dialogue.[25] Words are void and therefore unchanged, no matter who articulates them, and in what context. Regardless of the number of speakers, there are no diverse positions of meaning in the conversation. The unchanged position renders the words senseless: With no balance between the personal and the communal, difference and similarity, words serve no function but to point to the dialogue's monologism and stasis.

"Kids"—Splitting

This is one variation of what Ivone Margulies names "dialogue-qua-monologue."[26] Another variation requires a rereading of "Viewfinder," focusing this time on the dialogue between the photographer and his host. The conversation plays an important part in creating the impression of fragmentation and "fractioning" of the story's movement. Typical of Carver, the dialogue is both probable and out of the ordinary:

> I was trying to think of something to say.
> "Three kids were by here wanting to paint my address on the curb.

They wanted a dollar to do it. You wouldn't know anything about it, would you?"

It was a long shot. But I watched him just the same.

He leaned forward importantly, the cup balanced between his hooks. He set it down on the table.

"I work alone," he said. "Always have, always will. What are you saying?" he said.

"I was trying to make a connection," I said.

I had a headache. I know coffee's no good for it, but sometimes Jell-O helps. I picked up the picture.

"I was in the kitchen," I said. "Usually I'm in the back."

"Happens all the time," he said. "So they just up and left you, right? Now you take me, I work alone. So what do you say? You want the picture?"

"I'll take it," I said.

I stood up and picked up the cups.

"Sure you will," he said. "Me, I keep a room downtown. It's okay. I take a bus out, and after I've worked the neighborhoods, I go to another downtown. You see what I'm saying? Hey, I had kids once. Just like you," he said.

I waited with the cups and watched him struggle up from the sofa.

He said, "They're what gave me this."

I took a good look at those hooks.

"Thanks for the coffee and the use of the toilet. I sympathize."
(*WWTA*, 13–14)

As already noted, many of the gaps in the story were opened up only in its final version, while the earlier version is more coherent. Thus, for instance, the peculiar phrase "happens all the time" (what is happening all the time: that kids leave? That a person is in the back, or in the kitchen?) is clearer in the earlier, fuller version. Leaving aside the question of whose artistic vision these changes reflect—Carver's or Lish's—I would like to restate my view that these changes put to practice, or took to the extreme, the possibilities of the text. They highlight the peculiar nature of the conversation and the relationships between the characters.

In its present state, the conversation produces a double impression. On the one hand, it is autistic by nature, as are other conversations in Carver's stories, and especially in this collection. Even when responding to their interlocutor's questions, it seems that the speakers speak from entirely different worlds, with very little, if anything, in common. The ambiguous expressions "long shot" or "make a connection" allude to this aspect of the conversation. The dialogue lacks any balance between question and answer or a mutual elaboration of a common subject matter. The speakers raise several issues at the same time, and then drop them, the responses lack connection and even the connections in the discourse of one speaker are often tenuous. The connection between sentences, if any, is unclear and seems to refer to a previous personal context unknown to the interlocutor (in phrases like "Now you take me" or "Me, I keep a room downtown"). The impression is of a conversation starting in medias res, based upon a previous context, which the reader is not privy to. It seems the photographer expects to be understood; at the same time he unexpectedly understands his host's condition (in expressions like "hard, hard," "happens all the time," "sure you will," or "it won't work, they are not coming back"). The conversation between strangers is carried out along different channels and indicates a secret alliance between the two. As for the reader, he or she is outside the conversation, and at the same time, the story is told as an anecdote that the narrator shares with someone (in expressions like "you know" or "you see" and in many deictic expressions), thus assuming an inner listener.

This mysterious conversation thus subtly incorporates the stance of the reader—one of both strangeness (deprived of context) and familiarity (with the textual assumption that he is inside)—with the tension of strangeness-familiarity between the characters. Indeed, despite the inexplicable alliance between the two, the strangeness remains. It is manifested in the photographer's use of clichés, not necessarily reflecting true understanding; in the voyeuristic, suspicious stance of the narrator, who is not that impressed at the intuition shown by the chance visitor. All these question the very existence of a connection between the speakers. A similar encounter, with almost identical linguistic qualities, occurs in "Collectors," with a similar doubt as to its nature.

To track the origin of this doubt I will again focus on one substantial word in "Viewfinder"—the word "kids," which makes its first appearance in the narrator's words: "Three kids were by here wanting to paint my address on the curb" (13). It comes again in the photographer's speech: "Hey, I had kids once. Just like you" (ibid.). The third time the "kids" are referred to indirectly: "It won't work, . . . They're not coming back" (14). And on the roof, before the stone throwing scene, they are mentioned yet again:

> It was then I saw them, the rocks. It was like a little rock nest on the screen over the chimney hole. You know kids. You know how they lob them up, thinking to sink one down your chimney. (15)

The "kids" are mentioned then three times explicitly, one time indirectly, and every time the reference is to different kids. However, due the general nature of the reference "kids" and their not being present in the story, these different kids blend into one hostile, invasive, and painful entity. The conversation forms a uniform concept of kids, which bridges the gap between speakers, allowing for identification. The narrator explains his mention of the kids with reference to the photographer by saying: "I was trying to make a connection." He thus implies both his effort to connect the facts and reaching out to his interlocutor. Indeed, the kids are the link between the photographer and himself ("I had kids once. Just like you"), between the narrator and his assumed listener ("you know kids"), and kids help the reader make an analogy between the characters.

At the same time, here too the dialogue reveals its dual nature. On the one hand there is an abstract, uniform image of "kids," which has no presence in the story and merges into a single entity in the reader's mind. For the characters, however, this image splits into several others: the kids who wanted to paint the curb, the photographer's kids, the narrator's kids, the kids who threw rocks into the chimney. This tension between the abstract image and its different manifestations is partly responsible for the puzzlement in the first reading of the story, which I believe is contrived and represents the dialogue's duality. This is a dialogue in which even the point that connects, unites, and allows contact between speakers is, in fact, subject to refraction which threatens to sever the link between them and between the reader and the text. This bewildering impression of a talk about one and several things at the same time is another factor in the polarity of strangeness and familiarity in the encounter. *What We Talk about When We Talk about Love* is the name of the collection in which "Viewfinder" was published. Is it possible to talk of "kids," let alone of "love"? Can any of the speakers reach beyond his own private image of the subject matter, which is part of their "version of reality," or is he entrapped in it?[27] Do the interlocutors share the union imposed on them by language and the reader? Is there any movement in a dialogue whose continuum of meaning is so refracted? While the word "Alaska" passes, void and opaque, between the people who articulate it, "kids" is loaded with so many different meanings that any common ground might be lost. The impression of a dialogue-qua-monologue in "What's In Alaska?" is created by the stasis of the word and how it lingers in one standpoint in all of its appearances (the dialogue is monologic), while in "Viewfinder" this impression stems from the fact that the points of departure in the conversation can be so remote, that the possibility of any contact between the speakers and their perspectives is doubtful (the dialogue is really comprised of two monologues). It is no accident that the encounter culminates with a nonverbal interaction in the curious series of photos, discussed in the previous chapter.

In any conversation or expression in language, the subject matter is both shared *and* refracted in different meanings. Still, Carver succeeds in highlighting the ensuing vacillation of conversation between a void and a charged communication, familiarity and strangeness. These poles assume different manifestations, and they appear in different permutations and combinations. They both allow communication and create miscommunication. Words are simultaneously loaded with meaning and devoid of it. The sense of being charged stems from one unifying meaning and many split meanings. Unity of meaning is both a condition for contact and arrests the movement which enables it. Multiple meanings both allow for a dynamic in the conversation and threaten to disconnect it altogether. A state of strangeness breeds multiple meanings, but so does the state of familiarity. Thus in "Careful," Lloyd's wife, Inez, comes to visit him in his small apartment where he is trying to recover from his alcoholism. She wishes to speak to him, probably about a separation and her new life. This conversation never takes place and instead they have a typical Carverian conversation between husband and wife, both casual and laden with meaning. This conversation, which is carried out while Inez is trying to clean Lloyd's clogged ear with a pin, is doubtless influenced by Hemingway's dialogues and his use of generalization and ambiguous speech:

> "Anyway, we need to try *something*. We'll try this first. If it doesn't work, we'll try something else. That's life, isn't it?"
> "Does that have a hidden meaning or something?" Lloyd said.
> "It means just what I said. But you're free to think as you please. I mean, it's a free country," she said. (*WICF*, 269, Carver's emphasis)

"Does that have a hidden meaning?" is a typical question in a discourse burdened by too much familiarity, where nothing is understood at face value, and words have too many shared meanings.[28] Still, conversations between strangers carry the same burden of hidden, private meanings. With all the differences, these two types of conversations create—to use Sarraute phrasing in a slightly different meaning—a "stiff" dialogue, which "becomes stilted" and "adopts a cautious, slackened pace." What can we learn from the obsessive repetitions in a couple's conversation in "Preservation"? ("We lost our Freon. . . . The Freon leaked out. Something happened and the Freon went." *Cathedral*, 41). Are the repetitions a symptom of words being drained of any personal content, or of their being too full, in a way that does not allow it to proceed? Do they indicate strangeness and two separate monologues, or a single stance that leaves no space for progress in the conversation? The oscillation between fullness and void, familiarity and strangeness is reflected in the dual positioning of the reader, in the place of both the lover and the stranger. As an outsider listening to a lifelike dialogue, namely a dialogue with no context, the reader is both admitted into the circumstances and outside of them, tempted to read a "hidden meaning" in words, and yet suddenly left with only their literal meaning.

The drug-context situation in "What's in Alaska?" sharpens the sudden transformation of the conversation between an overdose of meaning to its total annihilation; between contact and disconnection. The laughter all through the evening (especially Helen's) is a causeless laugh. In the beginning, it seems to express a deep understanding between the participants. However, this understanding disappears or eludes them, as if it was never there ("That's funny.... What's funny?... God, I don't know."). The mental shorts created by the drug underscore the disconnections in any process of communication. They embody the unsteady current of conversation as such, wavering between contact and disconnection, the continuum of meaning and its fragmentation.

"Junk Language"

So, where should we look for "hidden meaning"? Carver lets us accrue phrases like "that's life" or "it's a free country," that is, clichés—"junk language," to use Arias-Misson's expression.[29] This language of "meat and potatoes," as others call it, is the main reason why critics describe Carver's characters as blue-collar people, somehow inarticulate, who lack the ability for introspection and to render their feelings in a rich, idiomatic style. Cliché, however, does more than typify the characters in terms of status or education, and as shown by Fabre-Clark, has diverse and dynamic functions in different stories.[30]

While imposing on its speakers a uniformity of style, cliché both unites them and secludes them, by robbing them of the ability to express their unique experience. Providing a mold in which an individual expression has to be cast, cliché is an extreme embodiment of the externality and uniformity of language as such. Erasing differences and nuances, it ends up by highlighting them and isolates its speakers. In the echoing conversation, language becomes looped because the speakers do not load words with any personal content, and words in their turn have no inner resonance, and are therefore passed on just as they were received. Cliché is another version of this process. However, while the echoing dialogue points at the nature of the contact between the characters (there is no diversity in the stances in the conversation), the use of cliché reveals the characters' struggle with the means of expression, which is not diverse enough to convey their situation. I do not share the view that Carver aims at describing a world or a society that has been pared down by the diminishment of language, and does it by convincingly mimicking the clichés of everyday speech.[31] This presentation implies a parody, which has no trace in the narrator's tone or his vocabulary, which are not so distant from his characters. Nor it is suggested in the approach to characters, which is never condescending or judgmental. Still, Carver's use of clichés hardly reflects a lack of awareness. There is no doubt that they are meant to be presented as such, and often the characters refer to their being clichés. Consider, for instance, the mother who loses her son in "A Small, Good Thing":

> "No, no," she said. "I can't leave him here, no." She heard herself say
> that and thought how unfair it was that the only words that came out

were the sort of words used on TV shows where people were stunned by violent or sudden deaths. (*WICF*, 397)

Or the man who is torn between two women in "Menudo":

> Then it struck me that what we were saying—the tense, watchful expressions we wore—belonged to the people on afternoon TV programs that I'd never done more than switch on and then off. (*WICF*, 456)

The monologue of the ex-wife in "Intimacy" is rife with clichés ("water under the bridge"; "you must have some other arrows in your quiver"; "that's the bone of contention here"). Nonetheless, while the representation of her speech verges on parody, she is well aware of its nature, as indicated in her amusing blend of clichés:

> And so there you have it on a nutshell. My eggs in one basket, she says. A tisket a tasket. All my rotten eggs in one basket. (*WICF*, 449)

Or in her improvisation on platitudes:

> Your heart is a jungle, a dark forest; it's a garbage pail, if you want to know. (ibid.)

> Time is a gentleman, a wise man said. Or else maybe a worn-out old woman, one or the other anyway. (451)

In fact, it is not only the limitations of clichés and their inadequacy in conveying a singular experience that the stories reveal. Sometimes, it is precisely their one-dimensionality and flat generalizations that allow characters to express themselves in situations of crisis, when suddenly clichés become meaningful, personal, and concrete. Such is the case in "Intimacy" ("I thought my heart would break. What am I saying? It did break." [ibid., 448]). Or in the speech of Holly, the wife whose husband cheats on her in "Gazebo" ("You were my everything, just like the song." [ibid., 145]). Other clichés in this story ("Holly was my own true love" or "You're still number one"), uttered by the husband—both broken-hearted *and* thinking of his Mexican lover—are not as convincing. Here the cliché is about to lose its power and become hollow and devoid of meaning again. These swift transformations reveal again the duality in Carver's dialogues and the way they sway between fullness and void, the personal and the shared.

Cliché is thus perceived as invasive, imposing a false union on its speakers, while at other times, it can be felt from the inside, a powerful, accurate means of expressing deep feelings. Either way, it becomes absorbed in its speakers' life and speech. This dominance of cliché begs the question of the text's approach, especially since it avoids parody. Do Carver's stories express an acceptance of clichés—an acknowledgment of their power and the way their use might prompt insight?[32] Moreover, can a text so full of clichés actually escape their influence and is it not in serious danger of becoming cliché-ridden itself? To answer this we should first distinguish between the narrow sense of cliché, namely the truisms and platitudes that characters use, and its broader sense, henceforth my focus: In its broader sense, cliché is part of a general disposition of uniformity, whereby differences are erased and a rigid mold is enforced automatically on a diverse, multiplied existence. On the basis of this distinction, I would like to suggest that while there is no escape from cliché at the level of word choice, Carver's dialogues do resist cliché at the level of representation. To clarify this observation, a digression is needed, back to the dialogue in "What's In Alaska?".

"What?"—Redundancy

For William Stull, Carver's dialogues, more than any other aspect of his writing, reveal his hyperrealism.[33] Indeed, exchanges of words of the sort we find in "What's in Alaska?" are common in "life" conversation, with or without the help of a water pipe filled with marijuana. Unlike the theater of the absurd, Carver is always careful not to violate probability. At the same time, he achieves an effect that Brooke-Rose defines as "the real as unreal," well known to viewers of hyperrealist paintings.[34] This effect consists of challenging the conventions of representing reality by using "reality" itself. This effect is achieved in various means, both simple and sophisticated, as, for instance, by the use of the question "what," which crops up so frequently in "What's in Alaska?". Here is one of its many appearances:

> "What did you read?" Carl said.
> "*What?*" Helen said.
> "You said you read something in the paper," Carl said. (*WICF*, 79–80, my emphasis)

And here's another:

> "Where did you get it?" Mary said.
> "*What?* That little place on Fourth Street, you know," Helen said.
> (*WICF*, 74, my emphasis)

These two appearances of "what" indicate the distraction typical of small talk that later will be intensified by the influence of smoking. Both contribute to the humorous impact of the conversation. In its first appearance, the word has a function, however minor, in the process of communication, since it is directed at an interlocutor and followed by an answer (the same as "What did you say?" in Hemingway). The second time it appears, it has no communicative function and is a result of the discrepancy between speech and thought. Both appearances point to the dynamic of the conversation rather than to its content. In these cases, this consists of dissonance and discrepancies in rhythm—both between speakers and between speech and thought. However, the second appearance of "what?", where it is followed by an immediate answer, is another symptom of the dialogue's adherence to the model of "life" dialogues. It conveys the impression of a transcript of a conversation recorded word for word. More than most literary dialogues, it preserves the traits of oral speech. While Hemingway is indeed a behaviorist writer whose dialogues would be considered by Sarraute as too "true to life," he would not go so far as to include the "what" that one mutters before fully absorbing an interlocutor's question. Carver has gone further, including superfluous elements of conversation: He includes the repeated and accompanying extra words which in oral dialogue are attached to the basic information.

According to information theory, redundancy is a condition for the transmission of information. While redundancy in fact diminishes the volume of information being transmitted, it facilitates its transmission by helping to overcome the noise inherent to any communication, namely all the factors that impede optimal reception.[35] The circumstances of communication in Carver's world are often disturbed by various noises. Consider, for instance, the noisy beginning of "Put Yourself in My Shoes" ("The telephone rang while he was running the vacuum cleaner" [*WICF*, 94]). The noise of the vacuum cleaner, even after it stops, seems to dictate the conversation between Meyers and his wife—a chain of miscommunications. These noises are all part of the fictional world. The communication between reader and text, however, is rooted in different conditions and entails different noises. Readers compensate for the noise surrounding their reading by rereading or by adjusting their rhythm of reading. Therefore, when a textual dialogue includes redundancy, without the noise it is meant to overcome, the effect is entirely different from an oral conversation: The superfluous elements are now redundant both in terms of the information and the inefficiency of its transmittal. We may even say that there is an inverse proportion between the communication *in* the text and the communication *with* the text. Indeed, the quantity is a crucial factor here: A certain amount of redundancy is necessary for the dialogue to sound realistic. However, when redundancy exceeds certain limits (which continually change, according to the conventions of the day), the noise-resistant redundancy in turn creates a new (metaphorical) noise. The excess of irrelevant elements distracts the reader from focusing his full attention on the overall impression of the story. Though "relevancy" or "function" of elements in the story is elusive and relative, there is no doubt that redundancy affects the coherency of the text. Much like actual noise, which prevents a listener from following a tune or a musical theme, redundancy makes the reader work harder in tackling the subject matter of conversations or themes and plots in a story.[36] According to Stirling Haig,[37] the lifelike, pseudo-oral literary dialogue burdens the reader in this way whenever it breaks the equilibrium between the demands of style and realism. The reader is then required to make an extra effort to decipher it, which would not have been required had he or she been present at the conversation, sharing its conditions and context.

Conveying dialogue "as is," including repetitions, silences, and phatic expressions, has been the trend in art and literature, challenging the conventions of representation and/or of signification. This has been expressed in the theater of the absurd, the *nouveau roman,* and the avant-garde cinema of Jean-Luc Godard and Jacques Rivette. As Rohmer rightly observes, avant-garde experiments bred "unreadable" dialogue and "unbearable" realism.[38] This came about both because "the real has killed the true-to-life" (as Rohmer said), and because it is difficult to follow a unifying line due to the plethora of details or the problem of distinguishing the hierarchy and importance of different kinds of information. Sometimes this effect of "noisy" redundancy pertains to a conscious use of the conventions of one media in the context of another. Thus, the minimalist movie-maker, Chantal Akerman, included information in her cinematic dialogues which is usually the preserve of theatrical dialogues, and which in cinema—with its visual images and technology—is superfluous.[39] The placing of these dialogues out of context results in a defamiliarization of both media and encourages their reflexive examination by the viewers or the readers.

Carver never reaches the unreadability of the *nouveau roman* or radically challenges conventions of representation. He consciously avoids a precise transcription of the way people talk lest the readers would just "snore away,"[40] yet his dialogues still create "noise" and defamiliarization. While in Akerman and Hemingway, defamiliarization is created due to decontextualization and the use of another media's conventions (that of the theater—in the context of cinema and literature correspondingly), Carver decontextualizes "life" dialogue.[41] Interpolating, as it were, lifelike dialogues within the context of fiction, he defamiliarizes both the conversation and its representation. It is not the realistic context that this dialogue reconstructs, as in Hemingway, but the literary one, even as it foreshadows the artificiality of the dialogue and reduces its transparency. By seemingly avoiding censorship, it reveals the selection that all literature in fact makes. The defamiliarization of literature is especially noticeable in dialogues, since, unlike other elements of the narrative, direct discourse seems to undergo no construction to be assimilated into the narrative's verbal representation of reality; yet, as Genette rightly observes, it is precisely direct discourse that might send the reader back to the text which quotes it, rather than to reality, when its over-accuracy breaks the convention of representation. For Genette this breaks "the contract of literalness" implied in direct discourse, whereby it is granted the status of true to life.[42] The often mechanical, sometime lifeless nature of Carver's dialogues are therefore not evidence of his failure to render convincing dialogue (as Sarraute might have said), but a conscious effect of its decontextualization. In addition to these meta-literary qualities, Carver's dialogues reflect the "actual" experience of his characters, their relationships, and the nature of conversation as such, which, as much as it is a means of communication, might also be read as evidence of its failure.[43]

In a subtle and disarming way, Carver's dialogue thus undermines the conventions of representation. By his seeming avoidance of selection, and his excessive use of words that merely "pad" discourse, his dialogues sabotage the reader's automatic process of digesting the text by absorbing the necessary while ignoring the waste of redundancy. He thus cracks the natural impression that representation achieves by concealing its work of selection and establishing hierarchies.

On several occasions, Gilles Deleuze points at the link between the principle of selection and cliché.[44] Cliché, he suggests, is based on omission of details, on a partial vision and a reduced image. The etymology of the word "cliché," originally referring to a hollow printing block, contains this aspect in its operation. One of the ways artists deal with a cliché-swamped world and resist the uniformity of this "rubber stamp" is to introduce "everything" in their representations. They thus recover the "lost parts" of the image and its literal fullness, redeeming them from the abstraction they underwent to comply with certain needs (ideological, economical, or psychological). Deleuze compares this method to experiments done in modern music, in works which resist selection and challenge the distinction between sound and noise.[45] Deleuze's theory will be fully explored in the fifth chapter. The main point I would like to stress at this juncture are the two opposite directions Deleuze indicates. There is "representation," including clichés that tend to reduce, make abstract, and erase differences in its object, in the service of some function. And then there is "expression," which "drills holes" in clichés by giving room to what is redundant, heterogeneous, literal, and serves no function.

Interestingly enough, Carver's dialogues pull in both directions, each work on a different dimension of his writing: The language of the characters teems with clichés. However, the dialogue's very representation, with its redundancy and the way it strays from any unifying theme, goes against the functional-reductive-unifying grain of cliché. This duality in Carver's cliché-ridden conversations is another version of the tension between lack and fullness that is manifested on the level of the dialogue's representation.

Clichés, like an echoing conversation, cause the dialogue to collapse. Failing to express themselves in homogenous molds, the characters lapse into total silence (thus in "Preservation," "Gazebo," "What We Talk about When We Talk about Love" and in "Vitamins"). However, does the reading experience, with its challenge of cliché via redundancy, compensate for this disconnection through its communication with the reader? Does the excess in the dialogue and the ensuing distraction actually result in miscommunication? Instead of answering this, we might as well point to the doubt that any attempt at characterizing Carver's dialogue reveals: Whenever this conversation suggests a contact or a movement through a conduit that might connect its speakers, it flickers unsteadily, remaining fragile and uncertain.

Conclusion

"I pay a lot of attention to trying to make the people talk the right way," Carver stated in an interview. "By this I don't mean just *what* they say, but *how* they say it, and *why*. There's never any chit-chat in my stories. Everything said is for a reason, and adds, I want to think, to the overall impression of the story."[46] Carver mentions "reason," and in this context the term seems to encompass both "reason" and "purpose"—both the realistic motivation for, or the psychological source of, a particular exchange of words and the artistic motivation, namely its contribution to the story's "overall impression." Either way, at first glance, these dialogues indicate no reason or motivation: They barely advance the plot, they have little of "the necessary," and one wonders whether the flat, overused words have anything to do with their speakers' real feelings. "The trivial speech rhythms exhaust the inner throat; their diction injures the inner ear like TV's spiel," says Arias-Misson in his insightful essay on Carver's "absent talkers." "Ellipsis contracts 'the speech muscles.' . . . The unsaid makes a vacuum in the middle of language into which the meaning of the talkers' existence is sucked." And the "characters are the pronouns and the proper names given existence by the verb 'said.'"[47]

Nevertheless, the dialogue in Carver's stories *does* have a reason, a source and a purpose. It fulfills a phatic function for the characters,[48] and its reason, or source, is "this terrible desire to establish contact." For the reader, its purpose is to illustrate the process of communication itself. This, more than any external reality, is the conversation's real subject. Regardless of its content, this dialogue mainly points at the way words cross over or pass between speakers—oscillating between sameness and difference, familiarity and strangeness, fullness and void. The fragility of this passage, the uncertain contact, the disconnections in communication are another version—at the level of meaning—of the "fractioned" continuity described in the previous chapter. The common phrases "he said" or "she said," which according to Sarraute staunch the flow of subterranean movements, help in emphasizing this discontinuation.

The struggle to communicate is reenacted within the process of reading, though not in direct proportion. The reader is more than an outsider listening to a failed dialogue. The difference between actual communication and the process of reading breeds new miscommunications and sophistically involves the reader. The decontextualization of a lifelike dialogue and its placement within a literary context shut out the reader from the context that the speakers share, and the redundancy aimed at overcoming noise is now experienced as—noise. The more the dialogue becomes true to life, the more its being an artifice is revealed and its transparency diminishes. The reader is thus brought up against an opaque text, which is self-referential, and defamiliarizes the representation of dialogue, as well as the very process of communication.

The continuum of meaning between reader and text—its vacillation between sameness and difference, redundancy and lack, realism and literariness—will be discussed further in the third part of this study, where I will again address the cliché and its interaction with all sorts of redundancy.

The force of cliché compels Carver's speakers to "extrude interiority into the shell of stereotype,"[49] as Arias-Misson puts it. The tension between inside and outside, suggested by this intriguing observation, underlies the next part of this study. Chapter 3 will be devoted to the one who is in charge of quoting the dialogues discussed here—the narrator.

Notes

1. In Nathalie Sarraute's essay "Conversation and Sub-Conversation," in *Tropisms and the Age of Suspicion*, trans. Maria Jolas (London: John Calder, 1963), 118.

2. Ibid., 113.

3. Sarraute, "From Dostoyevsky to Kafka," in *The Age of Suspicion*, 60.

4. Sarraute, "Conversation and Sub-Conversation," 119.

5. Katherine Mansfield's expression as quoted by Sarraute in "From Dostoyevsky to Kafka," 71.

6. Sarraute, "The Age of Suspicion," in *The Age of Suspicion*, 94.

7. On Hemingway's omissions in this story and others as an influence on Carver, see Arthur F. Bethea, "Raymond Carver's Inheritance from Ernest Hemingway's Literary Technique," *Hemingway Review* 26:2 (2007): 89–104.

8. Sarraute, "Conversation and Sub-Conversation," 112–13.

9. *The Short Stories of Ernest Hemingway* (New York: The Modern Library, 1938), 371–76.

10. Sarraute, "Conversation and Sub-Conversation," 114.

11. Eric Rohmer, "Film and the Three Levels of Discourse: Indirect, Direct and Hyperdirect," in *The Test for Beauty*, trans. Carol Volk (Cambridge: Cambridge University Press, 1989), 85.

12. See a useful analysis of the traits of literary dialogue versus dialogues in life, in Stirling Haig, *Flaubert and the Gift of Speech: Dialogue and Discourse in Four "Modern" Novels* (Cambridge: Cambridge University Press, 1986), 1–2. Among the traits of oral dialogue Haig mentions are redundancy, circularity, and repetitions, which also characterize the Carverian dialogue.

13. Gentry and Stull, 113, Carver's emphasis. See also page 208.

14. Ibid., 98.

15. Ibid., 17, 46.

16. Carver illustrates this quality in a manual gesture of two fingers missing each other, in Gentry and Stull, 208.

17. See David Boxer and Cassandra Phillips, "'Will You Please Be Quiet, Please?': Voyeurism, Dissociation, and the Art of Raymond Carver," *The Iowa Review* 10:1 (1979): 81.

18. Ibid., 80–81.

17. Arias-Misson's phrasing (on page 626).

19. On Carver's "wonderful loopiness" see Geoffrey Wolf's testimony in Halpert, 125.

20. On Carver's repetitious and circular dialogue see Chénetier, "Living On/Off," 174.

21. Roman Jakobson, "Linguistics and Poetics," in *Language in Literature*, ed. Krystyna Pomorska and Stephen Rudy (Cambridge, MA: Belknap Press, 1987), 64.

22. Compare to Sarraute's comparison of Dostoyevsky's typical dialogue to the way a needle of a galvanometer "gives amplified tracings of the minutest variations of a current," in "From Dostoyevsky to Kafka," 69.

23. Arias-Misson, 627.

24. Haig, 20.

25. According to Deleuze, following Bergson, movement depends on the tension between difference and sameness, unity and diversity. See Gilles Deleuze, *Bergsonism*, trans. Hugh Tomlinson and Barbara Habberjam (New York: Zone Books, 1991). On the polarity of sameness and difference as what lies beneath conversations and relationships in general (as manifested in the oeuvre of Nathalie Sarraute), see Ann Jefferson, *Nathalie Sarraute, Fiction and Theory: Questions of Difference* (Cambridge: Cambridge University Press, 2000).

26. Ivone Margulies, *Nothing Happens: Chantal Akerman's Hyperrealist Everyday* (Durham: Duke University Press, 1996), 53.

27. This is Jefferson's expression (on page 9), following Lyotard.

28. In this context, a very intriguing discussion is offered by Bramlett and Raab in their study of Carver's conversation, especially in "Intimacy." They use methods from discourse and conversation analysis to show, among other things, how the current conversation (*little-c*, in James Paul Gee's terms) is connected to, and echoes, the ongoing conversation that intimates continue throughout their shared history (*big-c*). They also show that the conversation—and the fluctuations in the intimacy between the speakers—interacts with the intimacy that the narrator gradually builds with the reader. See Frank Bramlett and David Raabe, "Redefining Intimacy: Carver and Conversation," *Narrative* 12:2 (2004): 178–94.

29. Arias-Misson, 626. On Carver's clichés see also Mullen, 110–11.

30. In her meticulous reading of Carver's last stories. See Claire Fabre-Clark, "The Poetics of the Banal in *Elephant and Other Stories*," in *New Paths to Raymond Carver: Critical Essays on His Life, Fiction and Poetry*, ed. Sandra Lee Kleppe and Robert Miltner (Columbia: University of South Carolina Press, 2008), 173–86.

31. This view is expressed in Barbara Henning, "Minimalism and the American Dream: 'Shiloh' by Bobbie Ann Mason and 'Preservation' by Raymond Carver," *Modern Fiction Studies* 35:3 (1989): 689–97.

32. As suggested by John Alton in his 1968 interview with Carver. See Gentry and Stull, 166.

33. Stull, "Beyond Hopelessville," 5.

34. Brooke-Rose, 291–310, with reference to Robbe-Grillet's fiction.

35. Deleuze describes the interaction between information-redundancy-noise in communication theories and suggests his own model in *Negotiations: 1972–1990*, trans. Martin Joughin (New York: Columbia University Press, 1990), 41.

36. On the noise in verbal communication versus "noise" in a literary system, see Jurij Lotman, *The Structure of the Artistic Text*, trans. Gail Lenhoff and Ronald Vroom (Ann Arbor, MI: University of Michigan Press, 1977), 75–77.

37. Haig, 1–2, 172.

38. Bal, *Narratology*, 106; Rohmer, 86.

39. Margulies, 55.

40. Gentry and Stull, 113.

41. Norman Friedman uses Hemingway's "Hills Like White Elephants" as an example of the "dramatic mode," (rather than "the camera" mode), thus suggesting his closeness to the theater. See Norman Friedman, "Point of View in Fiction," *PMLA* 70 (1955): 1178.

42. Genette, *Narrative Discourse Revisited*, trans. Jane E. Lewin (Ithaca: Cornell University Press, 1988), 57. See also in *Narrative Discourse*, 184–85.

43. As suggested by Flaubert, according to Haig, 172.

44. The following summary of Deleuze's theory is based mostly on Gilles Deleuze, *Cinema 2: The Time-Image*, trans. Hugh Tomlinson and Robert Galeta (Minneapolis: University of Minnesota Press, 1989), 21–22. See also Deleuze, *Negotiations*, 42–43. On Deleuze's concept of "expression" that avoids cliché, see André Pierre Colombat, "Deleuze and Signs," in *Deleuze and Literature*, ed. Ian Buchanan and John Marks (Edinburgh: Edinburgh University Press, 2000), 14–33.

45. On cliché as a way to avoid cognitive "noise," see Roland Shusterman, "Realism, Knowledge and the Cliché," in *Le Cliché: textes réunis par Gilles Mathis* (Toulouse: Presses Universitaires du Mirail, 1998), 152.

46. Gentry and Stull, 113.

47. Arias-Misson, 625–26. The title of his essay "Absent Talkers" seems to gesture toward Derrida's idea that any utterance whatsoever is a quotation of cultural clichés whose talkers are absent. This is indeed the spirit of Arias-Misson's essay.

48. Chénetier demonstrates "the absurdly extreme ingrowths of phatic conversation," in "Living On/Off," 175–76.

49. Arias-Misson, 626.

Part II
THE EYE OF THE CAMERA

CHAPTER 3

"Whoever Was Using This Bed"
VOICE

> I cannot conceive the necessity for God to love me, when I feel so clearly that even with human beings affection for me can only be a mistake. But I can easily imagine that he loves that perspective of creation which can only be seen from the point where I am. But I act as a screen. I must withdraw that he may see it. (Simone Weil, *Gravity and Grace*[1])

"Intimacy"—Distance and Closeness

More than any of Carver's stories, "Intimacy" yielded responses that may be seen as invasive or verging on the sensational. The striking resemblance between the characters of the writer and his ex-wife, who meet after many years, and Carver and *his* first wife, Maryann, have naturally given rise to all sorts of speculations and guesses. Sam Halpert, who edited Carver's oral biography, based on the testimonies of friends and family members, kept pressing his interviewees about "Intimacy," especially Maryann Carver. When it comes to this story, it seems that the two sides are battling over its status: Carver's friends try to deny any connection between the story and reality, whereas Halpert insists on finding clues to Carver's life in it.[2]

Years of literary criticism dominated by the New Criticism and structuralism no doubt have gone a long way toward lessening the importance we ascribe to the "truth" in the story or its link to the writer's own biography. Still, even if we prefer not to see this as an autobiographical story, which renders facts and events that have actually happened, this story embodies the position of the Carverian narrator with regard to his characters. In that sense, "Intimacy" tells Carver's story as a narrator and—perhaps more implicitly—as an author. This story is therefore a good starting point to discuss Carver's narrators, the nature of their connection to the characters, and the way his typical narrative voice echoes the characters' experience.

Told in the first person, "Intimacy" is about a husband who surprises his ex-wife with a visit after years of separation. Without delay, the wife directs accusations at him for the way he treated her while they were married and afterwards: not only that he cheated on her and hurt her in every possible way, but that he even revealed intimate details of their marriage in his stories, making her a laughing stock. The writer-narrator keeps silent all through the meeting, submissively accepting his wife's charges. Suddenly he kneels. This immediately cuts off the stream of blame. Bewildered at this unexpected gesture and eager to put an end to the uncomfortable situation, the wife promises her ex-husband that she forgives him, and everything is over and done with. The narrator remains silent, on his knees. In the ironic twist to the story, the wife understands that her husband asks for her forgiveness not only for using their life in his stories, but also for the use he will make of this very meeting in his future writing.

"Intimacy" has a special character. It is a scenic story, with a monologic dialogue. This is not a device in which the interlocutor's speech is omitted (as in Camus's "The Fall"). In "Intimacy" the narrator keeps silent most of the time, and when he responds, it is with phatic expressions such as "right as rain," "I'm all ears," or simply "I'm listening." This one-way conversation perhaps indicates the nature of their relationship or the personality of the husband, who, as his wife observes, will do anything "to avoid a fuss" (*WICF*, 446). His choice in keeping silent, in diminishing his presence and being entrenched in his passivity, seems to be reflected in the narration as well, and in the representation of the wife's discourse. While at the start of the meeting her speech is conveyed in indirect discourse ("She says I've caused her anguish, made her feel exposed and humiliated" or "She says, she wished I'd forget about the hard times . . ." [445]), soon enough the narrator ceases to synthesize her voice in his, and the story slides into free indirect discourse ("She's bored with it. Sick of hearing about it") and eventually into direct discourse ("Your private hobby horse, she says.").[3] Henceforth, the wife's speech is rendered verbatim, with quotes which invariably start with "she says."

For Nathalie Sarraute, phrases like "he said" or "she said" are one of the main obstacles of the behaviorists' representation of speech. She considers them a disturbance in the natural flow of feelings that keep the "novelist" away from his characters. In her view, the impression that a narrator allows characters to "live lives of their own" is simply a deception, while in fact, "he is keeping a firm hold on the reins."[4] Sarraute's diagnosis is particularly apt for the dialogue-monologue in "Intimacy"—although, unlike her examples, this is a first-person narrative. Though the husband assumes a passive "hands-off" approach, he is not as uninvolved as it might seem, in terms of his narratorial stance. The "she says" phrases keep barging into the ex-wife's monologue, in an arbitrary and inexplicable way. The very need for so many "she says" is dubious, let alone in a dialogue where only one speaker talks. The frequency of these reporting verbs is also striking: at the start and conclusion of every paragraph, and in short intervals. In addition, the layout of the story seems to underscore this arbitrariness with its one-sentence paragraphs. Why, for instance, do sentences like "she says, 'sometime I could scream'," or "she says, 'are you listening to me?'" deserve their own paragraphs? In this way, the constant interruption of the character's speech becomes so abrupt and out of place that we cannot see it merely as a necessary evil in narratorial mediation. Rather, the interruptions seem to be the way that the narrator insists, however awkwardly, on reminding the reader of his presence. Giving up some of his authority in his use of direct discourse, he seems to regain it through these reporting verbs and through the rhythm and layout of the text. The narrator's silence, both in the text and in the story's events, cannot conceal his "keeping a firm hold on the reins." In a sense, the frequency of reporting verbs, their monotony, and their arbitrariness create a similar effect to that of free indirect discourse: They distance the reader from the speaker and muffle her voice. This occurs precisely in the kind of narration that supposedly gives her room for expression by "introducing" discourse which is not "governed" by the narrator's voice.[5] Borrowing from the discourse of the visual arts, we may say that the reporting verbs provide a frame to the character's speech, and here this frame, like the frames in photography (and the style of painting that foreshadows it), creates the impression of an arbitrary cut, which paradoxically draws the viewer's attention to the very existence of a frame (a device that will be further discussed in the fifth chapter).[6]

This "passive-aggressive" stance of the narrator, shown in the level of speech representation, determines the nature of the meeting. The silence of the husband spurs the wife to keep up the flow of talk that will constitute the story ("When I don't answer, when I just keep sitting there, she goes on." [448]); the silent gesture when the husband kneels eventually grants him the freedom of narration ("You just tell it like you have to." [452]). Even his forgetting an incident when his wife once pulled a knife on him extracts this memory from her. In fact, the story suggests that the ex-husband recalls many things, but he chooses not to reveal his own memories which are painfully different from those of his wife (as are other husbands' memories in Carver's stories). Remaining silent, "forgetting," and stimulating his ex-wife's memories, are then a tactic of sorts, which serves this writer's hunt for "material."[7] The use of the word "tactic," however, should not lead to the conclusion that the husband-narrator is a cold manipulator who toys with his wife's feelings, or an observer with no emotional involvement in what is taking place. The emotions he expresses ("I laugh too, but it's nerves,"

[446] or "I might break into tears even" [452]) seem authentic, and so is the act of kneeling which is far from contrived. Possibly, there is some irony in the title of the story (assuming that it is the narrator's) or in his comment when the assault begins ("Make no mistake, I feel at home" [444]); yet this irony does not gnaw at real feelings.

As much as the narrator is both active and passive, both recalling and forgetting, his attitude toward the scene is ambiguous. It entails both detachment and involvement, distance and closeness. When the gush of accusations subsides, and the wife gives her ex-husband permission to tell all, she comes very near him: "She moves closer. She's about three inches from my face. We haven't been this close in a long time. I take these little breaths that she can't hear and I wait. I think my heart slows way down, I think" (452). This intense focus on the details of physical closeness is noticeable here as in other Carver stories. It is as if he is trying to create a literary equivalent of the theatrical mise-en-scène by drawing the reader's attention to the positioning of the characters and the way they face each other within the interior space (e.g., in "Careful," "Whoever Was Using This Bed," and in "Menudo"). The indication of closeness is especially interesting in a story, which despite its name, "Intimacy," embodies such ambiguity in the feelings of the narrator, who is both close to, and distant from, the other character, as well as to and from himself and his past.

The location of the narrator in relation to the character is a central issue which calls for examination beyond the special circumstances of this story, and in the way this touches upon other narrators and characters in Carver's stories.

Neutral Narrator—Dissociated Character

Passive both in the story and its narration, the first-person narrator conceals his knowledge, emotions, or memories; he lets the other character take the lead, even as he manipulates her behavior and the reader's response, yet betrays his own vulnerability and involvement. This description of the narrator in "Intimacy" also applies to other earlier Carver narrators. The narrators of "Viewfinder" and "Collectors" allow an occasional visitor to enter their territory, manipulate the other person with their passivity, and observe his behavior in a mix of curiosity and indifference. The host in "Viewfinder" explains why he has invited the photographer to his house with "I wanted to see how he would hold a cup" (*WWTA*, 11), while the host in "Collectors" just "sits there" and watches as his visitor shows him how a vacuum cleaner works, accompanied by philosophical comments. Still, the passivity and detachment cannot conceal the way these narrators are moved by their encounter with a stranger. This is also applicable to characters who lend their point of view to stories without being the actual narrators. Thus, "What's in Alaska?" and "Put Yourself in My Shoes" portray characters of men who, from a passive and uninvolved position, watch the scenes of the story with a sidelong glance, as if at a play they are both detached from and connected to.

In their essay "'Will You Please Be Quiet, Please?': Voyeurism, Dissociation, and the Art of Raymond Carver," Boxer and Phillips suggest an overall framework to understand the features of these narrators, while sketching a convincing profile of the characters in Carver's first collection.[8] According to Boxer and Phillips, this character is typically in an "in-between" state (between jobs, apartments, or stories). This vulnerable state, a kind of emotional limbo, allows the character access to the twilight zone between self and other—a voyeuristic glimpse into another person's life that is also one's own life. Then, the delusively peaceful surfaces of life break open, and the characters, who by now have become a sort of "other" to themselves, experience a painful awakening, which forces them to face the angst underlying their existence. The glimpse into another person's life, which involves a detachment from oneself, is reflected in the quality of the story and the interaction between the narrator and the reader. The detached, uninvolved tone of the narrator allows the reader to take part in the voyeuristic act. Boxer and Phillips link the covertness of the narrator to his standing alongside the reader and "peering into the disturbed lives of these unsuspecting characters" (80). For them, his passivity is that of the eavesdropping voyeur.

> Carver's characteristic short stabs of language convey panic, and the sort of detail of action that might be reported by an eyewitness. (77)
>
> Passivity is the strength of this language; little seems to be said, yet much is conveyed. If Carver's *eye* is that of the voyeur, his *voice* is that of dissociation. . . .
>
> Carver is the writer as voyeur, a chronicler of overheard conversations and secretly witnessed actions. (81, my emphases)

These quotes show how the states of voyeurism and dissociation—symbolized by the images of a window and a mirror—are correspondingly divided, on the narrative level, into Carver's "eye" and "voice." Still, since we're dealing with different aspects of one state of mind, it is not always a clear-cut division. The boundaries between narrator, character, reader, eye, and voice blur; together they form the mixture that this intriguing essay describes.

In the collection that Boxer and Phillips review, most of the stories are in the third person (the narrator is *extradiegetic-heterodiegetic* in narratological terms), yet, this fact is not as crucial as it may seem, since this narrator embodies, despite remaining external to the story's events, the same state of mind that the characters and the first-person narrators find themselves caught in—that of dissociation and otherness. In fact, this leads to an interesting paradox or reversal: The third-person stories embody, in their narration, the character's state of mind, and could have been narrated by the character, whereas the first-person stories undermine their own logic; they illustrate the same problem that Dorrit Cohn diagnoses in Kafka's early version of *The Castle*, and Gérard Genette addresses in his categorization of narrators—the improbability of an objective-neutral first-person narrator.[9] This narrator, who betrays no emotion in his narration, who refrains from judgment and who reveals no hindsight, is a kind of third-person narrator with regard to himself. This aptly describes some of Carver's character-narrators who attribute no emotional motivation to their actions or any after-the-fact reflection, as one might expect of first-person narrators. Why does the host in "Viewfinder" stand on the roof throwing rocks? Why does the ex-husband in "Intimacy" touch his ex-wife's sleeve and kneel? Why does the narrator in "Boxes" cover his face with his hands in front of his girlfriend and his mother? These actions are all probable within the context of the story, and they have a reason, yet the action seems dissociated from the context and the reason, and often the characters themselves wonder about them ("What am I doing on the floor? I wish I could say" ["Intimacy," *WICF*, 450]). Even such a simple action as laughing (in "Elephant") is presented as detached from its performer ("as if I read somewhere how to laugh" [*WICF*, 487]). In his *Cinema 1*, Deleuze describes a similar situation in postwar American cinema, where the characters experience their actions as someone else's and wonder at their meaning. For Deleuze, this is a symptom of the collapse of a "sensory-motor scheme," where the links between action and response are disconnected.[10] This situation, and its applicability to Carver's world and characters, will be further explored in the fifth chapter. As for the state of wondering or astonishment, it is often referred to in critical writing about Carver, both in reference to the man himself and to his fictional characters (especially in the early stories), who are described as acting unconsciously, without being aware of, or fully understanding, their feelings.[11]

As for narratorial choices, the tendency of Carver's narrators to give little information (*paralipsis*, in Genette's terminology) is psychologically motivated.[12] Thus, we could point to first-person narrators, who do not reveal the meaning of their actions, and to third-person narrators, who are dissociated from the characters (by remaining outside their consciousness) and from themselves (by avoiding judgment and revealing no emotion). Both types reflect the same state of mind, that of characters who are dissociated—or other—to themselves. Paradoxically, it is precisely the detachment of the third-person narrator from the emotions of the characters, his way in keeping away from them that brings him closer to the character whose experience of otherness he reconstructs in the process of narration.

Unlike Nathalie Sarraute, narratology sees the modus of "showing"—for example, the narratorial position whereby the narrator clings to the time, space, and point of view of the character, and avoids judgment and irony—as one of "closeness" to characters.[13] In Carver's case, this closeness is amplified by the similarity and interaction between experience and narration. Regardless, however, of the different meanings one can assign to "closeness" or "distance" in the context of narration, this discussion brings us back to "Intimacy." This story introduces a first-person narrator, whose distance from, and closeness to, the character is concrete, whereas a third-person narrator is only metaphorically close to, or remote from, his characters. Yet, though the ambivalent position of the narrator in "Intimacy" is rooted in this story's special circumstances, it still characterizes the unique voice of Carver's narrators in general. This voice, like the characters in their fragile state of crisis, is poised on the cusp between self and other. It is a silent voice, present in its very absence, both personal and impersonal, close to the characters and remote from them. These oxymorons, though pointing to the uniqueness of Carver's voice, can, at the same time be taken and expanded beyond it, because Carver brings to the fore tensions that lurk in the "neutral-objective" position as such. This position, which has been attributed to Robbe-Grillet, and to some extent to Hemingway and Camus, becomes concrete in his stories, and enmeshed in the experience of the characters. Furthermore, the type of neutral narration, *l'écriture blanche* as Barthes calls this brand of writing, has often been compared to the eye of the camera.[14] Insights that illuminate the art of photography might, therefore, be used to shed light on the literary "photographic voice" as well.

"His Side, Her Side," and the "Unoccupied Perspective"

In the course of Carver's career, the dominance of the neutral voice seems to diminish, possibly due to changes in his personal and creative life. However, the presence of this voice is strongly felt in the first two collections, culminating in *What We Talk about When We Talk about Love*. The opening of "Why Don't You Dance?", which appears in this collection, elucidates the nature of the neutral voice as well as its connection to the characters' experience, which goes even deeper than Boxer and Phillips have suggested.

"Why Don't You Dance?"—a story about a man who puts out in the open the entire contents of his house, and his encounter with a young couple who want to buy some of his furniture—is typical of Carver for several reasons. As in other stories from this collection, characters mutually reflect one another, while the story juxtaposes the "before" and "after" states.[15] A sense of "make believe" is created in the story and explicitly referred to: The furniture stands outside exactly as it was set in the house, and the young couple occupies the domestic setting as if they were living in the house. Indeed, Carver often depicts, or refers to, a state that resembles ordinary life, but for the slightest shift that makes it "as if" life. With this in mind, Larry McCaffery likens the experience of reading Carver to that of standing in a model kitchen at Sears, "where you experience a weird feeling of disjunction that comes from being in a place where things *appear* to be real and familiar, but where a closer look shows that the turkey is papier mâché, the broccoli is rubber, and the frilly curtains cover a blank wall."[16] The realization that things are not as they appear, which has been attributed to photography and hyperrealist painting and connected to their horrifying, rigor-mortis quality, partly explains their frequent comparison with Carver's writing. In "Why Don't You Dance?" this feeling strikes the reader right from the start:

> In the kitchen, he poured another drink and looked at the bedroom suite in his front yard. The mattress was stripped and the candy-striped sheets lay beside two pillows on the chiffonier. Except for that, things looked much the way they had in the bedroom—nightstand and reading lamp on his side of the bed, nightstand and reading lamp on her side.
> His side, her side.
> He considered this as he sipped the whiskey. (*WICF*, 155–56)

The feeling of "as-if-life" or "almost-life" is supported by the phrase "except for that," which points at the small difference (the sheets lay beside the bed rather than on it) in the otherwise perfect domestic setting. It shifts the reader's attention from the more substantial change: the placement of the bedroom outside the house instead of inside it. This sort of understatement is also evident in terms of word choice. Though Carver was rightly described as a writer "who never tried to achieve a beautiful line,"[17] an alliteration steals into this opening and connects the words "stripped" and "striped." The slight difference in spelling and pronunciation illustrates, by means of litotes, the unbridgeable chasm between the colorful, innocent state of "before" and the state "after," when one is stripped of everything.

The main impression left by the opening, however, is of a decontextualization which creates defamiliarization. Both are responsible for the hyperrealist effect of the story. Moreover, the dislocation of the furniture from its domestic context is reflected in the narration. The neutral voice, taking no stand toward the events, also avoids giving any context and starts in medias res, without filling in the gaps later, not even through dialogue, as in "Viewfinder." All that the reader might conclude is that the man had a spouse and that he is alone now. Even the use of his point of view ("his side, her side") does not inform the reader about the circumstances. The context of a yard sale is not grounded either. There is no background to the fact that the entire bedroom set stands outside, and no reason is given for this peculiar act. The young couple assumes that they are at a yard sale, but the landlord is indifferent to the transaction, and the description is of an entire room, and not pieces of furniture offered to buyers. The germ of this story was indeed an anecdote Carver heard about a drunken couple who moved all their furniture out onto the lawn until the neighbors called the police.[18] This knowledge supports the feeling that Carver was interested in this curious scene, detached from any reason and circumstance, rather than an actual yard sale.

The power and uniqueness of Carver's openings have been noticed by some of his critics. Carver's openings, with their "paradoxical immediacy," says Martin Scofield, "take us into a world which is either strange or banal, or both at the same time." According to Geoffrey Wolff they throw the reader "off guard," while for Marc Chénetier, these openings kick the reader onto the stage in medias res, "as Carver, using imperative and *unjustified deictics* bludgeons presence upon the reader." And these "sudden entrances upon the page point to the characters' absence of control over lives consistently rendered through a language of vagueness and pointlessness" (my emphasis).[19] The deictic situation that Chénetier points to is indeed present in the opening of "Why Don't You Dance?". The second paragraph opens with "*that* morning," and it introduces personal and possessive pronouns (he, his, her), without specifying a name or describing a character.

However, do deictics need to be justified? In ordinary speech they do, no doubt, require a consent between the addressor and the addressee as to the meaning of the "here" or "now" or the identity which fills the "he" or "she." Without this known context (*origo*) deictics are indeed unjustified. The case is different in literature, however, as the literary and linguistic scholar Ann Banfield has shown.[20] Banfield's continuous exploration of the language of fiction in general and of deictics in particular could be expanded beyond their linguistic dimensions. Thus, although Carver does not use deictics in any unusual manner, Banfield's ideas can throw some light on his narrators' position, especially with reference to his characters' experience. This calls for a digression from "Why Don't You Dance?" to introduce Banfield's theory.

According to Banfield, only in the "strange" language of fiction, essentially different than the language of speech, deictic words appear in third-person expressions. They thus create free indirect speech and "unspeakable" sentences. This argument is central to her concept of literature and the language of the novel, which she has refined and elaborated on over the years. Banfield argues for a duality in free indirect discourse. On the one hand, it is a personal discourse, which is connected to consciousness and experience—henceforth the use of deictics. At the same time, it is impersonal due to its use of the third person and the past tense. Yet, she concludes, this duality results not from the combination of consciousnesses—of the narrator and of the character. Rather, it is a linguistic trait, inherent in fiction. The language of fiction is unique in its combination of the objective sentence of narration with a sentence that expresses speech and consciousness. This subjective sentence undergoes objectification, since it includes both reflexive layers that the character has formulated and unformulated layers whose very inclusion in fiction has promoted them to the status of thought. Therefore, Banfield sees no need for the term "narrator." It is not the narrator who expresses both objective reality and different layers of the character's consciousness, but rather the language of the novel.

Over the years, Banfield has become even more extreme in her renunciation of the traditional duo of narrator-character. She argues that free indirect discourse is free of the character's voice, as much as it is from narratorial mediation. It is only in the language of fiction, she maintains, that one can find deictic words which pertain to no subject in its linguistic manifestations (proper name, adjective, or pronoun). These words point to a minimal subjectivity, reduced to "private" space and time. By "private," Banfield refers to positions in time and space that are not personal, for example, pertaining to no specific consciousness, and at the same time are not the "public" time and space of Newtonian physics. Banfield draws most of her examples of unattached deictics, which are not connected to an actual observer or to a human subject, from the works of Virginia Woolf. These linguistic forms are symptomatic of Woolf's interest in the possibility of representing the visible world with no mediating self.

The capacity to convey a visible world with no self is for Banfield what the eye of the camera embodies. A self might be involved in its operation, yet is not responsible for everything that the camera captures, and is not indispensable. Indeed, Banfield links the development in the language of fiction to the progress of technology, which introduces devices such as the telescope and the microscope. These optic devices allow humanity an access to places and times where no human has ever ventured. However, if a person had been given access to them, this is how he or she would have seen them. Recording what a person could have seen, but *had* not necessarily seen, they suggest a possibility that sensory data would gather around an "empty" center, containing no consciousness. These data were given the name "sensibilia" in Bertrand Russell's theory, and Banfield demonstrates their embodiment in the language of fiction. In her 1991 essay, in which she interprets Roland Barthes's seminal book on photography, *Camera Lucida* (*La chambre clair*), Banfield fully formulates the connection between the language of fiction and photography.[21] Photography, she suggests, pointed to the possibility of an "unoccupied perspective" (Russell's term, following Leibniz), which is bound to a specific "here" and "now," yet unoccupied by a subject and a consciousness. The language of fiction, with its special use of deictic words and pronouns, gives voice to this perspective. Like photography, fiction indicates a neutral in-between reality that, being rooted in a specific time-space slot, is not objective and public, and is not subjective either, since it is not subjected to a certain consciousness. In Barthes's essay, photography has a very close connection to death, and Banfield explains this connection. The unoccupied perspective that photography embodies is a reminder to the viewer that one's stay in a specific time and space is random and interchangeable. It shows—as do the deictic words—that the consciousness which occupies any time-space perspective is as unnecessary and ephemeral as the one that occupied the eye of the camera (or was captured in it) when the photograph was taken.

In the following discussion I will draw on Banfield's concepts: the possibility of "non-subjective subjectivity," the unoccupied perspective, the neutrality of fiction, the connection of fiction to photography through deixis and the way both are reminders of death. My use of Banfield will be partial, however, in the sense that I have chosen not to give up on traditional terms like narrator or character. This anthropomorphic inclination of mine clashes with Banfield's focus on the impersonal aspect of language, yet this very tension is inherent to my argument concerning Carver. My use of Banfield is also partial in the sense that I will use her concepts to analyze Carver's narration and themes rather than his language. Indeed, Banfield's theory has implications beyond the aspect of language, and the fact that she draws insight from thinkers such as Bakhtin, Blanchot, Deleuze, Foucault, Lacan, and Barthes sets it in the broader context of subjectivity in general. Similarly, when Barthes resorts to the linguistic term of deixis in his discussion of photography, he reaches beyond the narrow linguistic sense of this concept. It is this broader sense that I will use too.

In applying Banfield's "unoccupied perspective" to Carver's narratorial stance, let us start from the basic experience of the characters, which is reconstructed in narration. The characters in "Why Don't You Dance?" and "Viewfinder" are both depicted in a state of staring at a slot of space. One is looking through the door and "considers" "his side" and "her side," while the other character looks at the picture of his house:

> I looked a little closer and saw my head, *my head*, in there inside the kitchen window. It made me think, seeing myself like that. I can tell you, it makes a man think. (*WWTA* 12, Carver's emphasis. This paragraph is missing from the manuscript version.)

"It makes a man think," says this observer without sharing his thoughts with the reader. While the concealment of thoughts here seems like a deliberate choice, in other stories it might suggest a character that is basically not inclined to introspection. The main point, however, is that in Carver's visible world, where characters think mostly through seeing, this act often consists of capturing the surrounding space and the possible locus of the onlooker inside it. The series of photographs that the host in "Viewfinder" wants to take in different locations of the house is another example of the desire to see oneself in space. In each of these instances, a character looks at, or expresses a desire to see a slot of space, which he once occupied, and through which he might see himself. The space thus reflects some aspect of the self, from which the character is now detached. Here is another example from one of Carver's last stories, "Whoever Was Using This Bed." Here the recently occupied space is the marital bed, and the people who occupied it are the narrator and his wife, who after a hectic night of talking about death, look at the bed in which they had lain:

> We're sitting together looking at the headboard and at the nightstand. The clock's there, too, and beside the clock a few magazines and a paperback. We're sitting on the part of the bed where we keep our feet when we sleep. *It looks like whoever was using this bed left in a hurry.* I know I won't ever look at this bed again without remembering it like this. We're into something now, but I don't know what exactly. (*WICF*, 439, my emphasis)

Is there a better way to defamiliarize a familiar space than to look at it from the wrong side?[22] Still, the focus of this paragraph is not the familiar-strange space, but the self-other who occupied it—"whoever was using this bed." The space will preserve the presence of its occupants through their memory ("I know I won't ever look at this bed again without remembering it like this"), even as it points at their absence from it ("left in a hurry"), an absence that is also hinted at in the neutrality of "whoever." This story has another bed: the hospital bed which the narrator conjures up, envisioning himself dying from a terminal disease. This bed is also empty, "just a bed" (441). Is it because it waits for the narrator, or because he is already dead? In both these cases the bed contains his possible death, and it brings to mind the marital bed, which, whoever was using it, "left in a hurry," while the narrator's glance moves between these two beds, along with the story.

What then is the significance of this gaze? Why does the loner in "Why Don't You Dance?" consider "his side" and "her side"? What is the meaning of the gaze of the mother, who's about to lose her son in "A Small, Good Thing," when she looks at the chairs that a bereaved family just left in a hurry? As indicated, the chair or the bed might be occupied or unoccupied. They thus suggest the possibility of a human presence that might (but does not have to) be actualized. The way that a character looks at the space that had, or will be, occupied by him or her, is a look at a self-less self. The self is thus reduced to the space he or she occupies, but the connection to it is somewhat arbitrary, since this space also contains the self's absence from it, or its replacement by another person—as is the case in "Why Don't You Dance?".

Indeed, this reduced concept of self is also applicable to the other, who is also reduced to his position in space. "Neighbors" illustrates this very clearly. It is the story of a couple who takes care of the neighbors' apartment while they go away, and is said to be based on an experience in Carver's life, while some see it as epitomizing his work as a whole. Indeed, this is a key story in understanding the mirror relationships between characters (as observed by Ron), their voyeuristic inclination (as diagnosed by Boxer and Phillips), which make them "third parties . . . glimpsing what seems to be real life in progress" (as formulated by Ford).[23] In fact, this story is, in a sense, the reverse of "Why Don't You Dance?". In "Neighbors," Bill, whose point of view dominates the story, occupies other people's space by using their furniture, wearing their clothes, and living their presumed life, whereas in "Why Don't You Dance?" the abandoned person fills the "his" and "her" sides with an analogous couple. In stories such as "They're Not Your Husband" and "The Idea," the two possibilities intertwine, such as when a husband peeps at his wife, while occupying another person's position, and at the same time considers "his side" beside hers. Either way, all these possibilities involve an empty space, from which the self or the other is absent, while potentially being occupied by another self and other. This "existential shell" is hollow, yet it preserves a possible presence of a subject, even when the subject is not actually present.[24] It is a space in which the characters see themselves or another person as stripped of any attributes but the space they have occupied or will occupy. This kind of perception of the self or the other, by definition, entails no introspection, which accounts for its rarity in Carver's work. The reduction of the self and other to a slot of space could also account for their interchangeability in Carver's doppelganger plots. The unoccupied space thus opens up an opportunity for identification and communication, as Carver's later work illustrates. At the same time, it indicates a contingent existence, where the connection between a person and his presumed place is arbitrary and entails the possibility of his or her absence.[25] Many of Carver's characters who are expelled from their homes aptly demonstrate this possibility. The angst which is inherent to this experience had been pinpointed in "Whoever Was Using This Bed," where the emptiness of the marital bed foreshadows the emptiness of a death bed, while the withdrawal from the space in favor of "whoever" implies its terminal, post-death evacuation.

"Narrative Voice That Comes from the Furniture"

The horrifying, substantial experience that has been depicted here is almost inseparable from Carver's unique narratorial voice. Adam Mars-Jones's description of it as a "narrative voice that comes from the furniture" seems to capture its essence perfectly.²⁶ One should not conclude from this brilliant characterization that Carver's narrator adopts the furniture's point of view or takes its position in space. Rather, it suggests that the furniture—a complement of the human body, a negative space which outlines the characters' contours from outside, an empty "shell of existence," indicating both presence and absence—fleshes out the narrator's stance vis-à-vis his characters. The precision of this metaphor lies in being drawn from the stories' material, and its actualization in the characters' experience renders it almost literal.

The deserted bed or the empty chair are not connected to any optic device like the camera, the telescope, or the microscope, yet for me they are the embodiment in space of the "unoccupied perspective," which Banfield finds in photography. The unoccupied perspective pertains to a conception of subjectivity which was formulated by Russell and Whitehead. Here subjectivity is, in fact, a consciousness-free time-space slot, which could be occupied by a particular consciousness, or remain unoccupied. This minimal conception of subject, where there is a private entity though not necessarily a personal one, is part of those thinkers' concentration on the viewer's body rather than on his or her mind, and of their noncognitive conception of a physical subjectivity. Moreover, Russell expands "perspective" to include the dimension of time, in the sense that subjects in the present are also private with regard to their past and future.²⁷

Furniture as such occupies a position in space, yet its representation in Carver includes the various presences which occupied this limited space at different times. It thus expresses the characters' experience of their—or others'—reduced subjectivity, which is reconstructed in narration. Carver's narrative voice, which clings to the physical conditions of the characters, namely the place they occupied in a certain time, rarely exploits fiction's privilege to penetrate a character's mind, and as a covert narrator, he conceals his own consciousness. In light of this, we may say that the narrator remains (much like his characters) in a liminal space: poised on the cusp between the personal (being limited in time and space) and the impersonal (devoid of consciousness); between the subjective and the objective, in the space that Banfield, following Blanchot, calls "the neutral." This space has its linguistic expression in deixis, and for Blanchot (with reference to literature) and Barthes (with reference to photography) it is closely bound up with death.²⁸

The placement of the narrator in the characters' space rather than in their consciousness is well illustrated in "Why Don't You Dance?". The man whose perspective dominated the beginning of the story leaves the scene, yet the narrator sticks to the character's (now) unoccupied perspective, and a couple arrives on the scene. The character is thus reduced to the space he or she occupied at a certain time. When he or she is gone, another character occupies this space as well as the narratorial position. Sticking to space and time, rather than subjectivity, the narrator shifts to another person who occupies this perspective, yet the space somehow preserves the presence of its previous occupants by way of analogy—the crack in the young couple's relationship suggests a similar fate to that of the house's former tenants. In addition, in this story, as in "Viewfinder" and "Collectors," the space not only gestures to the absence-presence of the man who lives in it, but also to the woman who has left it. While she is not present in the story, the story implies her presence-absence—"her side."

"The Real Story"

The state of gazing at the unoccupied space encapsulates the characters' angst. Suddenly, they no longer experience themselves from the inside, via their consciousness, but from the outer boundaries, or "shell," of their existence. They thus confront the void and contingency at the foundation of their existence. The reverse side of this experience, where the self is perceived as other, is the penetration into the shell of the other, who turns out to be another version of the self. The narrator, who avoids any representation of thoughts, reconstructs this experience by adopting an unoccupied perspective, devoid of consciousness. However, this eye-of-the-camera type of narration is more than poetics to suit the experience of the characters. It also suggests a statement about the nature of stories and storytelling as such. This will be shown by a brief reading of one of Carver's few stories to deal with writing and writers: "Put Yourself in My Shoes," from the early collection *Will You Please Be Quiet, Please?*

Myers, an out-of-work writer, who is now "between stories" and therefore feels "despicable" (*WICF*, 96) visits the Morgans with his wife. The couple does not know the Morgans, but by the end of the story, during which the visit attains an inexplicable tension, we learn that Myers and his wife lived at the Morgans' house for a while, and the Morgans accuse them of having taken personal belongings from their home. Up to this point, however, the visit consists of stories that the hosts tell their visitors. They are presented as raw material for Myers to build a story with, and they are accompanied by all sorts of clichés about writing and literature:

> It's a horrible story. . . . But maybe you could use it. . . . Grist for the mill, you know, and all that. . . . The power of the pen. I'll go right to the climax, as you writers say. (*WICF*, 101, 106, 108)

The stories that the Morgans tell verge on the macabre. The husband tells of a married college professor who fell in love with a student, and when he was about to leave his wife and house, his son threw a can of tomato soup at him, giving him a severe concussion. The wife tells of a woman who arrived at their house in

Germany in order to return a lost purse but suddenly passed away on their living room couch. The stories are full of details, and are no more than sensational anecdotes, for "it would take a Tolstoy to tell" them right (103). Myers' gift as a writer is thus challenged here, while the storytelling Morgans expect him to breathe life into the stories, to speculate on what took place in the "mind" of the angry son, the young lover, the treacherous father, and the deserted wife. He is expected to "put himself in the shoes" of the characters. When Myers fails to do so, and starts to giggle instead, Mr. Morgan blows up at him:

> If you were a real writer, as you say you are, Mr. Myers, you would not laugh. . . . You would not dare laugh! You would try to understand. You would plumb the depths of that poor soul's heart and try to understand. But you are no writer, sir! (110)

And while he is at it, Mr. Morgan reveals what for him is "the real story," which "lies right here, in this house": the story of three couples, whom he names X, Y, and Z. He tells how X offered Z to take care of Y's apartment, without there having been a chance for the couples to meet each other. He reveals that Z not only slept in Y's bed but violated their agreement by bringing a cat into the house; that they also opened closets, used linen, opened boxes of kitchen utensils, used personal possessions and bathrooms accessories, and even poked around the attic, looking at personal effects.

There are, then, stories which need a Tolstoy to tell them, by fathoming the characters' depth of feelings, and there is a "real story," which "doesn't need Tolstoy to tell it" (111). It is precisely the "real story" that replaces the participants' names with X, Y, and Z (once Mr. Morgan even confuses the "Z" with the "Y"). The anonymity of the participants is necessary, of course, for the dramatic revelation that Y and Z are in fact the Myerses and the Morgans, and real stories indeed call for discretion. This is, however, merely a partial explanation. Within the broader context of Carver's work, the participants in a "real story" indeed face a situation whereby they are variables in an empty equation, representing interactions and replaceable positions, rather than possessing substance and identity.

In the "real story," where the characters again occupy each other's space, the phrase "Put Yourself in My Shoes" loses the metaphorical sense that the Morgans have given it, namely as a poignant gaze at the other's inner self. Rather, the real story entails an invasion of the empty slot that the other used to occupy, into his or her empty shell of existence, to the intimacy of his bathroom accessories and his vacant bed, and most of all, "his side" in relation to "her side." It means putting oneself in the other's shoes, without his being there. Accordingly, the narrator of "Put Yourself in My Shoes" is Carver's usual behaviorist one, who avoids revealing the characters' inner reality but rather depicts them outwardly.

Both the character and the narrator remain anonymous. While the story is told from Myers' "shoes," there is almost no trace of his individual consciousness. He remains basically an "other," opaque in his speech, gestures, and sudden laugh, which though precisely rendered, remain unmotivated and inexplicable.

This is indeed Myers'/Carver's "real story": the meeting point of the most personal with the impersonal and anonymous, which for Blanchot is indeed "the space of literature."[29] It is precisely the interchangeable shell of existence, which in its contingency points to the possibility of death, that becomes the truest expression of the self, rather than the flux of consciousness that is captured from the inside.

This is tightly connected to the act of narration, which is an act of placing a frame and a context, while, at the same time, a process of decontextualization and externalization. This act substantially changes the story's inwardness, and inserts otherness into it, where—to put it in Shoshana Felman's words—"No one is left in the 'outside' of the story, except the story's inside."[30] Myers seems to overcome his writer's block in the end and realizes that he is "at the very end of a story" (112), but he reaches this point only after the "real story" has been told, with his real name replaced by an anonymous letter.

This inherent externalization of narrative is, in fact, also expressed in "Intimacy" and "Why Don't You Dance?". The echo of one story is heard in the other, for what is the husband-writer accused of but of laying his marital bed out in the open? And what is being displayed for all to see in the yard sale but "intimacy"? The story that the writer will tell of his ex-wife and the furniture in the yard embodies the laying out of what is, by definition, inside, while "the inside" as such is beyond reach. This realization is reflected in the nature of the narration, which is always from the outside. The story of "whoever was using this bed" will be told by the one who already "left in a hurry" and now is left to look at "his side." When the girl in "Why Don't You Dance?" tries to tell the story of her meeting with the lonely man, she feels that "there was more to it, and she was trying to get it talked out" (*WICF*, 161). After a while, she stops trying, since one's own story can never be told. There is always more to tell, or too much already told, as the narrator in "Fat" feels. The story will be told by the voice that chooses to tell it by *showing*, and thus will tell of the inside which is now an outside, where the self is accessible only as other.[31]

The writer Richard Ford recalls his first encounter with "Intimacy":

> I said to him after I read that story, "Jesus, Ray, I read your story about Maryann." That's very unlike me because I recognize and I insist in my own work that direct correlations between life and what gets represented in stories are impossible, untrue. And I didn't even know Maryann, but this remark just leapt out of my mouth. I said, "I read the story about Maryann." And he said in a very guarded way,

"That wasn't about Maryann." And then I thought to myself after I said that, well, that's right. Even if it's not right, it's right.[32]

On second thought, as Ford realizes, Maryann's story is indeed not *her* story.

And this is how "Intimacy" ends. The narrator, who accepted his ex-wife's permission to tell the story of their meeting, is about to leave: "So she walks me to the front door, which has been standing open all this while. The door that was letting in light and fresh air this morning, and sounds off the street, all of which we had ignored" (*WICF*, 452). He steps outside and sees children playing in the street, "but they aren't my kids, and they aren't her kids either" (453). Fallen leaves pile up on the sidewalk: "I can't take a step without putting my shoe into leaves. Somebody ought to make an effort here. Somebody ought to get a rake and take care of this" (ibid.).

It seems indeed that the outside—"all of which we had ignored" is eventually the space of the story, where the kids are not "his" or "hers," and a neutral "somebody" ought to take care of the leaves. "Except for that"—as in "Why Don't You Dance?"—things looked much the way they had inside. The story is the outside, and it will be told from the outside. Paradoxically, this is precisely what makes it "the real story."

Conclusion

In a 1945 lecture, Merleau-Ponty points at the interaction between the cinema and what he terms "the new psychology."[33] The new psychology, he contends, brought a new conception and understanding of the world and its perception. Besides the realization of the crucial role that configuration has in organizing our knowledge, and in the importance of bodily experience and positioning, it brought a new conception of the others. It made us notice that "in reality introspection gives me almost nothing" (ibid., 52). Love, anger and hatred are no longer perceived as inner realities accessible only to the person who experiences them. Rather, they are "types of behavior or styles of conduct which are visible from the outside. They exist *on* this face or *in* those gestures, not hidden behind them." A feeling is understandable when we succeed in seeing it as the "modification of my relations with the other and with the world, because I have managed to think about it as I would think about the behavior of another person whom I happened to witness." According to Merleau-Ponty, this behaviorist assumption informs both modern psychology and the cinema. Unlike the novel, where we expect thoughts to be revealed to the reader, in the "new psychology" as well in the cinema—"dizziness, pleasure, grief, love and hate are ways of behaving" (ibid., 58). For Merleau-Ponty, both fields confirm Goethe's phrase, "What is inside is also outside" (59).

The cinema has undergone many transformations since Merleau-Ponty addressed it in his lecture, and the psychology he describes in no longer "new." However, the behaviorist assumption which underlies his observations could still illuminate Carver's poetics. Carver admitted that he is not as interested in his characters' thoughts as in their behavior and speech.[34] He shows love, hate, and sadness through behavior and gestures, and the speech he gives them is rarely introspective. This inclination, no doubt, supports his poetics' connection to the cinema and photography. Thus, his poetics not only coincides with Goethe's insight, but reveals new meaning through his use of the eye of the camera.

"What is inside is also outside" is applicable to photography because it captures characters from the outside, unlike literature, which penetrates their consciousness. However, it is true mostly because through its deictic stance and its empty center, the eye of the camera—as well as its literary expression—suggests a conception of the self as outside, as a shell determined by time and space, rather than by any specific consciousness. This painful realization might explain the immanent fragility in Carver's voice, which seems to be present in his absence, and whose ambivalent position was concretized by the narrator of "Intimacy." This silent, self-reductive, passive narrator reconstructs the conditions of the unoccupied perspective—a negative space, devoid of consciousness and words. It is precisely this quality that makes him so intimately close to his characters—characters caught in a crisis, in which they are dissociated from their life's continuity and experience themselves as stripped of everything except the awareness of death, which makes them more themselves than ever.

In the sixth chapter I will return to this point from another angle, in the context of Barthes's reflection on photography. But this idea will also recur, though in a different guise, in the next chapter, which introduces one of Carver's most impressive and moving characters—Claire from "So Much Water So Close to Home." In this story, he not only revealed his tremendous empathy as a writer by "putting himself in the shoes" of an agonized woman, but also portrayed a character whose total empathy for another person, the way she puts herself in another woman's shoes, occurs through death. The next chapter will resume the discussion of the eye of the camera. While in this chapter this metaphor was used to investigate Carver's narrative voice, in the next it will help explore his treatment of description. Whereas the conclusion here was that "the inside is outside," the next chapter will explore the possibility that the outside is inside.

Notes

1. Simone Weil, *Gravity and Grace*, trans. Arthur Wills (New York: G. P. Putnam's Sons, 1952), 88.

2. See, for example, in Halpert, 141–42 (Maryann Carver), 159–66 (Richard Ford).

3. Bramlett and Raabe, in their brilliant discussion of this story, argue that the narrator employs free indirect speech to build his intimacy with the reader. See p. 190.

4. Sarraute, "Conversation and Sub-conversation," 112–13.

5. See Genette, *Narrative Discourse Revisited*, 57, where he discussed this quality of direct versus indirect—or free indirect—discourse. Here, due to the special use of "she says" and layout of the speech, the effect of direct discourse is similar to free indirect discourse in that it both gives a voice to the character and expresses a narratorial stance.

6. Martin Jay discusses this quality of photography. See "Scopic Regimes of Modernity," in Hal Foster, ed., *Vision and Visuality* (Seattle: Ray Press, 1988), 3–28. He draws on Svetlana Alpers and her view of the connection between photography and Flemish painting in her book *The Art of Describing: Dutch Art in the Seventeenth Century* (Chicago: Chicago University Press, 1985). See discussion here, in the fifth chapter.

7. In Halpert's *Oral Biography*, Chuck Kinder describes this dynamic in the relationship between Raymond and Maryann Carver. Carver used to interrogate Maryann about events he forgot in his drunkenness, and the story was "taking root in Ray's mind as Maryann would plumb her memory about events" (Halpert, 38).

8. Boxer and Phillips, 75–90.

9. Cohn, who bases her understanding of the logic of literature on Käte Hamburger's theory, analyzes this "illogical" type of narrator while comparing the early (first-person) version of Kafka's *The Castle* to its final (third-person) version. See Dorrit Cohn, "K. Enters *The Castle*: On the Change of Person in Kafka's Manuscript," *Euphorion* 62:1 (1968): 28–45. Genette (in *Narrative Discourse Revisited*, 121–27) admits that he could not find a pure example of this type of narrator (homodiegetic narrator with external focalization), but he still assigns it a category of its own, which so far is still unfilled. On the complexity of the notion of "neutral narrative" and its manifestations see Monica Fludernik, *Towards a 'Natural' Narratology* (London: Routledge, 1996), 172–77.

10. Deleuze, *Cinema 1*, 207.

11. See, for example, Richard Day's testimony in Halpert, 145, or his introduction to Carver's early play, in Raymond Carver, *Carnations: A Play in One Act*, ed. William L. Stull (Vinebury, CA: Engdahl Typography, 1992), iii.

12. Genette discusses *paralipsis*, or "hyper-restriction of field," in *Narrative Discourse*, 52, 205.

13. On the closeness and distance in mimesis and diegesis, see Genette, *Narrative Discourse*, 162–64, and in *Narrative Discourse Revisited*, 44–49.

14. See Roland Barthes, *Le degré zéro de l'écriture* (Paris: Editions du deuil, 1953), 108. Arias-Misson describes Carver's narrative voice as a "*voix blanches* turned inside out like a glove" (627), which is enmeshed with the voice of the anonymous characters who struggle to express themselves vis-à-vis silence and clichés. Genette (in *Narrative Discourse*, 187), following Friedman (1178–79), distinguishes the eye-of-the-camera category from Hemingway's "dramatic mode." In my opinion, Carver's writing is closer to the former technique than the latter. Of Carver's fondness for Flaubert's impersonal voice, see Gentry and Stull, 67, 126.

15. This state of affairs was analyzed by Moshe Ron in his epilogue to Raymond Carver's *Last Stories* (Tel Aviv: Hakibuthz Hameuhad, 1998), 181–95 (in Hebrew).
16. Gentry and Stull, 98.
17. As Tobias Wolff puts it in Halpert, 155.
18. See William Kittredge's testimony in Halpert, 146. In his poem "Distress Sale" (*AOU*, 5–6) Carver does treat a yard sale situation.
19. See Scofield, "Negative Pastoral," 245; Geoffrey Wolff, in Halpert, 125; Chénetier, "Living On/Off," 166–67. Frank Kermode also quotes some of Carver's openings in his review of Carver's *Call If You Need Me*. See Frank Kermode, "No Tricks," *London Review of Books*, 19 October 2000. http://www.lrb.co.uk/v22/n20/kerm01_.html (accessed January 30, 2008).
20. Ann Banfield, "The Name of the Subject: The 'il'?" *Yale French Studies* 93 (1998): 93; *The Place of Maurice Blanchot* (1998): 169. Henceforth, the summary of Banfield's approach is based on her works: *Unspeakable Sentences: Narration and Representation in the Language of Fiction* (London: Routledge & Kegan Paul, 1987); "Describing the Unobserved: Events Grouped around an Empty Centre," in *The Linguistics of Writing: Arguments between Language and Literature*, ed. Nigel Fabb and others (Manchester: Manchester University Press, 1987), 265–87; "L'imparfait de l'objectif: The Imperfect of the Object Glass," *Camera Obscura* 24:3 (1990): 64–87; *The Phantom Table: Woolf, Fry, Russell and the Epistemology of Modernism* (Cambridge: Cambridge University Press, 2000). For an analysis of Banfield's concept of an "empty center," see Fludernik, 192–98.
21. In the essay, "L'imparfait de l'objectif," Banfield elaborates on Barthes's approach, which viewed photography as concretizing a deictic stance. On deixis in photography as representing the turn toward contingency in the concept of vision in Western art and thought, see Jay's discussion (following Norman Bryson and John Berger) in *Downcast Eyes*, 134–35.
22. This situation may gesture to a similar one in Hemingway's story, "Cat in the Rain," which Carver mentions in Gentry and Stull, 17.
23. See Ron's Epilogue; Boxer and Phillips; Richard Ford in Halpert, 163. About "Neighbors" see also in Raymond Carver, "On Neighbors," *CIYN*, 177–78, and the interpretations of Douglas Unger and Robert Stone in Halpert 124, 130–31.
24. Ron in a series of radio lectures on "The Voice of Israel" in May-June 1999 (in Hebrew).
25. This element of contingency is what drew Altman to Carver when he adopted his stories to the screen in *Short Cuts*. See David Sawyer, "'Yet Why Not Say What Happened?' Boundaries of the Self in Raymond Carver's Fiction and Robert Altman's *Short Cuts*," in *Blurred Boundaries: Critical Essays on American Literature, Language, and Culture*, ed. Klaus H. Schmidt and David Sawyer (Frankfurt: Peter Lang, 1996), 195–219.
26. As quoted by Scofield, "Negative Pastoral," 252.
27. Banfield, "Describing," 217.
28. Maurice Blanchot, "The Space of Literature," trans. Ann Smock (Lincoln: University of Nebraska, 1982); "The Narrative Voice," *The Infinite Conversations*, trans. Susan Hanson (Minneapolis: University of Minnesota Press, 1993), 279–87. Banfield draws on his insights mostly in her essay "The Name of the Subject."

29. Blanchot, ibid.

30. Shoshana Felman, "Turning the Screw of Interpretation," in *Literature and Psychoanalysis: The Questions of Reading: Otherwise*, ed. Shoshana Felman (Baltimore: Johns Hopkins University Press, 1982), 124. In this essay, Felman analyzes James' *Turn of the Screw*, a novella in which the frame story pulls the reader inside and at the same time externalizes its inner content with "a voice whose intrusion compromises the tale's secret intimacy and whose otherness violates the story's presence to itself" (123).

31. Cf. Elliott Malamet's interpretation of "Where I'm Calling From"—a story in which the narrator chooses to tell his story through another person's story—in "Raymond Carver and the Fear of Narration," *Journal of the Short Story in English* 17 (1991): 59–72.

32. Halpert, 159–60.

33. Maurice Merleau-Ponty, "The Film and the New Psychology," in *Sense and Non-Sense*, trans. Hubert L. Dreyfus and Patricia Allen Dreyfus (Evanston: Northwestern University Press, 1964), 48–59.

34. Gentry and Stull, 146.

CHAPTER 4

"Why Do I Notice That?"
VISION

> Werther is telling his story, and speaks in the present tense, but his scene already has the vocation of a remembrance; in an undertone, the imperfect tense murmurs behind this present. (Roland Barthes, *A Lover's Discourse: Fragments*[1])

The Direct Look

Carver "knew more than anyone where his characters should look," says Geoffrey Wolff. By look, Wolff clarifies, he does not mean the characters' point of view, but "where their eyes fall, what they see and what they don't see." As with other aspects of Carver's writing, here one has to take note of the influence of Hemingway.[2] Wolff offers this observation with reference to the early "Will You Please, Be Quiet, Please?" but it is also applicable to the later "So Much Water So Close to Home." As in other stories by Carver, this one has two versions that open in the same way:

> My husband eats with good appetite but he seems tired, edgy. He chews slowly, arms on the table, and stares at something across the room. He looks at me and looks away again. He wipes his mouth on the napkin. He shrugs and goes on eating. Something has come between us though he would like me to believe otherwise.
> "What are you staring me for?" he asks. "What is it?" he says and puts his fork down.
> "Was I staring?" I say and shake my head stupidly, stupidly. (*WICF*, 213)

A direct, confronting look; an evasive looking away; a denial of the very look—this variety of looks encapsulates the relationship of the couple in this story: Stewart, the husband, who went fishing with his friends, found the body of a dead girl floating in the river, and decided to ignore it; his wife, Claire, who is deeply affected by the incident, and consequently alienated from her husband.

The woman's direct look is merely implied in this opening. She denies it ("was I looking?"), and ironically describes her husband's response to her with a "meaningful look." However, later, when the couple goes out for a drive, and finally confront each other by a roadside stream, the husband will find no escape from the direct look: "I look at him across the picnic table with such intensity that his face drains" (221). Claire's annihilating gaze—an other's gaze, as Sartre describes it—is judgmental and seems to petrify its object. However, it is not only its intensity that makes the husband's face "drain," as we learn from the previous paragraph:

> I look at the creek. I float toward the pond, eyes open, face down, staring at the rocks and moss on the creek bottom until I am carried into the lake where I am pushed by the breeze. (ibid.)

The identification with the dead girl is evoked physically. Very casually, with no preparations, this disturbing vision, in which Claire and the girl share the same body, slides into the otherwise factual, realistic report, which resumes right after this description. Similarly, in the shorter version, during forced sexual intercourse with her husband (in which Claire refuses to participate in the longer version), she suddenly starts to talk in her dead double's voice: "He says something else. But I don't need to listen. I can't hear a thing with so much water going" (*WWTA*, 88). The intensity of these words, says Arias-Misson, is "so alien to the flow of the voice . . . that the reader checks back to see if the faucet has been left running in the kitchen."[3] The even tone blurs the boundaries between vision and reality, metaphor and literal meaning. It places these hallucinations on the same level as reality: Claire *is* the girl who floats over the water.

No wonder that this double-layered look of the woman, whose depth expresses the dead girl's vacant stare, drains life from the husband's face. Is it the impact of the poignant, judging, living look, or of the dead unseeing look?

The absence of sight in looking is indeed crucial to this story, where a deflected gaze is as powerful as a direct look. Thus, Stewart deflects his look when his wife stares at him, and refuses to acknowledge the change that has overturned their life; the fishermen leave the river without so much as another look at the dead girl; Claire pretends to be asleep when her husband looks at her, and when a truck driver approaches her car on her way to the girl's funeral, she shuts her eyes.

Carver's stories almost obsessively recall the theme of the relationship between men and women, and this story is no exception. The recurrent images of water (so common in Carver's second collection) suggest the archetypical triangle of femininity-water-death, as this story explores, through a woman's prism, a collective feminine experience.[4] Claire's crisis results partly from her realization of the potential of the male gaze to be so destructive—a gaze which has myriad expressions in this story: the look of her husband, the look of the occasional men who scan her body, of the man who raped and murdered the girl, of the fisherman (her husband, perhaps) who casts light on the girl's body with his flashlight, and the looks of the coroners who probe her body with their instruments. However, the male gaze and its immanent violence is only part of Carver's approach to the issue of looking. Stories like "The Idea" or "They're Not Your Husband" similarly explore the male gaze, but overall, Carver's stories introduce us equally to men and women, strangers and lovers, who look at each other in a way which constitutes—alongside their failed verbal communication—a language of looks that carries its own codes.

The issue of looking is broader, though, for this plethora of looks draws one's attention to the way in which this fictional work "looks"—namely approaches visible reality and implicitly "sees" it. As a realist and a behaviorist, Carver seems to claim a discussion of his "eye" and "vision," yet the use of these terms raises many questions, among them: Is it possible to talk of seeing in a text, which regardless of its mimetic qualities is always diegetic, for example, mediated by language? Is the issue of seeing synonymous with that of description? Is it the visualization of a text in the reader's mind, and how do we approach this process? Does a text which we call "visible" or "descriptive" present the reader with specific content, such as static objects or fragments of scenes in which movement has been suspended, or can it also include movement and action? Is seeing in the context of textuality equal to fictional space? How does it relate to time and to the characters' point of view? The continuous effort to define the concept of description illustrates all these difficulties.[5]

The notion of seeing is equally problematic: Does "seeing" refer to any encounter between the eye and external reality? Is there a pure optic element in seeing that might be isolated from language or interpretation? Do recognition, generalization, and the organization of the field of vision constitute an inseparable part of seeing? Some of these questions will be addressed, though not exhaustively. Nor do I offer an unequivocal answer. For now, however, let us simplify this intricate issue and address the first impression that Carver's fiction produces—writing focused on vision, both by referring to the act of seeing and by promoting visualization. Carver explicitly stated his commitment to show a "visible" action, and the responses to his fiction indicate that he achieves this goal.[6] "His eye is set on describing and revealing the world as he sees it. His eye is so clear, it almost breaks your heart," says one critic.[7] Such responses regard Carver's writing as straight forwardly "looking" at reality, where the mediating "eye" (is it really *Carver's* eye?) is clear, allowing the reader to "see" reality as is, without denial, and therefore it "breaks one's heart."

Claire's direct look at the beginning of "So Much Water . . ." is thus a suitable metaphor to describe Carver's look, even as it informs the way reality is perceived in this particular story. I will use this way of looking to examine and challenge accepted notions of Carver's writing and "seeing." Thus, in this chapter, the stories under discussion ("So Much Water . . . ," "Cathedral," and excerpts from other stories) will not only illustrate Carver's poetics, but will also be used as a pool of metaphors to characterize it. This method is consistent with what has already been restated in the course of this study—namely, that Carver's stories tell their own poetics, and that the meta-fictional dimension is an integral part of the world and experience that they convey.

"So Much Water . . ." presents several ways of looking, through which I will investigate the issue of visibility in Carver's world. Four different ways of looking (the direct look, the sidelong look, the glimpse, and eyes shut) will allow me to explore the Carverian "look," each revealing another facet. Thus, the structure of this chapter is somewhat spiral. It is important to qualify, however, that by analyzing these looks I do not mean to explain their individual appearances in the stories, but rather to employ them as general metaphors.

There seem to be two reasons for the impression of clarity, or directness, in Carver's representation of reality. One is his lucid language and its absence of embellishments and devices, which usually draw one's attention to their fabric as much as to their "reality." Carver's language has almost been purged of metaphors, except for well-worn ones. In one of his stories ("A Small, Good Thing") the movement of a child's legs, after his injury in an accident, is compared to a climbing motion. In another story ("Neighbors"), a man and a woman lean into a door "as if against a wind" (*WICF*, 93). However, even these simple images are the exception. Similarly, a direct look implies minimal intervention between the fictional reality and the text, even as the observer and object are totally separated. It is as if the observer (be it the narrator *or* the character) is determined not to taint sight with his presence, as revealed by language. Even when the textual reality is mediated by a character's "eye," it is rendered in the most immediate manner, and seems to be issued from what Edward Casey terms the "surface of consciousness."[8] As demonstrated in the previous chapter, the subject refrains from infusing into the description of the object (assumed to be totally external) an interpretation, or memories and feelings.

This aspiration, to eliminate the distance between "world" and text at the level of language, is also shown in the choice of tenses, which contributes to the impression of lucidity. Present tense dominates the majority of "So Much Water . . ." and is used in other Carver stories. As narratology has acknowledged, the present tense never stands for a realistic situation, since one cannot both experience and narrate at the same time. Still, writers keep investigating the possibilities of the present tense, either by providing realistic motivation for its use and making it plausible all the same, or by using it to challenge the conventions of narration.[9] However, even when there is no completely realistic motivation for the use of the present tense, its effect is of immediacy—and this is indeed the case in "So Much Water . . .". Claire's look seems to be reported in real time, freed from the distortions of time and memory, and it thus involves the reader in the act of looking. In fact, the choice of tenses coincides with the structure of the story. It begins in medias res (and in the present tense) and then the story returns to Stewart's fishing trip, his confrontation with his wife, and the harassing phone calls in the wake of the publication of the incident in the press, which are all reported in the past tense.

However, inside the analepsis to the near past, there is also (in the story's longer version) an analepsis to the distant past: the circumstances under which Claire met her husband, was "tempted" and married him, their marital problems, her illness, her hospitalization, and her reconciliation with her husband on her return home. The report of past events supplies the biographical, perhaps psychological, background to the fishing incident and illuminates the present. As a result, the violence in this version is more concrete, and its precedents (though not its reasons) can be found in the past. However, those past events, unlike the fishing incident and what followed, are told, like the opening ("My husband eats"), in the present tense: "She is in another town working as a receptionist for an electronic parts firm and becomes acquainted with one of the engineers, who asks her for a date. Eventually, seeing that's his aim, she lets him seduce her" (223). When she recalls her past, Claire refers to herself in the third person, and this device is motivated by feeling dissociated from her past: "The past is unclear. It's as if there is a film over those early years. I can't even be sure that the things I remember happening really happened to me" (ibid.). In fact, the elusiveness of the past is something that was felt even then: "After a short while they decide to get married, but already the past, her past, is slipping away. The future is something she can't imagine. She smiles, as if she has a secret, when she thinks about the future" (ibid.).

For Roland Barthes and Alain Robbe-Grillet, the past tense, the oppressive *Demiurgos* of writing, goes hand-in-hand with an authoritarian third-person mode.[10] Here, on the other hand, the third person combines with the present tense. Moreover, the present tense is used both in the moment of looking, where a woman watches her husband "with his hands on the table," and in the description of a long-forgotten past, when things seem to be happening to someone else. How can the present tense serve both the direct look, where there may be a link between the times of looking, narration, and reading, and the experience of recalling an obscure past with many missing details? Do these opposite uses of the present tense only indicate the flexibility of this tense, or do they also indicate a connection between the contrasting states of looking and recalling?

While addressing these questions, it is interesting to recall Carver's early story, "Furious Seasons," where there is also a special use of tenses: The events of the present are told in the past tense, whereas memories from the past are told in the present tense. This Faulknerian confusion of present and past could also illuminate our story in its connection to the theme of looking.[11] We have seen how Claire's direct look encapsulates another look, from a different time—the look of the dead woman. Similarly, it seems that in the depth of sheer observation, in the present, there lurks another eye, both seeing and unseeing, taken from a different time. Indeed, observation bears the traces of memory, while the use of the present tense points to their connection.

Again, the use of the present tense is helpful in clarifying this paradox. In relation to the past, the present tense is used to evoke Claire's elusive past, as if it is happening to someone else. It is the present tense of someone who narrates a dream. Claire admits that "it's as if there is a film over those early years," and that she "can't be sure that the things" she "remembers happening really happened" (223). Had Claire used the past tense, it would validate and bestow on this tenuous past the false firmness of truth.[12] Claire, who imagines herself floating over the water expresses, through her sympathy with the dead girl, a sense of *herself* as rootless and dissociated. Here, the present tense illustrates the feeling of living on isles of the present that are detached from the past and the future. In a moment of grace, Stewart says to Claire that "from now on" they're going to live in the "here and now." Ironically, he unintentionally describes her nightmarish experience of life in an eternal present, in which she cannot imagine the future, and the past is unclear: This present is devoid of continuity and the insight that retrospection could bestow upon it. If she ever had any insights, Claire has already forgotten them ("She remembers having an insight about the seduction, but she can't remember what it was." [223]) Instead, all that are left are fragments, which for no obvious reason have remained. At the same time, the present tense represents the will to get a grip on what is lost and blurred, making it present and visible. It compels direct observation to tap into the act of recalling by its very longing for immediacy and the presence of looking.

But is there a substantial difference between the description of the past and the present? At first glance, Claire's sight of the present seems immediate and concrete. The sight of the husband who eats and smokes, or the details Claire has glimpsed from the window on her way to the funeral, appear to be present and fully tangible, and the use of the present tense supports this. Yet, as much as these descriptions convey what Claire sees in the present, in the most direct manner, they also summon memory. Memory is present in the form of an aspiration, because the precision of the details conceals a desperate attempt to get a grip on what constantly threatens to slip away and become obscure and intangible. Memory is also present in the fragmentary nature of these descriptions, regardless of how detailed they are. It is as if the sights are preparing themselves to become a memory, thus making memory already present.

This lack of distinction between the nature of observation and memory is also evident in the absence of a clear principle of selection. The shreds of past events which flicker in Claire's mind—her playing in the sandbox with her son, her severe headaches, her lying near her husband while telling him a sexual anecdote in order to please him—seem preserved for no obvious reason, with no particular insight to accompany them. "The past is unclear"—no matter what significance the reader may draw from this selection of incidents. Similarly, when referring to Claire's perception of the present, she already wonders what causes her to notice these particular details, and she ponders their significance. Thus, for example, her observation of her husband who has just heard her smashing the dishes in the kitchen:

> He waits a minute, then draws on his cigarette and leans back in the chair. I pity him for listening, detached, and then settling back and drawing on his cigarette. The wind takes the smoke out of his mouth in a thin stream. *Why do I notice that?* He can never know how much I pity him for that, for sitting still and listening, and letting the smoke stream out of his mouth. (*WICF*, 214–15, my emphasis)

"Why do I notice that?" What make this moment, these details, special? Why do they capture her gaze, evoking such feeling? The drift of the cigarette smoke, which embodies that which is ephemeral and elusive, makes an imprint on her mind, arousing intense and unclear emotion. Fixating on a random fragment, charging it with feelings once it has been captured, prepares it, as it were, for memory. Memory is inscribed in the act of observation, and as in memory, a detail is snatched from a whole, makes one wonder at its meaning, wavering between the random and the significant.

It is important to note that the memory discussed here in relation to observation is a memory that has undergone no processes of organization, filling in of gaps and rationalization, to the extent that this is possible in narrative. This approach to past events is grounded in Claire's experience, even as it represents a general inclination of Carver's characters. The past of these characters—if evoked at all—is rarely an organized, well-made story. Usually, only few images surface: a bulldog dragging a chain that the kids found in "Careful"; a boy throwing some beans out a window in "After the Denim"; "very carefully combed hair and loud half-baked ideas about life and art" in "The Student's Wife" (*WICF*, 37).

In that sense too, memory bears the imprint of observation in real time, which only labels objects, without integrating them into an overall structure that will provide them with meaning—without telling a story. The gaps in this initial phase of observation seem to foreshadow gaps in memory eroded by forgetfulness, since even in the present there is a lack of connection between the details. Deep inside the living eye lurks the dead eye. As in memory, so too in observation: The eye which does not see is as active as the one which sees. The descriptions are produced by a gaze, which consistently clings to the sight—an eye that "sees everything," as Carver often says of his characters (e.g., in "Neighbors" and "Put Yourself in My Shoes"), yet that eye is already dotted with blanks similar to the forgetfulness that surrounds the isles of memory. The description of the funeral of the murdered girl is in fact a collection of impressions laconically rendered—a boy in flared pants and a yellow shirt who bites his lips, the flash of the parking lot which for a minute reminds Claire of a meadow. This type of description is rooted in Claire's experience. Claire, like other characters, desperately seeks to draw connections: "There is a connection to be made of these things, these events, these faces, if I can find it. My head aches with the effort to find it" (234).

Many of the descriptions of space in Carver's work illustrate an almost obsessive listing of objects, which still fails to produce a whole space. Here are some of the more typical ones:

1. There was a little rectangle of lawn, the driveway, the carport, front steps, bay window, and the window I'd been watching from in the kitchen. So why would I want a photograph of this tragedy? ("Viewfinder," *WWTA*, 12)
2. There was a bed, a window. The covers were heaped on the floor. One pillow, one sheet over the mattress. ("Collectors," *WICF*, 117)
3. I got up and looked into the hallway, where I slept on a cot. There was an ashtray, a Lux clock, and a few old paperbacks on a table beside the cot. ("Night School," *WYPB*, 100)
4. He saw ashtrays, items of furniture, kitchen utensils, the clock. He saw everything. ("Neighbors," *WICF*, 90)
5. His eyes skipped around the kitchen—stove, stove, napkin-holder, stove, cupboards, toaster, back to her lips, back to the coach in the tablecloth. ("Will You Please Be Quiet, Please?" *WICF*, 90)
6. Something took him when he saw the lighted windows, saw snow on the roof, saw the station wagon in the driveway. ("Put Yourself in My Shoes," *WICF*, 98)

Ignoring the different realistic motivation for some of these descriptions (watching a photograph in description 1, entering a room in description 2, a marital crisis in description 5), there are striking similarities. All of these descriptions are from direct observation, although they are not written in the present tense.

In addition, an observer is present, who sometimes also narrates the story, and his immediate point of view dominates the scene. More important, the level of detail and organization of the field of vision might vary, but the impression is invariably of fragmentation. A sense of wholeness is created, says Slavoj Žižek, not because everything is present, but rather when an illusion of continuity is created.[13] As in the representations of movement, discussed in the first chapter, the items are adjacent in space, they belong to the same semantic field (house, furniture, street), and they embody an urge to see and describe "everything"; yet they do not create continuity in the field of vision. Moreover, most of these descriptions do not mention the relation between the items in space, which is an important factor in reconstructing a three-dimensional space in the reader's mind.[14] The space they depict is therefore two-dimensional, as if it were meant to illustrate the flatness of a photographic sheet, rather than an actual three-dimensional space.

Indeed, as far as the reader's eye is concerned, a list of items is not enough to create an impression of an entire space. Thus, G. E. Lessing and Georg Lukács—each from his ideological point of departure—both maintained that the linearity of language dismembers the simultaneity of space, and demand that description be banished from literature, unless it is integrated in action.[15] Modern description treats the inevitable fragmentation by a type of synecdoche, using a few fragments to represent a whole. However, Carver's descriptions do not try to overcome the limitations caused by the linearity of language, and the impression of randomly chosen fragments makes it difficult to treat them as synecdoches. Instead, the monotonic rhythm of these descriptions, recalling item after item, seems to underscore the arbitrary dismembering of space when it meets the eye. Thus, it is hardly the space that is the core of these descriptions but rather the very act of seeing. Sight, it appears, is partial and limited, regardless of the insistence on grasping the space, and despite the desire, expressed by one character, "to see everything, save it for later" ("Put Yourself in My Shoes," *WICF*, 96). More than making present the objects one sees, these descriptions illustrate how desperately sight strives to grasp something that eludes it, "to get a fix on it" (again, Carver's words).[16] In a sense, observation is already a memory, with its fragmentation, its seeming lack of selection, its fixation on detail—which appears to be both meaningful and random—rightly begging Claire's question: "Why do I notice that?"

At this point, a discussion beyond Carver's corpus is required: Consideration of two major writers with a special interest in description will help me demonstrate Carver's connection to a tradition of description, as well as his unique treatment of it. The standard-bearer of modern description is, naturally, Flaubert, with his endless catalogues of items—furniture, articles of clothing and animals, and his meticulous depiction of interior spaces. Flaubert represents the attempt to liberate description from cultural allusions, colorful metaphors and embellishments, and search for an impersonal, direct look at space as it is. His declaration "I am an eye," which suggests both immediacy and poignancy, reveals, according to some critics, the influence of photography.[17] One typical description is that of the house of Madame Aubain, the landlady of Félicité, the protagonist of "A Simple Heart" ("*Coeur simple*").

> This house had a slate roof and stood between an alley-way and a lane leading down to the river. Inside there were differences in level which were the cause of many a stumble. A narrow entrance-hall separated the kitchen from the parlor, where Mme Aubain sat all day long in a wicker easy-chair by the window. Eight mahogany chairs were lined up against the white-painted wainscoting, and under the barometer stood an old piano loaded with a pyramid of boxes and cartoons. On either side of the chimneys-piece, which was carved out of yellow marble in Louis Quinze style, there was a tapestry-covered arm-chair, and in the middle was a clock designed to look like a temple of Vesta. The whole room smelled a little musty, as the floor was on a lower level than the garden.[18]

This laconic, typically Flaubertian description sketches, in lucid language, free of metaphors, the outline of the house, the interrelation between its parts, and an incomplete list of its furniture, in whose midst the landlady sits as motionless as the house's furniture. This seemingly simple description attracted the attention of both Roland Barthes and Ezra Pound. In his seminal essay "The Reality Effect," Barthes mentions the barometer on top of the piano as an example of an item which cannot be integrated into the story's nets of plot and symbolism, and therefore serves only to point at its "being there" and producing a "reality effect." In Canto 7, Pound quotes a few lines of this description in homage to Flaubert's genius, which could keep the "dead weight" of objects from arresting the "subjective movement of the mind."[19]

Unlike Carver's descriptions, quoted earlier, in Flaubert's text there is no identifiable observer who watches this space, yet the space seems to be visible in real time, and there is no linguistic or temporal barrier to the act of description. Nonetheless, this space is imbued with memory and consciousness—probably that of Félicité, the maidservant, who had to leave the house after the death of her mistress, and nostalgically preserves its objects in her mind, just as she will keep some of them in her room. There are signs of the presence of memory: First of all, a close reading reveals that the description is not of the house as such, in a typical state, unbound to specific time, but pertains to specific times that its objects have been projected onto the "mental retina" of its tenant.[20] It could thus be compared to a photograph, not only because it is direct and laconic, but also because it preserves a moment where the space was transformed into an image. Secondly, the description mentions the interconnection between the inner and outer parts of the house ("between an alley-way and a lane"; "Inside, there were differences in level"). This quality endows the space with a depth which Carver's descriptions lack; it embodies the movement of the body within it, as, for example, in the differences being "the cause of many a stumble." The measurements of the house are those that Félicité sensed while moving within it, and thus they are preserved in her memory and in the text. Finally, within this envisioned net of coordinates that the memory of the body sketches, only a few segments of the house are embedded. As in Carver's description, memory is present in the space's fragmentation, in the way its objects hang on a thread, surfacing from the void, as they must have surfaced in Félicité's recollection. The latent reference in this description is therefore not the space as the character sees it, but the space as it is *present* in the character's mind. In fact, it is not the space which is rendered here, but rather its sensory imprint and the sediment it leaves in memory. Here lies the melancholy atmosphere of this description, which, despite the excess of objects, succeeds in preserving the "subjective movement of the mind."

This latent pull of the Flaubertian description toward inwardness and consciousness has been traced by Genette in his fine essay "Flaubert's Silence."[21] This essay's point of departure is not Flaubert's descriptions of outer reality, like the house in "A Simple Heart," but his representation of daydreaming and memory. Genette shows, with the help of linguistics, the way in which subjects of imagination have a surprising realistic quality, and the way they can be integrated in the story's "real" events (much like the imaginings of Carver's Claire, when she feels her own body merged with the dead girl, or in her factual report of the fishing events which she had not witnessed). In fact, the sense of reality in the representation of consciousness, as well as the presence of consciousness in the description of reality, are two sides of the same coin—the blurring of the internal and external in our experience of the world. Dream and imagination, says Genette, following Bachelard, create in us a memory of an imaginary past, which makes us respond to spaces as if we were already there.[22] Flaubert had indeed reported a "Proustian" feeling he got in encountering a new space. The multiplicity of descriptions in Flaubert, rather than indicating his love of facts, reveals his fondness of contemplation and introspection, attuned as he was to the echoes of inner and outer space with each other. "Have you ever believed in the existence of things?"—he writes to Maupassant in 1878—"Isn't everything an illusion? Only so-called relations—that is, our ways of perceiving objects—are true."[23]

This effect—the presence of memory in observation and of inner space in outer space, is different in Carver, and in a sense even opposite. Flaubert's descriptions reveal that observing is recollection, as an imaginary or actual past is evoked by the space when viewed, whereas Carver's descriptions—the products of observation in real time—suggest their future state as memory. They illustrate Deleuze's statement that "It is in the present that we make a memory."[24] Moreover, memory is present as a lack. In Flaubert, the act of recollection adds inner resonance to outer space, while the interconnections within the space endow it with depth, whereas in Carver's two-dimensional space, the sense of wholeness diminishes as it is consumed by forgetfulness as soon as it is observed.[25] The present tense of this text points at a basic lack, and the present's threatening similarity to a fragmented past. Claire lives in a constant present, unable to achieve a retrospective distance and perceive herself in a temporal continuity. Paradoxically, this experience stems from what is missing in the present, already experienced as partial and intangible. While the present in Flaubert is always a memory, in Carver's present it is already forgetfulness.

The delusions of the present tense and its inherent paradoxes were noticed by the writer and literary theoretician Alain Robbe-Grillet. Carver may have paid homage to Robbe-Grillet in the experimental, tense-confusing "Furious Season," in which a woman who repeatedly brushes her hair brings to mind the portrayal of "A" in *Jealousy*. In this novel, for example, Robbe-Grillet uses the present tense to blur the distinctions between the present and memory, reality and imagination. Robbe-Grillet took the complex structure of temporality and the blurring of present and past, only latent in Flaubert, to the extreme. Yet while in Flaubert's work the description is multilayered and a chink in the present opens up into a reverberating depth of time, in Robbe-Grillet the characters are trapped in a flat, homogenous dimension, where past, present, and future and reality and imagination are all entangled. This use of the present tense is part of Robbe-Grillet's overall effort to change the status of description in fiction. Its function, he maintains, should not be to establish the real and to support the outdated distinctions between different times and different layers of reality. The cinema marked a turn in this regard and should inspire what Robbe-Grillet calls the "new novel." Henceforth, description should sabotage vision, blur the familiar contours of the objects, and borrow from the cinema the equal status it gives to subjective experience, which—like reality in the present—is always in the visible "front" of the film. The image in cinema "keeps us from believing at the same time what it affirms, just as description kept us from seeing what it is showing."[26]

Robbe-Grillet's arguments are confusing and paradox-ridden. In the effort to banish man from the object of description, he declares war on metaphors and "animistic adjectives." He thus inhibits the reader from fitting the object within any grid of signification, and hampers the projection of an "interpretive screen" on space, which, in the old novel, was imbued with human time and faith. However, at the same time, Robbe-Grillet restores the human by the very "movement of the description":

> It is no longer a question here of time passing, since gestures, paradoxically, are on the contrary shown only frozen in the moment. It is matter itself which is both solid and unstable, both present and imagined, alien to man and constantly being invented in man's mind. The entire interest of the descriptive pages—that is, man's place in these pages—is, therefore no longer in the thing described, but in the very movement of the description.[27]

At first glance, it seems that the only point of contact between Carver and Robbe-Grillet is their interest in an outer, concrete reality at the expense of introspection. It is hard to see any other similarity between the unidentified fragmented objects of Robbe-Grillet and Carver's swift labeling of items in space. The former defamiliarizes the object by showing it in a way that prevents its identification, while the latter merely identifies the objects allowing only a general, crude visualization. If we measure them by Shklovsky's standards, when defining the effect of defamiliarization, Carver's descriptions do not allow the reader to really "see" the object (in the visionary sense Shklovsky gave to seeing). Rather, his economical use of everyday language does not show reality in a fresh, unfamiliar way, and merely spots and points to objects by their "positioning in space."[28]

However, these two opposite ways—the omission of nouns in order to show the object by itself (in Robbe-Grillet) and the replacement of the particular object by a general noun (in Carver)—meet in this vague yet rich concept of "the movement of the description." Robbe-Grillet has not explained this phrase, and its significance (or significances) may only be inferred from his work and critical writings. The movement of the description is first of all a result of the fact that the description follows an act of observation which infuses time and human touch into space.[29] The movement of description also pertains to the movement of the descriptive language. And both these movements are actualized in the act of reading, since, according to Robbe-Grillet, the time of reading is the only time of the text. In addition to these possible meanings, note that for Robbe-Grillet the object is an integral part of its description. Henceforth, the movement of the description is also the movement of the grist of description, which is "both solid and unstable, both present and imagined, alien to man and constantly being invented in man's mind." The object eludes description, constantly changes shape, and moves between dimensions of time and levels of existence and inhibits vision (i.e., recognition). In that sense, the movement of description is the core of description rather than a mere dimension of it, and it is precisely the present tense, which is inherently impossible, that allows Robbe-Grillet to express this dynamism. The present tense tries to become one with the visible, to make it present, yet at the same time fixates it. It is therefore always one step behind. Being a kind of stationary post, which the object evades, it embodies the movement of reality, which is inseparable from the movement of observation and description.

The way in which Carver's characters try to fixate their surroundings by the use of general nouns reflects a similar tension. It is not the visible that these descriptions make present, but its disappearance in the moment of seeing. The rapid automatic labeling of objects, which indicates no real "seeing," underscores it. They illustrate fragmentation in the very first encounter with space. Much as this visible reality seems immediate and present, and the look seems direct and frontal, the space cannot be contained, and the description is a "description of an effort"—the effort of consciousness to grasp a continuity which eludes it in the very encounter with the world.

This is the tragic side of seeing, as expressed in some of Carver's stories—a gnawing of continuity and of meaning, and an acute sense of loss—no doubt a substantial experience in Carver's world, as he often acknowledged.[30] The last section of this chapter will explore the brighter side of seeing, and the "solution" Carver finds to its problematic nature in one of his more optimistic stories. At this stage, I would like to conclude that Carver is connected to the writers discussed here both by his manifest passion to see and to describe, *and* by revealing the tensions inherent in seeing and description as such. Given the differences between Flaubert, Robbe-Grillet, and Carver, they all embody an aspiration for a "pure" vision in their immediate representation of impersonal space, freed of meanings or interpretation. They all reintroduce consciousness to this seemingly neutral description—be it by the resonance of memory, the movement of the description, or the fragmentation brought on by forgetfulness. They all contain an element of non-seeing in the act of seeing—in the way the unseen lurks in the heart of the seen, the sabotaging of visualization, or the elusiveness of the sight. Finally, they all present a description which illustrates—sometimes latently—an experience of movement and of time.

The Glimpse

Claire goes out for a drive with her husband. They stop briefly, and she notices two details: "I notice a great stack of papers just inside the door. On the top step a fat woman in a print dress holds out a licorice stick to a little girl" (*WICF*, 220). Naturally, any realistic text has details whose only purpose is to produce the "reality effect." However, in a text which displays almost no effort to create a sense of wholeness in the fictional world (especially in the abridged version of this story), these details stick out on account of their lack of connection to the plot, the atmosphere of the story, or any symbolic net. They are motivated by the glimpse, a swift look which captures a spark of reality or an isolated fragment. This kind of look is delineated by time and has a double connection to movement. One often glimpses while moving (and the era of the car has doubtlessly refined this kind of looking at the American space). However, the swiftness of this gaze does not allow one to take in the entire field of vision. Thus, while the observer is moving, the details under observation become detached from their dynamic continuity, and their movement is truncated midway.

The direct look—by which I began to characterize Carver's manner of description as a way of looking which seems to diminish temporal or verbal intervention—is revealed to be a look permeated with consciousness and memory and consumed by forgetfulness. The glimpse is another metaphor by which I will modify Carver's direct look, and explore its features from another angle.

Carver's corpus abounds with glimpses. It is with this look that Claire sees the symbolic river while driving to the funeral. The waitress in "Fat" glances at the fingers of a fat man, with whom she will sense a bond of identification and reflection. The passengers of a train are glimpsed by Meyers when he rushes through the carts (in "The Compartment"), and the everyday gestures and details of landscape are glimpsed by Al in his drive to find the dog that he abandoned (in "Jerry, Molly and Sam").

The effect of the glimpse is also striking in the "Will You Please Be Quiet, Please?". Like "So Much Water . . . ," this story focuses on a marital crisis. Ralph, following the discovery of his wife's unfaithfulness, has a night of drunkenness and violence. The crisis, which cuts off any sense of continuity in Ralph's life, is embodied in the nature of his movement in this nightmarish night—a fragmented movement of wandering, rendered by broken sentences, vague images, and gestures accompanied by an inexplicable fear:

> Ralph glimpsed shadowy figures of men and women talking, their heads close together . . . The door opened behind him and they go into a car parked at the curb and Ralph saw the woman toss her hair as she got into the car: He had never seen anything so frightening. (*WYPB*, 240)

Runyon explains Ralph's reaction to the tossing of hair in Freudian terms as indicating a fear of the feminine, also evident in the description of Ralph's wife. According to Runyon, the hair of the female figure suggests the hair of the Medusa who petrifies anyone who looks at her.[31] While this allegorical reading is intriguing, I believe that the impression left by this gesture is not necessarily a result of specific symbolic content. The very isolation of a detail from a continuum of space and movement—via the glimpse—is sufficient for this angst. It exposes the observer, stripped of all defenses and denials, to immediate contact with raw reality, with no context to mitigate its influence.

The intimidating detail which sticks out from a field of vision while disturbing its homogeneity suggests Lacan's concept of the "gaze." This element in the field of vision observes the observer, contains the very act of sight, and constitutes a "blot" or a blind spot—inaccessible and intimidating. Lacan's conception may also shed light on the end of "What's in Alaska?" where the gaze is in the form of two eyes peeping out at Jack—another one of Carver's voyeurs. In "Where Is Everyone?" the narrator, who sleeps in his mother's bed, wakes in horror to the sight of white light and roaring sound. This scene seems to demand that it be read in the spirit of Lacan (as interpreted by Slavoj Žižek), to whom this kind of phenomena—the dispersion of an amorphous substance and a bodiless voice or gaze—signify the presence of the "real": one of the more mysterious dimensions of Lacanian existences which is also connected to the mother.[32]

Whether or not we adapt these possible psychoanalytic readings, undoubtedly Carver has an interest in an initial sense of threat, which he expresses in his essay "On Writing":

> I like it when there is some feeling of threat or sense of menace in short stories. I think a little menace is fine to have in a story. For one thing, it's good for the circulation. There has to be tension, a sense that something is imminent, that certain things are in relentless motion, or else, most often, there simply won't be a story. What creates tension in a piece of fiction is partly the way the concrete words are linked together to make up the visible action of the story. But it's also the things that are left out, that are implied, the landscape just under the smooth (but sometimes broken and unsettled) surface of things. (*Fires*, 26)

For Carver (whose style as an essayist is as colloquial as in his fiction), menace is a condition for the movement and tension of the story. However, this somewhat technical explanation "leaves out"—to use his words—the existential aspect of this feeling, which is explicitly stated in "Will You Please Be Quiet, Please?": "Yes, there was a great evil pushing at the world, he thought, and it only needed a little slipway, a little opening" (*WYPB*, 241). In Ralph's life, evil pushes after a crack opened up in the tranquil surface of his marriage, and this crack is manifested in his way of looking and its textual expression—a series of glimpses which crumble the false wholeness of the field of vision.

Beside this intimidating fragmentation there is, however, another implication to the glimpse: It is a way of looking that entails an intricate relationship between the present and memory, another variation of the complexity that we found in the direct look. In a sense, the glimpse stands for pure vision. Modern art, with its yearning for capturing the "moment" prior to any processing, verbalization, or interpretation, has taken special interest in the concept of the glimpse or a blink of the eye. Yet, this was followed by the realization (as formulated by Derrida) that "there is duration to the blink, and it closes the eye."[33] Being an extreme manifestation of the ideal of pure, preverbal visibility, the blink of the eye embodies the impossibility of such vision and an "innocent eye"; for even in a glimpse one cannot achieve a pure encounter with reality, which is not extended over time and mediated by language or memory. These elements usher in a momentary non-seeing (the instant of the closing of the eye) to sight.

Moreover, what meaning does the glimpse hold outside memory? More than any other look, this look encourages a post-factum observation, within consciousness and away from the object. Just as in the development of a negative, the swiftness of the glimpse requires a delayed reaction and it is dependent on memory to unfold the results of observation.

This quality of the glimpse is often revealed in Carver's stories, as in a simple sentence from "How About This?" where the impression of a casual detail sinks in only later ("He suddenly recalled the mattress in the kitchen. He understood that it made him afraid" [*WYPB*, 193]). However, the inevitable extension of the glimpse beyond its time, even as it embodies immediacy, is especially interesting when Carver ponders his own craft. Following his observation about menace in the short story, and using V. S. Pritchett's definition, Carver sees the glimpse as a metaphor for the short story, which enables only a quick look into fictional reality:

> V. S. Pritchett's definition of a short story is "*something glimpsed from the corner of the eye, in passing.*" Notice the "glimpse" part of this. First the glimpse. Then the glimpse given life, turned into something that illuminates the moment and may, if we're lucky . . . have even further-ranging consequences and meaning. The short story writer's task is to *invest* the glimpse with all that is in his power. (*Fires*, 26–27, my emphases)

Thus, Carver finds that the widening circles around the glimpse and the way it gradually accumulates life and meaning make it a suitable metaphor for the short story. The plethora of glimpses inside the reality of his stories may be seen as a meta-fictional gesture toward the genre that accommodates them. However, they can also be seen as a factor in the process Carver describes, which another short story writer, Tobias Wolff, clarifies, while emphasizing the reader's part in it. For Wolff, short stories weave "their images through your memory," and some passages, which are "often no more than a glimpse through an open door, inscribe themselves forever on the reader's moral being, and bring the world into sharper focus."[34] In Wolff's observation, as in Carver's craft, the two meanings of the glimpse—a metaphor to characterize the short story as well a way of looking *in* the stories—collaborate. The glimpses of Carver's Claire or Ralph are the spots where the reader is summoned to integrate his or her memory with that of the character, and complete, or process, that which the characters capture in their glimpse without really deciphering. The reader thus treats the images as if they were derived from his or her own experience and memory. They seem to waver between the significant and the random, rather than being parts of a constructed scheme intended to produce meaning. In this way, readers integrate themselves actively in the text. The glimpse is a result of swift movement in the fictional world, which inscribes images in the memory of both the character and the reader. In addition, the reader's quick passage through the short story is also a kind of "glimpse" at a slice of reality.

All these forms of movement and activity compensate, as it were, for the stasis of movement in the glimpse. This occurs both at the level of meaning (to be discussed further in chapter 6) and at the level of visualization. Indeed, as Elaine Scarry's cognitive findings show, the unfinished, interrupted, broken-off movement, or the partially-seen detail, tends to create an effect of movement in the reader's imagination.[35] Thus, it is not their symbolic or informative content that makes these details significant, but the dynamic process which they generate—what Slavoj Žižek calls "the movement of interpretation."[36]

Still, the content of these details is what distinguishes Carver from other modern and modernist writers who have taken interest in the glimpse and its parallels: the blink of the eye and the fraction of a moment. For Henry James, the glimpse stands for the moment when a random, concrete scene becomes archetypical and universal. Virginia Wolff's "moment" is one of intensity and utter concentration. William Faulkner's blink of an eye has a mythic dimension; it wavers between reality and imagination, and encapsulates different levels of time.[37] These features could hardly be attributed to Carver's glimpsed details, which stick to the everyday and the marginal, and challenge the process of the production of meaning. In the next section—and the next mode of looking—I will explore this quality of Carver's vision and its thematic implications.

The Sidelong Look

When Carver selects materials for his fictional world, he turns to the most mundane and banal aspects of everyday reality. What is more banal than a car mirror? Still, this ordinary object, serves him in "So Much Water . . ." to introduce another variation of a look, and another aspect of the Carverian look. When Claire and her husband return from their ride, Stewart watches Claire apprehensively through the mirror, and she watches him looking at her. During the ride to the girl's funeral, a truck driver stalks her, using the same mirror, and she uses the side mirror to avoid him. This look is indirect, self-denying. It is directed at one area of the field of vision, while secretly scanning another. These aspects (rather than the exact location of the pupil) are what make the look in the mirror a sidelong look. However, Carver's stories abound with actual sidelong looks. Lloyd scans, his head tilted, all "the objects of his life" in the corner of the room (in "Careful"); Lee squints at the fishing net in "Sixty Acres." The very same word is used to describe Jack looking at his wife embracing his friend in "What's in Alaska?".[38] And we are still in the realm of jealousy and a marital crisis when a whole scene is rendered through a jealous husband's "corner of the eye" in "Signals." All these instances involve an intense way of looking, which breaks the habits of automatic observation and results in defamiliarization.

What is the significance of the sidelong look? What are its implications? There is a familiar connection (especially in cinema) between a sidelong look and the sense of menace which Carver sees as indispensable to a story. In addition, this look has been thoroughly explored in the writing of Lacan when he discusses vision and the device of anamorphosis.[39] Lacan analyzes a painting by Hans Holbein, "The Ambassadors" (1533), which has an unidentified object in the foreground of the picture. Only a quick and sidelong look, when one exits the room, allows the viewer to make out the form of a skull. The viewer thus unexpectedly confronts the presence of death and of the "real" that lies beneath the surface of the tranquil and orderly world of the ambassadors, as well as in his own world—the "real" which cannot be accessed through a direct and frontal look. Again, this concept of the sidelong look, which Lacan (like Pritchett) combines with the glimpse, aptly describes the disquieting encounter of Carver's characters with a raw reality that resists symbolization, and confronts the viewer—as well as the reader—when he or she is off guard.

In Lacan's writing, the sidelong look pertains to a complex conceptual framework which will not be discussed here. For our purposes, it is important to note that according to Lacan, with this look the viewer disarms, for a moment, the ordinary patterns of understanding, by which one organizes the world, makes sense of it, and reinforces his mechanisms of denial. These patterns are symbolized by the direct look, which fails to see Holbein's skull. When the object of observation is a person, he or she is may not be aware of the look which involves no eye contact and communication. In terms of the viewer, as intense as this look might be, it is "in passing," in the margins, outside of the awareness and the fully articulated areas of consciousness. In fact, there is a mutual act here: The person who is being viewed unknowingly does not comply with another person's look, and the viewer is set to see the other in a way which is free from the usual patterns of seeing.

To further explore the sidelong look in Carver's works (again, as a metaphor rather than an actual element in the fictional world), I would like to use some analogies from photography, and elaborate on what had been already mentioned in the first chapter. In American photography in the fifties, there was a trend characterized by what is often called "the sidelong glimpse."[40] Photographers—among them Robert Frank (especially in his influential "The Americans"),

Bruce Davidson, and Lee Friedlander—abandoned "the decisive moment" (of coincidence, of standing at a junction or a turn) in favor of the marginal moment and "non-events" of life. The sidelong glimpse expressed these photographers' attempt to avoid selection, centralization, and the setting of hierarchies, since their photographs do not comply with an abstract scheme which emphasizes certain crucial events and ignores others. In fact, photography had this potential from its early days. As Deleuze has observed, the chronophotographers Edward Muybridge and Étienne-Jules Marey contributed to the concept of movement by representing it through equidistant snapshots rather than by "poses or generalized postures," in which "the remarkable or singular instant remains any-instant-whatever among the others."[41] Walter Benjamin's famous insight about the power of photography to capture "the optical unconsciousness"—for example, the fraction of movement unknown to the pre-camera era—also points to the fact that a photograph often captures the "right detail" of movement rather than the representative one.[42] This detail might contradict the preconceptions of the way movement should be. However, despite this quality—or maybe because of it—this detail plunges into subjectivity, and finds "shelter in daydream."

In Carver's work, there are some poses that imitate photography's "decisive moment": a sort of theatrical "tableau" that freezes characters in a significant gesture; often they constitute a "pregnant moment," which encapsulates a whole series of previous and future events. Such is the throwing of the stone in "Viewfinder," or the way Bert, in "A Serious Talk," strikes the pose of a *discus* thrower, thus revealing his inability to *discuss* his marriage with his wife.[43] Such is also the standing of a woman on a beam in "How About This?" which embodies the fragile equilibriums between the couple in the story. However, for many of the gestures which describe Carver's characters, such an interpretation would be over-reading. It seems that they signify nothing except for the character's physicality: They roll their tongues behind their teeth, they scratch their necks, touch their lower lip, narrow their eyes, and pat their chin. Carver describes all sorts of gestures and expressions which are neither decisive nor representative. These are the gestures that characterize the sidelong photographic glimpse, which refrains from showing people in a moment which complies with an abstract idea that the viewer or the reader has, but portrays them as a physical body, focusing on their concrete otherness.

As with Carver's other aesthetic choices, the casual gesture, implying a sidelong look, has thematic implications. These are clearly shown in "So Much Water . . .". Claire looks at her husband with a mix of astonishment, alienation, judgment, and revulsion. His physicality is crucial in this story, since much of what Claire feels has to do with him being a body—a male body. Their physical interaction is a disturbing reminder of the abuse inflicted on the murdered girl. Claire winces at the sight of Stewart's legs, and notices in repulsion his hairy knuckles and broad fingers "that had moved over me, into me last night" (*WICF*, 218). Nonetheless, this look at the husband's physical presence is far from being one-sided, and it is here that the effect of this story can be located, with its powerful combination of contradictory feelings. The fishing incident unleashes in Claire the anger and violence incipient in her marriage. At the same time, it evokes a radical empathy, through which she almost merges with the body and the gaze of the tortured girl. This empathy with another woman brings with it resentment of the entire male sex, as well as a suspicion toward sexuality in general, which the story poignantly expresses, albeit sometimes heavy-handedly.

Surprisingly, the empathy is not reserved for the dead girl. Claire, who winces in bed to avoid her husband's body, also notices his tiredness and edginess and is filled with compassion. This empathy is motivated by gestures which cannot be channeled—either by her or the reader—toward a specific, clear characterization: him smoking a cigarette, putting his arms on the table, staring vacantly in the dark, or the way he suddenly and unwillingly sobs. While her feelings toward the girl are complete identification, similarity and even symbiosis, the feelings toward the husband are stimulated by total otherness. It is as if she is facing an opaque being, whose expressions and gestures signify both an otherness which cannot be reduced and a sense of vulnerability. It is precisely these gestures of otherness which stimulate her empathy. These are captured in passing, in a sidelong look, absentmindedly, without her knowing why she noticed them. They steal in from the margins of the direct look. They are gestures that elude patterns of meaning or preconceived notions about the nature of the other-male. The empathy created by these postures is the opposite of the empathy she feels for the girl, since it involves an awareness of otherness and an unbridgeable gap. Yet this very empathy constitutes a breach in the barrier between man and woman, self and other. In both versions, the story does not suggest a real conciliation between Claire and Stewart; still, it is far from offering an unequivocal view of their conflict.

Thus, in an integrated work, Carver's different, yet similar, ways of looking create his special mix of lucidity and compassion. It is harsh in its directness, and sees "everything" with pitiless transparency, yet it is aware of its own blindness, limitations, and blind spots—everything that eludes sight and sinks into forgetfulness. It is a look which reaches for the space as such, yet it illustrates the effort (and mostly the failure) of consciousness to find continuity and meaning in the world of things. It captures, in passing, an immediate detail, dissociated from any meaning, yet it calls for its deciphering in memory. And indirectly, through the margins, beyond the range of preconceived meaning, it allows for emotional contact with the other. This look meticulously registers external reality, yet it reveals the invisible, interior, and personal levels of reality. Borrowing from the insights of Roland Barthes, when speaking of the nature of looking at a photograph, we may say that the act of seeing occurs in Carver mostly with closed eyes, when the look does not confront the object of sight.[44]

I will try to elucidate this argument through a reading of one of Carver's most well-known and popular stories, "Cathedral," where a closing of the eyes actually occurs.

Eyes Shut

In many of the interviews conducted with Carver in the wake of his success, he emphasizes the importance of humor in his stories.[45] It does seem, however, that the very life of the characters who populate them, with their marital crises, divorces, drinking problems, and precarious work situations, sometimes prevent readers from enjoying or even noticing the flickers of humor—black humor mostly. "Cathedral" is different in that sense, as it is in other senses. Carver admitted striking out in a new direction in this story, and it is usually viewed—along with the collection in which it was published—as a turning point. Critics argue that in this collection Carver moved toward "fuller" prose, and started portraying a richer—more optimistic—reality than that in his earlier stories.[46]

"Cathedral" is a first-person narrative, opening with the narrator who is preparing—somewhat nervously—for a visit by his wife's friend and former employer, a blind man who has recently been widowed. We know little of the narrator-host, not even his name, yet his presence is perceptible. The way he tells his story, as well as the story's comic tone, characterizes him vividly. Thanks to him, the humor, which might be overlooked by readers in other stories, becomes accessible and noticeable. Just to mention the amusing dinner ("We ate like there was no tomorrow. . . . We didn't look back." [*WICF*, 364]) or the way the narrator uncomfortably refers to his wife's past love life or describes her hobbies: listening to her blind friend's tapes and writing one poem a year.

Since humor is an important factor in rendering this story so effective and characterizing the narrator, it is useful to use it as a point of entry for this text. What is it, for instance, that makes the narrator's portrayal of Robert, the blind man, somewhat grotesque?

> As I stared at his face, I saw the left pupil turn in toward his nose while the other made an effort to keep in one place. But it was only an effort, for that eye was on the roam without his knowing it or wanting it to be. (363)

And why does this description of the host, his wife, and the blind man entering the house seem ridiculous?

> We began to move then, a little group, from the porch into the living room, my wife guiding him by the arm. The blind man was carrying his suitcase in his other hand. My wife said things like, "To your left here, Robert. That's right. Now watch it, there's a chair. That's it. Sit down right here. This is the sofa. We just bought it two weeks ago." (361)

Eyes which fail to serve their owner call for a comic-grotesque description, where a detail may detach itself from the whole, take on a life of its own, as the organ becomes a malfunctioning machine. However, the unique nature of the object of description is but partly responsible for the comic effect, and it owes just as much to the particular viewer in this story. The narrator-viewer uses sight mostly to fragment and disintegrate what he sees, while "the marvelous independence of the human gaze," which—as Proust puts it—is "tied to the human face by a cord so loose, so long, so elastic that it can stray, alone, as far as it may choose," serving him well in his tendency to distance and dissociate himself.[47] These qualities of his look, which produce a comic effect, are also shown when he sees himself from the outside as part of "a little group" that makes its way in a cumbersome manner into the house, or when he accurately repeats his wife's well-meant words of guidance. In fact, the wife, who unintentionally uses a verb pertaining to sight ("watch it!"), or seems to forget at some point that she is guiding a blind man, and starts to "show" the house itself to the guest ("This is the sofa. We just bought it two weeks ago") betrays a reaction similar to her husband's. When he asks the blind man if he sat on the side of the train that has the view, covers his wife's bare thigh, or nods at his unseeing interlocutor, he, like his wife, reveals the difficulty of sighted people in imagining a world without sight.

Indeed, sight is the narrator's active sense, and the humorous tone is enhanced by the meticulous rendition of the visible, static, and moving elements of the visit, as—in one more example—the "tic" of the blind man tugging at his beard. In the first part of the story, the narrator is introduced to other sensual options—touch and hearing. His wife tells him of her unforgettable sensation when the blind man felt her face, and suggests that her husband listen to the tapes that her friend sent her. However, he fails to share her feelings about the physical contact and is glad when their listening to the tapes is interrupted midway, especially when his own name is mentioned. It seems that the narrator invariably chooses the position of the observer—with regard to himself and to other people—and preferably from a safe distance, as when he looks at the blind man and his wife from the window. This explains his strong aversion to blindness as such, and his difficulty in accepting a man who does not see, all the more one who does not see *him*. We learn from the narrator's words about Beulah, Robert's late wife: "And then I find myself thinking what a pitiful life this woman must have led. Imagine a woman who could never see herself as she was seen in the eyes of her loved one" (360). Or from what he says of the look of his own wife: "My wife finally took her eyes off the blind man and looked at me. I had the feeling she didn't like what she saw. I shrugged" (362). Both the way the narrator experiences the world and his personal contacts are based on seeing and being seen. It is not without significance, therefore, that the transformative process he will undergo concerns vision. This process culminates when he and his guest stay awake, watching television, and the blind man asks him to draw him a cathedral that appeared in a TV show. There are some phases in this process of drawing-description which gradually introduce possible approaches to visible reality to this skilled voyeur.

The first appearance of the cathedral is during a documentary about the history of cathedrals. Later the narrator will say that as far as he is concerned, the cathedral is merely "something to look at on late-night TV" (372). Indeed, for now, the cathedral (in fact, there is more than one) is a mere part of the endless stream of images that the television issues—one image among many one encounters randomly during zapping. Still, this first appearance of the cathedral foreshadows an important distinction—between sight and sound—that will acquire meaning later in the story. A narrator with a British accent ("the Englishman"), whose commentary accompanies the photos, stops talking every once in a while, and lets the camera roam over the cathedral, showing it from different angles. These two approaches to the object—*diegesis* and *mimesis*, if you wish—will be employed by the blind man and his host in their shared effort to represent the cathedral. Regarding representation, this effort clearly has implications for the work of the one who's in charge—as Carver says in his essay "On Writing"—of linking "concrete words . . . to make up the visible action of the story," namely, the writer of fiction.[48] There is a similarity between the effort to describe a physical object to a blind man and the work of fiction in facilitating visualization (with the difference that, unlike a blind man, the reader already has a stock of images to draw from). Moreover, here Carver revives the old connection between the modus of description and texts which deal with various architectonic structures.[49] In fact, when tracking the phases of the drawing or the description of the cathedral, one should alternate between two levels: the level of the story, where a character undergoes a psychic and moral process, and the meta-literary level, in which the mimetic task of creating and representing visible reality is being thoroughly explored. These two levels do not exclude each other, but are interwoven and illuminate each other.

The act of description is launched when the narrator feels that, as a host, he should report to his guest on what he sees when the show is not accompanied by a commentary. From the outset, he encounters a problem: Has he any base for description? Does a blind man know what a cathedral is? The replay of the blind man is telling. He repeats what he has just heard from the commentator, but selects the details that concern the process of building the cathedral:

> I know they took hundreds of workers fifty or a hundred years to build, he said. I just heard the man say that, of course. I know generations of the same families worked on a cathedral. . . . The men who began their life's work on them, they never lived to see the completion of their work. In that wise, bub, they're no different from the rest of us, right? (370)

It is only natural for a blind man to select details which have nothing to do with the cathedral's appearance, and specifically those that encourage identification ("In that wise . . . they're no different from the rest of us"). When he talks of the cathedral as a creation by many people, Robert thus foreshadows his own collaboration with the seeing man in "building" the cathedral on a paper. Also, by referring to the life and work of the builders rather than to the cathedral itself, he intuitively follows Lessing's suggestion when discussing the limitations of literature in representing objects.[50] According to Lessing, in a media which is marked by linearity, in which it is impossible to represent objects simultaneously, it is better not to describe an object, but to "tell it" by incorporating it into a plot and into actions which unfold in time. Therein is the greatness of Homer: He describes Achilles' shield through the story of its construction by Hephaestus and the plots he spins from its engravings. Yet this method indicates less of Robert's skill in the art of description, and more the general inclination which he tries to share with the narrator: He tries to incorporate visible reality into human time and human experience. Later, he will specifically ask to add people to the drawing of the cathedral. It seems that his attitude echoes the words of Emerson when speaking of a gothic cathedral that "affirms that it was done by us" only if we "apply ourselves to the history of its production," and "put ourselves into the place and state of the builders."[51]

Eventually, the blind man admits that he does not know what a cathedral is, and challenges his host by asking him to describe it. The task is difficult, practically impossible. Like other Carver's characters, this observer looks "hard" at the cathedral on the screen, but comes up with only a lame description. He repeats, in different variations, the adjective "big" ("tall," "reach high up," "massive"), but these synonyms are empty, and keep him away from the object. He tries analogy: The cathedral's buttresses remind him of viaducts, but he realizes that in this case, both the vehicle and the tenor are unfamiliar to his interlocutor. The two basic means of description, adjectives and metaphors, which this amateur describer intuitively chooses, fail him. Similar means were rejected by Robbe-Grillet in his theory of description. It was his aspiration to unlink the object from its human connotations, to impede the reader from seeing it, and thus, paradoxically, to rebuild it in his subjectivity.[52] In "Cathedral," on the other hand, the usual means of description will not serve because the seeing man is banned from a shared stock of visual images. However, whether through intentional sabotage (as in Robbe-Grillet) or through inevitable limitation (as in "Cathedral"), the result is the blockage of automatic visualization. In both cases, one should look for another way to access the object, and to start from scratch—to create the object even while describing it.

The next step in the narrator's effort to illustrate the height of the cathedrals is to emphasize the importance of God at the time these huge edifices were built. In response, Robert asks him if he is religious, and again draws his host toward a more personal experience of the object. In fact, this space in particular seems to call for it, being a structure that overtly expresses ideas and feelings. Yet the narrator is not ready for this option. He does not believe in God, and for him, the cathedral is but an image drawn from the media's flat world, devoid of any meaning or feeling: "Something to look at on late-night TV" (372).

The blind man then asks him to draw the cathedral. Of all the efforts to reach this structure—through personal time, the process of building, adjectives, metaphors, religious and personal experience—this phase, an amateur's drawing, with rough lines, on a brown paper—is for me the most accurate metaphor for Carver's style of description:

> First I drew a box that looks like a house. It could have been the house I lived in. Then I put a roof on it. At either end of the roof, I drew spires. Crazy.... I put in windows with arches. I drew flying buttresses. I hung great doors. I couldn't stop.... I'm no artist. But I kept drawing just the same. (371–72)

It is easy to imagine this simple drawing—some basic lines ("box that looks like a house"), with no perspective, drawn on a supermarket bag's brown paper—and to be reminded of Carver's descriptions. These are indeed a "beginners' mimesis": "an ashtray, a Lux clock, and a few old paperbacks on a table beside the cot"; "The driveway, the carport, front steps, bay window," and another window—a bland list of nouns, with only few adjectives and prepositions, and no metaphors. They do not create a sense of a particular space, no matter how detailed they are. They remain anonymous and yet familiar ("It could have been the house I lived in"), the kind of depiction that might explain why it so natural to compare Carver to Edward Hopper, with his all-American landscapes and wooden houses.[53]

This is the time to digress from "Cathedral" and quote Carver when he discusses the writer's task in showing things in reality "like no one else sees them":

> And this is done through the use of clear and specific language, language used as to bring to life the details that will light up the story for the reader. For the details to be concrete and to convey meaning, the language must be accurate and precisely given. *The words can be*

so precise they may even sound flat, but they can still carry; if used right, they can hit all the notes. (*Fires*, 27, my emphasis)

We can only guess what Carver means by "flat words." He thus expresses his desire to reach visible reality in the most direct way. The language which aspires to precision and concreteness should be therefore "flattened," for example, emptied of extra meanings, subdued of any resonance—referential and plain. Nonetheless, Carver's choice of the word "flat," which is fairly bold, and certainly not obvious, brings to mind the sparse two-dimensional space he depicts with these flat words as well as the fictional reality he creates: a world ridden by clichés and overused images, dissociated from the values that once gave them depth and resonance. Is there a connection between these different meanings of "flatness"? I believe so, especially when dealing with Carver, whose works shifts with great sophistication between different meanings of the concept of flatness.

Robbe-Grillet, who systematically undermines the concept—or "myth"—of depth, sought to link the object's surface and the surface of consciousness. In his descriptions, he brings together the "suchness" of objects, freed from metaphysical significance, and a fresh vision which avoids attributing additional significance to it. In the fictional space of Robbe-Grillet, he likewise undermines the illusion of depth. Similarly, Carver's descriptions often resist multidimensional vision, in the physical sense (depth in the field of vision), the metaphysical sense (meanings ascribed to the object), and the psychological sense (projections of the viewer). However, unlike Robbe-Grillet, this does not bring him closer to the object as such, or to a fresh vision, freed from familiar patterns of perception and signification. Rather, we have seen how Carver's vision is often no more than automatic recognition, with overused, everyday language and stock phrases. As in his dialogue, it seems that rather than undermine a vision suffused by cliché, he uses cliché's very methods: He rarely shows what makes an object particular, he shuns personification, and he uses a standard stock of images. His fondness for the surface of things, as well as his fondness of "flatness," thus brings him dangerously close to a one-dimensional vision of cliché—a claim that was made in its day against photography.[54]

So what *is* the advantage that flat words and one-dimensional space carry over the stock images of popular culture? Or—in our story's terms—how could such a crude drawing succeed in infusing life into a cathedral from a "late-night" show? Come to think of it, how can it be that of all the possible ways to represent reality, a drawing penetrates the darkness of a blind man? The answer to these questions unfolds later in the story: The blind man does not *see* the cathedral but rather feels its outlines when he lets his hand "ride" the hand of the seeing man. Actually, this gesture is far richer than a practical solution to blindness, as shown later, when Robert asks his friend to close his eyes and keep drawing.

The end of the story has been justly interpreted by critics as the final step in the protagonist's process of *bildung*, when he learns to share and feel empathy, and succeeds in experiencing another person by "testing his blindness."[55] It is important to note, however, that this process involves the sense of sight and the issue of representation. This tightens the connection between the psycho-moral process and the meta-literary level of the text, while the poetic issues are endowed with a broader moral resonance.

As the protagonist learns to put himself in the shoes of another man, he learns to give up, for a short while, on sight. His work of visual representation is totally dependent on the sense of touch: One hand rides another, a hand experiences the cathedral. It is common to attribute to the sense of touch the power to annihilate the distance that sight requires. This is a feminine sense, says Luce Irigaray, implicitly defying the patriarchical tradition of representation, based on the Cartesian concept of distance and separation between subject and object.[56] Similarly, for Emmanuel Levinas, touch stands for "the impingement of the world as a whole upon subjectivity."[57]

We have seen how the narrator of "Cathedral" consistently capitalizes on the distancing quality of sight. It is therefore crucial that the transformation he undergoes involves the sense of touch, both with regard to space and to another person. He thus reveals another aspect of the "surface"—it is not only the exterior of things, or lack of depth. It is also that which can be touched. Moreover, the blind man does not touch the cathedral itself or even its drawing. He visualizes it through the moving hand of the seeing man. In fact, it was already during the appearance of the cathedral on television that the withdrawal from words, the commentary, was made in favor of an image (the camera's work) which entailed movement—that of the camera around its object. This combination of movement and touch paves the way for the last phase of the encounter in "Cathedral"—the closing of the eyes.

To further understand the connection between touch, movement, and the eyes shut, let us return—from a different angle—to Robbe-Grillet and his theory of description. Robbe-Grillet, with his vision of a "new novel," turned his back on the traditional novel (mostly Balzac). He saw himself as carrying on "a line of descent" from Flaubert to Kafka—writers driven by "a passion to describe."[58] However, as mentioned, Robbe-Grillet's descriptions work to sabotage vision, and systematically destroy the visual image. In fact, he destroys the object by detaching it from the human "tyranny of signification" while at the same time, he rebuilds it in the reader's experience. The time of the object's existence becomes the time of viewing and reading, and the "movement of the description" brings back the human. Robbe-Grillet thus challenges the traditional opposition between story and description, time and space, which led thinkers like Lessing and Lukács to resist the modus of description. For Robbe-Grillet, description sets no obstacles to temporality, and it is suffused with its own time and movement. In addition, Robbe-Grillet annihilates the traditional dichotomy of subject and object, which underpins traditional description. Personification is impossible because the subject has no dominance in the field of vision, being an integral part of the object and of the act of seeing. "The movement of the description" thus becomes the dynamic existence of the object as such, *and* as part of the subject, who both grasps it and loses it, sees it and is kept from seeing it.[59]

It is only natural, then, that "the movement of the description" of the cathedral, the movement of the man who draws it, entails, and results in, closing one's eyes. The act of drawing for a blind man, which involves touch and movement, already challenges the status of the object as separate, external, and static. And the boundaries between the seer and the seen, the inside and the outside, keep eroding when the seeing man draws with his eyes shut, with no object in sight, and allows the cathedral to be "seen" inside him:

> Then he said, "I think that's it. I think you got it," he said. "Take a look. What do you think?" But I had my eyes closed. I thought I'd keep them that way for a little longer. I thought it was something I ought to do.
> "Well?" he said. "Are you looking?"
> My eyes were still closed. I was in my house. I knew that. But I didn't feel like I was inside anything.
> "It's really something," I said. (375)

Unexpectedly, this transitory blindness brings with it a total openness. The man whose house was his fortress, who had said that "a blind man in my house" (356) was not something he looked forward to, succeeds, momentarily, not to be "inside anything." And not being "inside" also means not being outside, when one gets to know a different kind of sight, a touch-like sight, which transcends the boundary between inside and outside.

This epiphany at the end of "Cathedral" is exceptional in Carver's oeuvre, and he testified to a sense of "opening up" when he wrote it.[60] However, Carver's entire work leads to this end, which can be seen as the essence of his poetics, or better, its aim. Indeed, Carver's rough mimesis, and his essential descriptions, which often verge on clichés, aim to create "a kind of closing one's eyes" (as Kafka had said of photography and of his own stories).[61] This enigmatic metaphor suits Carver's writing for various reasons. First of all, in his fictional field of vision, which is as fragmentary as an image in memory, the invisible is present as much as the visible. And then vision in these stories is, in fact, never in the present, but occurs after one has averted one's eyes, in order to see a detail that had been inscribed on the "mental retina"—a detail made to sink into the depth of consciousness. It is in this subtle way that his stories internalize visible reality, and direct themselves to the "blind man" of the text, to the one who indeed sees the story with his "eyes shut," inside his or her consciousness—the reader. This reader not only visualizes the text, since these stories—with all their effort to show reality—succeed mostly in their "movement of description." Through this movement, the reader experiences the process of seeing and all that comes with it: seeking continuity in the elusive field of vision, capturing details that will sunk into memory and pondering their meaning and emotional impact. In fact, the text relays to the reader to complete these processes.

The only way that a literary work and everything it contains could penetrate the mind of the reader, says Proust, is by the novelist's substitution of the opaque sections of reality, which are "impenetrable by the human spirit," by their "equivalent in immaterial sections . . . which the spirit can assimilate to itself."[62] Similarly, approaching this from a different angle, Elaine Scarry speaks of the way a text facilitates visualization by "drawing on the imagination's own properties," and "capitalizes on, rather than disavows, the ordinary feebleness of the imagination."[63] Carver's stories are reality-oriented, yet they are marked by the presence of consciousness, and are therefore directed to it. His stories begin with a vision that captures the surface of things, and end with a melting of boundaries and with touch—a touch that is made possible by this very surface. Rarely does he allow touch between the characters in his stories as he does in "Cathedral." However, touch does take place with Carver's readers, who can track, through "the movement of the description," the moves of consciousness in the text, and thus absorb them in their own consciousness.

And the opening to the space and to the other in "Cathedral," the opening of the text to the reader, suggests a tension that will unite the chapters of the next part of this discussion—the tension between the opened and the closed.

Notes

1. Roland Barthes, *A Lover's Discourse: Fragments*, trans. Richard Howard (New York: Hill and Wang, 1978), 216.

2. Halpert, 126. See also Decker's essay, in which he characterizes three types of looking in Carver: the narcissistic, the televisual, and the cinematic gaze.

3. Arias-Misson, 628.

4. See discussion of the connection between these three elements in Gaston Bachelard, *Water and Dreams: An Essay on the Imagination of Matter*, trans. Edith R. Farrell (Dallas: Dallas Institute for Humanities and Culture, 1983), 86. Sandra Lee Kleppe discusses this story in the context of violence against women in America during the years it was written and the area in which the story takes place. See Sandra Lee Kleppe, "Women and Violence in the Stories of Raymond Carver," *Journal of the Short Story in English* 46 (2006). http://jsse.revues.org/index497.html (accessed January 30, 2010).

5. See in an issue devoted to description in *Yale French Studies* 61 (1981): *Toward a Theory of Description*, especially the opening essay of Philippe Hamon, "Rhetorical Status of the Descriptive."

6. Carver, *Fires*, 26.

7. This is taken from the review in the *Washington Post Book World*, as quoted on the cover of *Where I'm Calling From*.

8. Edward S. Casey, "Literary Description and Phenomenological Method," *Yale French Studies* 61(1981): 199.

9. See discussion in Genette, *Narrative Discourse*, 215–27 (mostly on page 218). Cohn, *Transparent Minds*, 217–65.

10. Roland Barthes, *Writing Degree Zero*, trans. A. Lave and C. Smith (New York: Hill and Wang, 1968), 30–31.

11. See analysis of this story by Richard Day in Halpert, 145.

12. Of this quality of past tense see Émile Benveniste, "The Correlation of Tense in the French Verb," *Problems in General Linguistics*," trans. Mary Elizabeth Meek (Miami: University of Miami Press, 1971), 205–15.

13. Slavoj Žižek, *Looking Awry: An Introduction to Jacques Lacan through Popular Culture* (Cambridge: MIT Press, 1995), 89.

14. According to Gabriel Zoran, an effect of depth is created when there is a pronounced relationship between objects in the field of vision, which suggests the presence of an observer/perspective. See Gabriel Zoran, *Text, World, Space* (Tel Aviv: Tel Aviv University-Hakibbutz Hamehuchad, 1997), 113–14 (in Hebrew).

15. G. E. Lessing, *Laocoön: An Essay on the Limits of Painting and Poetry*, trans. Edward Allen McCormick (New York: Bobbs-Merrill Company, 1962). George Lukács, "Narrate or Describe?" in *Writer and Critic and Other Essays*, trans. Arthur D. Kahn (New York: Grosset and Dunlap, 1970), 110–48. See discussion of the ambivalence toward description in Hamon, "Rhetorical."

16. In Gentry and Stull, 156.

17. See discussion of Flaubert in Cesar Grana, *Modernity and Its Discontents: French Society and the French Man of Letters in the Nineteenth Century* (New York: Harper and Row, 1967), 131. See also Spiegel, especially in pages 28–39. Flaubert also influenced photography, as may be seen in the work of the American photographer Walker Evans.

18. Gustav Flaubert, "A Simple Heart," in *Three Tales*, trans. Robert Baldick (London: Penguin, 1987), 17–56.

19. Carroll F. Terrell, *A Companion to the Cantos of Ezra Pound* (Berkeley: University of California Press, 1980), 30.

20. "Mental retina" is Jean Hagstrum's expression. See Jean H. Hagstrum, *The Sisters Arts: The Tradition of Literary Pictorialism and English Poetry From Dryden to Gray* (Chicago: University of Chicago Press, 1987). I use this term with a slightly different meaning.

21. Gérard Genette, "Flaubert's Silence," in *Figures of Literary Discourse*, trans. Alan Sheridan (New York: Columbia University Press, 1982), 183–201.

22. Bachelard, *Water*, 4.

23. Gustav Flaubert, *The Letters of Gustav Flaubert 1857–1880*, trans. Francis Steegmuller (Cambridge, MA: Belknap Press of Harvard University Press, 1982), 293.

24. Deleuze, *Cinema 2*, 52.

25. Genette, "Flaubert," 192.

26. Robbe-Grillet, 151. This discussion of Robbe-Grillet is supported by Deleuze's commentary in *Cinema 2*, 44–45, 68, 101–5.

27. Robbe-Grillet, 148.

28. Victor Shklovsky, "Art as Device," (1925), in *Theory of Prose*, trans. Benjamin Sher (Elmwood Park: Dalkey Archive Press, 1991), 5. Of "description" as opposed to "identification" see Hamon, "Rhetorical," 3.

29. As other writers of the *nuevo roman*, Robbe-Grillet took to the extreme—even to the point of parody—the use of an observing eye as a motivation for description. See Ball, *Narratology*, 38.

30. Carver sees the severe tone of his stories as compatible with the sense of loss which informs them and the swift passage of time that precludes a chance "to get a fix" on things (Gentry and Stull, 156, 184).

31. Runyon, 80–83.

32. This (simplifying) note on Lacan is based on Jacques Lacan, *Four Fundamental Concepts of Psycho-Analysis*, ed. Jacques-Alain Miller, trans. Alan Sheridan (London: Hogarth Press, 1997), especially on the chapters "The Gaze" and "What Is a Picture?" It is also based on the interpretation of Žižek to Lacan in *Looking Awry*, especially in the fifth chapter, "The Hitchcockian Blot." Žižek explains that the object which belongs to the order of the "real" is invariably captured too slowly or too fast, as indeed is the case with a glimpse.

33. Jacques Derrida, *Speech and Phenomena*, trans. David B. Allison (Evanston: Northwestern University Press, 1973), 65. For a discussion of the "blink of the eye" in modern art, see Rosalind Krauss, "The Blink of an Eye," in David Carroll, ed., *The States of "Theory": History, Art and Critical Discourse* (New York: Columbia University Press, 1990), 175–99. For a Lacanian reading of Carver's fiction see William L. Magrino, "American Voyeurism," in *New Paths to Raymond Carver: Critical Essays on His Life, Fiction and Poetry*, ed. Sandra Lee Kleppe and Robert Miltner (Columbia: University of South Carolina Press, 2008), 75–91.

34. Tobias Wolff, Introduction to *The Vintage Book of Contemporary American Short Stories* (New York: Vintage Books, 1994), xiii–xiv.

35. Elaine Scarry, *Dreaming by the Book* (New York: Farrar, Straus & Giroux, 1999), 107–8.

36. Žižek, 91.

37. Henry James, "The Art of Fiction," in *The Art of Fiction and Other Essays* (New York: Oxford University Press, 1948), 11.

38. Runyon too has noticed (in pages 30–31) this repetition of the word "squint" in Carver's first collection.

39. Lacan, "What is a Picture?" in *Four Fundamental Concepts of Psycho-Analysis*, 105–19.

40. Thus, for example, in *The Art of Photography*, ed. the editors of Time-Life Books (New York: Time-Life Books, 1971), 134–44.

41. Deleuze, *Cinema 1*, 5–6.

42. Walter Benjamin, "A Short History of Photography," in *Classic Essays on Photography*, ed. Alan Trachtenberg (New Haven: Leete's Island Books, 1980), 203. Rosalind

Krauss points at the basic difficulty in applying the notion of unconsciousness to vision in *The Optical Unconscious* (Cambridge, MA: MIT Press, 1993), 178. Of the discrepancy between the seen detail and the truth, see also de Duve, 115, and the discussion here in chapter 1. See also Jay, *Downcast Eyes*, 133–35.

43. Moshe Ron noticed this verbal connection in a talk at the Hebrew University's Conference for the honor of Shimon Sandbank, 8 December 1999.

44. Roland Barthes, *Camera Lucida: Reflections on Photography*, trans. Richard Howard (New York: Hill and Wang, 1981), 53.

45. See, for example, Gentry and Stull, 58, 131, 155, 156, 199, 246.

46. See references to *Cathedral* in Gentry and Stull, 29, 44, 56, 101, 199. For a review of this common approach to *Cathedral* and a contradictory view, see Bethea, *Technique*, 6, 133–61.

47. Marcel Proust, *Swan's Way*, trans. C. K. Scott Moncrieff (London: Penguin Books, 1957), 207.

48. Carver, *Fires*, 26. See also a meta-literary reading of "Cathedral" in Scott, 59.

49. Hamon, "Rhetorical," 4.

50. Lessing, 78–84, 98–103.

51. Ralph Waldo Emerson, "History," in *Essays: First Series* (New York: AMM Press, 1968), 11–12.

52. See the essays "A Future for the Novel" (1956) and "Time and Description in Fiction Today" (1963) in Robbe-Grillet, *For a New Novel.* Robbe-Grillet allows only the use of adjectives pertaining to vision and forbids animistic adjectives, which embody the effort to contain the world and control it.

53. This comparison appeared for the first time in Le Claire. Another similarity to Carver is Hopper's conception of his painting as representing mental images, rather than actual space. This inevitable transformation of an image taken from reality into memory and thought is called, in Hopper's terminology, "decay." See Rolf Güter, *Edward Hopper, 1882–1967: Transformation of the Real* (Köln: Taschen, 1993), 65, 86.

54. See in the introduction, note 20.

55. Such are the interpretations of William Kittredge in Halpert, 147; Ron, Epilogue.

56. Luce Irigaray, *The Sex Which Is Not One*, trans. Catherine Porter and Carolyn Burk (Ithaca, NY: Cornell University Press, 1985), 25–26.

57. Edith Wyschogrod, "Doing before Hearing: On the Primacy of Touch," in *Textes pour Emmanuel Levinas*, ed. François Laruelle (Paris: Editions Jean-Michel Place, 1980), 199.

58. Robbe-Grillet, 22.

59. In that respect, Robbe-Grillet's concept offers an alternative to the Cartesian "scopic regime," which is based on the subject's dominancy and its basic separation from the object. This subject sees everything with no blink. See Jay, "Scopic Regimes of Modernity." Robbe-Grillet's approach coincides with other theories of sight in the twentieth century. Among these conceptions is Merleau-Ponty's, which sees in the body and its movement a substantial element in the experience of sight, where there is a constant, "chiastic" blending of sight with vision itself. We may also mention Lacan, who argues

that there is already a "gaze" in the field of vision, while visibility is part of the act of seeing. See Jay, *Downcast Eyes*, 298–325, 344–97.

60. Gentry and Stull, 44.

61. Gustav Janouch, *Conversations with Kafka*, trans. Goronwy Rees (London: Derek Verschoyle, 1953), 34. Barthes borrowed this definition to characterize photography in *Camera Lucida*, 53.

62. Proust, 101.

63. Scarry, 23.

Part III
SEEING AND MEANING

CHAPTER 5

Raymond Carver's "Man in a Case"
FRAME AND CHARACTER

> Look at the faces of people in the bus
> windows.
> The bus sentences the faces to death.
> You're living on borrowed time, says the frame.
> Your neck is
> Cut off
> (Yoel Hoffman, *How Do You Do, Dolores?*[1])

"Once, it was important to see myself as a writer from a particular place," Carver admitted in an interview. "I think I've moved around too much, lived in too many places, felt dislocated and displaced, to now have any firmly rooted sense of 'place.'. . . [T]he majority of my stories are not set in any specific locale . . . they could take place in just about any city or urban area. In any case, most of my stories are set indoors!" On another occasion, when asked why his stories usually take place indoors, he said: "The stories have something to do with the engagement or involvement between men and women, and these moments or little dramas are better played-out indoors than outdoors. It's healthy out-of-doors, and there are always some vapors hanging around indoors—fetid air."[2]

One has only to read Carver's "Little Things" (or "Popular Mechanics"), with its description of the tussle over a baby, to realize that inner space has a power so potent that it brings the conflict between husband and wife to a head and capitalizes upon its terrifying intensity. The story is indeed a mini-drama, in which the incipient violence in the relationship between men and women is highlighted by positioning the characters in an ever-darkening room. The interior space is delineated from an external point of view in the opening, which refers to the street outside the house, and in the terrifying finale which concludes the event—a kind of contemporary "Judgment of Solomon." The text thus demarcates its own boundaries, creating a frame that illustrates the entrance into and exit from the room that has turned into a boxing ring. However, the interior space itself is also a kind of frame; seeking to achieve a "unity of impression" and create an "insulated incident," Edgar Allen Poe suggests a "close circumscription of space" in a poem or story, because it possesses, he argues, "the force of frame to a picture."[3]

Carver stories present a complex relationship between interior spaces and all kinds of textual frames. The next two sections of this chapter will explore the nature of this relationship, and will address the varied meanings that the concept of "frame" has acquired in literary discourse. This will be done while sketching, as it were, a typical Carverian character. This character, whom I'll name (for reasons to be clarified later) "a man in a case," makes various appearances in different guises in several stories, and reflects some of the attributes of other Carver characters. For me, this character fleshes out the essentials of Carver's poetics. I have discussed some of these from different angles, in previous chapters. Most of this chapter will be devoted to a reading of stories by Carver where this "man in a case" appears, showing his tight connection to the inside-outside issue. In the realm of fictional space, this issue involves interior spaces, whereas in what I metaphorically will call the textual space, it involves the concept of frame. Later in the chapter I will address the "man in a case" from a different angle—his relation to movement and action; and by bringing together some theoretical texts, I will attempt to clarify the role allocated to him in Carver's short fiction.

The story with which I will begin delineating the character of the "man in a case" is "Careful" (from *Cathedral*). Naturally, this story takes place in an interior space.

A Man in a Case

The title of the story "Careful" appears in the text in different contexts, always integrated into the flow of the story or dialogue, and in each context its meaning is slightly different. At times it means "careful," and at times "caution," and at still other times, "take care." In fact, given the story, the title "Careful" is typical of Carver, who often centralizes a marginal word or sentence by placing it in the title, thus shifting the reader's attention from the more overt themes of the story. Moreover, at first glance, the theme and symbols of "Careful" seem transparent, even banal. Lloyd is paid a visit by Inez, his estranged wife, who comes to talk to him. That very morning his ear had gotten clogged up with wax. Inez helps him unblock the clogged ear; yet despite that, throughout the visit, Lloyd is unable to hear (or actually, manages *not* to hear) what his wife has come to tell him. Temporary deafness is an understandable psychosomatic reaction in a husband who refuses to "hear about" the new life of his wife—standing in the doorway wearing a spring outfit and holding a new handbag—a life which appears to exclude him. The theme of hearing and communication indicated by the ear incident and supported by other symbols (a silent television, to name only one) is therefore much more overt than the theme of carefulness implied in the title. However, thanks to this title, a net of thematic links surfaces, and the interior space is appropriate in this story.

The interior space of "Careful" is the small flat where Lloyd lives, separated from his wife, attempting to overcome a drinking problem.

> After a lot of talking—what his wife, Inez, called assessment—Lloyd moved out of the house and into his own place. He had two rooms and a bath on the top floor of a three-story house. Inside the rooms, the roof slanted down sharply. If he walked around, he had to duck his head. He had to stoop to look from his windows and be careful getting in and out of bed. (*WICF*, 264)

The space of Lloyd's apartment is described through his body movements. It is demarcated with respect to the restricted movements of the person living inside, who is forced to "duck his head," "stoop," "bend over," "almost get down on his knees" (265), and in general—"be careful" (264). The laconic description is of a specific space—two rooms and a bath on the top floor of a three-story house. Carver's friends testify that he had lived in an apartment like that on Castro Street in San Francisco when he was trying to stop drinking.[4] However, here too, there is no sense of place as a physical and social concrete environment, of which the character is both a product and a representative. It is an anonymous space, mostly used to describe the character in this strained body position. At the same time, it may be said (borrowing from Sherwood Anderson) that the story is "the story of a room almost more than it is the story of a man."[5] Very little is said of Lloyd in terms of character or biography; he is defined mostly by his relationship with the space he occupies, and marked by the body position that this space enforces on him. Moreover, the very anonymity of this space is what enables us to expand its meanings metaphorically and deduce other "spaces" which the character occupies: his body, his psychological state, and mostly the story which accommodates him. Some of Carver's poems similarly present an anonymous space which can also expand its significance to denote an existential place or stance vis-à-vis the other or the world. Such is the empty house in "Luck"; the other part of the house in "The Other Life"; or the little room in "Company." This sense of space is compatible with the perception of the self or the other as the equivalent of a slot of space, as already discussed. However, from now on I will elaborate mostly on the analogy between the fictional space and textual space, in other words, the story which "accommodates" the character.

There is a radical attempt to gain control, a lack of spontaneity, a certain stiffness, or merely carefulness—these are the psychic postures which Lloyd embodies through his body position. These states of mind, however, offer only a partial description, since the concrete world Carver depicts often resists being reduced to a finite psychic equivalent. In fact, this body position will undergo varied transformations throughout the story, each revealing a different facet. The first variation is in the description of Mrs. Matthews, Lloyd's landlady, whom Lloyd notices in passing through her open door. He stands on the landing to look at her:

> He saw the old woman lying on her back on the carpet. She seemed to be asleep. Then it occurred to him she might be dead. But the TV was going, so he chose to think she was asleep. He didn't know what to make of it . . . it was then that the woman gave a little cough, brought her hand on her side, and went back to being quiet and still again. Lloyd continued on up the stairs and unlocked his door. (264)

Standing in a liminal space, looking through a window or a door which frames a slice of reality, peeping at another person who reflects some aspect of oneself—these are familiar elements in Carver's world, and have been discussed in this study. The landlady episode diverts the reader from the plot. It emerges incidentally, from the description of the house, which is subjected to Lloyd's point of view and associations. To Randolph Runyon, Carver's critic, it seemed so out of place and disturbing that he chose to regard it as a "day residue"—something left over from a previous story in the collection.[6] Still, however tenuous the connection of the episode to the plot, one cannot ignore its dynamic, mirror-like connection to Lloyd's portrayal in the story. The space of the room, which enclosed Lloyd's body in the opening of the story, is analogous to the frame of the door which demarcates the landlady's body, while her supine posture—perhaps asleep, possibly dead—intimates an image that will develop over the course of the story: the image of the living-dead body of Lloyd which the space encloses like a coffin.

It seems superfluous to recall that Carver's glance at a highly external reality in fact constitutes a gaze into an inner reality, and that the window or the door represents a kind of threshold to the secret anxieties and desires of his characters. Such is the scene where a son peers through an open door to see his mother kissing a stranger ("Mr. Coffee and Mr. Fixit"). Such is also the case in "Careful." While peeping at his landlady's apartment, Lloyd confronts an anxiety that will surface later in the story. The landlady episode is a floating image, loosely connected to plot, and this contributes to its nightmare quality, as if it were the detritus of Lloyd's tortured inner reality. This reality is fully revealed when his wife, who eventually succeeded in unclogging his ear, is about to leave:

> He began to fear the moment he would begin to make his preparations for bed and what might happen afterward. That time was hours away, but already he was afraid. What if, in the middle of the night, he accidentally turned onto his right side, and the weight of his head pressing into the pillow were to seal the wax again into the dark canals of his ear? What if he woke up then, unable to hear, the ceiling inches from his head?" (275)

Lloyd's claustrophobic fear of waking in the middle of the night with a clogged ear, "the ceiling inches from his head," no doubt echoes the fear of being buried alive—a fear that, in Poe's works, is tightly linked to closed spaces, frame stories and framed "pictures of reality" (in stories such as "The Pit and the Pendulum" or "The Fall of the House of Usher"). Moreover, the ear incident suggests that the restricted space, with its low ceiling, externalizes, as it were, the boundaries of the body; and both threaten to close in on Lloyd. This analogy is reinforced by the diagram of an ear which Lloyd remembers from his childhood, presented as ramified, pipe-like space with canals, passages, and partitions. The word "careful" helps to form this conception of the body as a narrow space—prone to clogging and needing to be opened. Repeated, this word draws an amusing analogy between the bottle of champagne, which Lloyd "carefully" opens and closes with measured movements, and Lloyd himself, who is clogged up with a "plug" of wax (273, 276), urging his wife to be "careful" when she opens his ear (271), while in his head he hears the sounds of liquid and a cork popping (268, 274, 276). A person who drinks from morning to evening may indeed come to have a bottle-like view of reality. However, it seems that in addition, Lloyd himself has become a kind of receptacle for fluids (e.g., he feels "he is awash with fluids" [268]; he is reminded of the "pleasant sensation of water running out of his head" when he was a child [268]; and his wife carefully pours oil into his ear and tells him to "tilt his head" so that he will not spill it [273]). It may seem far-fetched, even ridiculous, to base an interpretation on the conception of "a man as a bottle." Nonetheless, Carver often tackles weighty and complex issues with humor or offhandedly, and "Careful" proves to be no exception. In a sense, it is a story of a man as a receptacle—both stiff and fragile, "plugged" and "careful," trying to preserve himself within his boundaries, and at the same time—prone to leakage.

Before dealing with different aspects of this conception of the body (which expresses a personality concept), and mostly its connection with the text's formal qualities, I would like to mention the last transformation of the body image in the story. Lloyd, fearing that his ear will clog up again, decides to sleep on his back, and he practices this position while he is awake:

> After he'd put on his shoes and tied the laces, he lay down on the bed and pulled the covers up to his chin. He let his arms rest under the

covers at his sides. He closed his eyes and pretended it was night and pretended he was going to sleep. Then he brought his arms up and crossed them over his chest to see how this position would suit him. He kept his eyes closed, trying it out. All right, he though. Okay, if he didn't want that ear to plug up again, he'd have to sleep on his back, that was all. (276)

Lloyd's position, lying on his back, with his arms straight at his sides and later crossed on his chest, is, in fact, a superimposition of the image of the landlady lying supine on the image of the man imprisoned in a coffin, alluded to in the opening lines. Here, Lloyd employs a paradoxical defense tactic. He defends himself against the threat of the stoppage of the ear and its "dark channels"—suggesting death and burial—by simulating the posture of a dead man. He is much like a person feigning death so as not to be killed—an analogy which is repeated in descriptions of obsessive neurosis. Although I am not inclined to diagnose Lloyd (or any other literary character) clinically, more than one of his characteristics brings to mind the rigid figure of the obsessed. While Lloyd's rigidity in the position of the dead expresses this symbolically, his behavior may also be interpreted as obsessive: the disturbing thoughts from which he cannot rid himself, his addiction to unconventional personal rituals, and the lack of spontaneity he shows throughout the story.

A psychological diagnosis is one way to shed light on the character of Lloyd, trapped in a rigid body position. A literary analogy is another. The next few pages will be devoted to a reading of a story by Anton Chekhov that will provide insight into the significance of this character as it is embodied in a body position, and link it to the structure of the story.

Carver has often been described as the "American Chekhov."[7] He has acknowledged his debt to the Russian author in interviews, essays, in his story "Errand," and in some of his poems. There are diverse reasons for this notion of similarity: the humanism and empathy both writers express in their stories; their compassionate approach to simple, poor people; their mastery of the short story genre; or their preference for the quotidian and the banal. Nevertheless, I find it difficult to pinpoint exactly how Chekhov has influenced Carver or even to point to this influence directly (the traces of Hemingway or William Carlos Williams are much more discernible). Let us consider Chekhov's story "A Man in a Case," which seem to have had a thematic—conscious or unconscious—influence on "Careful" and other stories by Carver. That story will be used as a point of departure and a frame of reference since the aim of this comparison is to shed light on Carver's works, rather than to form any sweeping conclusions on Chekhov's body of work or to define the nature of his influence.

The protagonist in "A Man in a Case" is Byelikov, a recently deceased Greek teacher and colleague of Burkin, the narrator. Byelikov is portrayed as an archetype of the kind of people who are "solitary by nature, who try to retreat into their shell like a hermit crab or a snail" (250).[8] He is a person who is always covered in layers: a cloak, a warm wadded coat, boots, and all kinds of coverings. "He stuffed up his ears with cotton-wool," travels in a covered wagon, lives in a house with blinds lowered and bolts locked, in a box-like bedroom, sleeps in a bed covered by a curtain, a blanket covering his head. Even his belongings are covered: his watch, umbrella, and penknife are "in a little case" (ibid.). This is a man in whom the narrator diagnoses "a constant and insurmountable impulse to wrap himself in coverings, to make himself, so to speak, a case which would isolate him and protect him from external influences" (ibid.), since reality irritates and frightens him. Threatened by the present, Byelikov prefers the past and dead languages. He is at home with rules and prohibitions, and feels agitated by any deviation from the norm. Byelikov's friends, depressed by his behavior, urge him to get married to a lively woman. The engagement, however, fills him with anxiety and leads to his eventual death. Byelikov is dead, and Burkin's impression is that "now, when he was lying in his coffin, his expression was mild, agreeable, even cheerful, as though he were glad that he had at last been put into a case which he would never leave again. Yes, he had attained his ideal!" (265–66).

The case motif is prevalent in Chekhov's works, Nilli Mirsky points out. It symbolizes a state in which one is imprisoned in a persona which is a kind of "sealed wrapping," annihilating all real feelings and spontaneity. This persona sucks the life out of Byelikov, making him a kind of "stuffed animal, devoid of authenticity."[9] The story suggests a similar line of interpretation, expressed by a listener, Ivan Ivanovitch. For him, Byelikov, no matter how extreme his portrayal, is an emblem for any person who has been trapped in a false life imposed on him or her by society: "And isn't our living in town, airless and crowded," he asks, "our writing useless papers, our playing *vint*—isn't that all a sort of case for us? And our spending our whole lives among trivial, fussy men and silly, idle women, our talking and our listening to all sorts of nonsense—isn't that a case for us too?" (251).

Setting aside this interpretation, the aim of my borrowing Chekhov's image of "a man in a case" is not to characterize the relationship between the individual and society; Carver's approach to this is indirect. Like Poe, he prefers the delimited space, where exterior reality has no tangible presence. It also seems that he adopted an observation made by Frank O'Connor (one of his favorite writers), that the short story was about human loneliness.[10] In fact, the presence of society in his stories is felt mostly in the economic influence that the capitalist way of life has on the lives of his underdog characters. The similarity between Byelikov and Lloyd lies, therefore, in their characterization or psychic condition, rather than as an allegory to an inauthentic existence. Both instances involve people beset by petrifying fear (comic in Chekhov, threatening in Carver), people whose defense mechanism entails stiffness, a kind of rigor mortis, which is concretized in their frozen body posture as well as in their narrow coffin-like space. There are, of course, differences: Byelikov is afraid of life, while Lloyd is afraid of death; Byelikov chooses to be enclosed and clogged up, while the narrow space and the ear incident are forced on Lloyd, resulting in a claustrophobic fear; Byelikov is afraid of any encroachment upon the normative, always preferring prohibition and permission, while Lloyd, the alcoholic, who breakfasts on champagne and doughnuts, has, in his isolation, lost any sense of what is customary and normative. Nevertheless, in Carver's story, these differences lose their significance since, at the end, is fear of life essentially different from the fear of death? ("No!" Carver says in his poem "Fear"). If anyone has decided, like Lloyd, that "being alone was the thing he needed most" (*WICF*, 266), or, has chosen, (to quote Carver's poem "Luck") to be in "the house where no one / was home, no one coming back / and all I could drink" (*AOU*, 3), has not that person also chosen the bottle-like–case-like existence to seal himself within? And does not the free life of isolation ultimately mean entrenchment in no less paralyzing personal boundaries?

My composite profile of the "a man in case" is thus a cluster of opposite reactions—the fear of death and fear of life; claustrophobic horror and agoraphobic self-imprisonment (which, as case studies show, are often enmeshed in one another); the breaching of boundaries and the collapse of those boundaries. This duality of the man in a case is especially evident in its Carverian version, where the loss of freedom is a result of an extreme attempt to gain control, as when Lloyd decides to sleep only on his back. In fact, the very imprisonment in the rigid borders of carefulness stems from the will to be alone and free. Carver is indeed an American writer, and as Tony Tanner has observed, American literature is torn between a yearning for freedom, a rejection of any limit or restriction, and the fear of "liquidity," the total blurring of the contours of identity. This is a fear which pushes one back to stiff boundaries and to the horror of rigor mortis.[11] This national inclination is compatible—at a personal level—with the tension Carver has often described in interviews: the tension between the total control he tried to actuate in his art and the chaos of his private life. In any event, this ambivalence of the man in a case toward his boundaries and the space in which he is enclosed does have an interesting manifestation in the realm of form. I will try to illustrate this through a further comparison with the Chekhovian "source."[12]

Different manifestations of the image of the case, consolidated in the coffin image, enclose Byelikov in Chekhov's story. Some formal devices also combine to reinforce this confinement, the most conspicuous of which is the frame story. "A Man in a Case" is indeed part of a trilogy: three stories told during a hunting trip, of which Byelikov's story is the first. The outer story, which wraps the story of the man in a case, detaches the reader from the actual person, and contributes to the shaping of Byelikov as an archetype. This effect is compatible with the general nature of the story, which is written in the tradition of the "portrait"—a subgenre of the short story, associated mostly with the French writer La Bruyère and his *Caractères*. "A Man in a Case" *has* a plot—Byelikov's engagement and his ensuing death. However, it centers on the description of a person as an archetype: At the start of the inner story he, and another character, are portrayed as examples of the kind of people who lead the life of a "hermit crab or a snail"—possibly a vestige of the early days of humankind. In the end, Ivan Ivanovitch's commentary interprets Byelikov as an allegory for the state of man in society. The word *anthrōpos*, which is associated with him, also supports this general portrayal, as well as the story's title. However, as so often in a "portrait" or a fable, Byelikov is merely a man-shaped trait. As in a fable, he is associated with all kinds of animals (a polecat is added to the hermit crab and the snail), and the text prompts the reader to visualize him as one-dimensional. The story also mentions an actual picture: an amusing sketch, made by his students and named "Anthrōpos in Love," which, like most caricatures, reduces its object to its most striking and typical traits. Byelikov could be defined then as a static character, not only because of his rigid nature, or habits that are compared to lying immobile in a coffin, but also because of his literary classification. He is portrayed as a simple character who undergoes no development and reveals one characteristic all through the story. Regarding this, let us remember the metaphor that the critic Bakhtin uses to describe a character solely designed by a narrator, in a monologic, definitive, closed manner, rather than through his or her dynamic self-consciousness:

> In the monologic design, the hero is closed and his semantic boundaries strictly defined: he acts, experiences, thinks, and is conscious within the limits of what he is, that is, within the limits of his image defined as reality; . . . The self-consciousness of the hero is inserted into this *rigid framework*, to which the hero has no access from within and which is part of the authorial consciousness defining and representing him—and is presented against the firm background of the external world.[13] (My emphasis)

It is not only the frame of characterization which enhances Byelikov's static nature, but other frames as well: the frame story, the frames of mental and actual pictures described in the story, and mainly the frame which circles the story as such, which in a literary "portrait" is indeed comparable to a picture's frame.

For the members of the semiotic school, Jurij Lotman and Boris Uspensky, the frame is the border between the inner space of the fictive world and the real world surrounding it. This border is in fact the beginning and the end of the text, where the reader enters fiction and exits from it.[14] However, besides being the actual borders of the text, which determine its composition, the frame often suggests the *process* of framing, namely the selection principle that any text appears to make while deciding, as it were, which details to include in its boundaries and which to exclude. The frame as a selection process also supports Byelikov's characterization as an archetype of "a man in a case." The text is condensed and tight in terms of theme and meaning; all of its details serve the theme of the text, declared in the title, which seems universal in their application to all humankind. In this sense, the different frames mentioned above coincide with the outlines of the overt theme of a story. The frame fits the portrait, since every element in the story helps to build the duplicable pattern which the portrait draws. This accord between the character and its different frames is reflected in the relationship between Byelikov and the varied cases closing in on him. The cheerful and agreeable expression he has in the coffin, his final case, indicates the sort of harmony and comfort one normally feels within the case most suitable to one's body, namely—the womb.

By contrast, the relationship of Carver's Lloyd with his apartment/case has nothing to do with comfort and harmony, as his wary gestures reveal: his stooping, bending over, ducking. Lloyd has to conform to a rigid, nonelastic space that enforces itself on him, and he reacts with rigidity. However, can this lack of harmony be said to be reflected in Lloyd's relationship with the "space" of the story which he occupies? How do the boundaries of this space, its frame, express this relationship? Is this assumed metaphorical link between interior spaces and all kind of frames applicable to other stories by Carver? These questions require an exploration of Carver's general approach to frames and to narrative frames in particular.

The Frame

While discussing the frame story in "Fat," Carver admitted his interest in "the idea of people looking on, or people looking *through* something at something else—a real and a metaphorical frame for the story."[15] Indeed, Carver has written three frame stories, and his stories are rife with all sorts of *mise en abyme* (anecdotes, dreams, and photos). However, the element that sheds light on his approach to the framing process is mainly the frames within the fictional world, those which "frame the signified," to use Brooke-Rose's term.[16] These frames are created by windows, doors, and peepholes, through which people look or are looked at (their prevalence in Carver's stories is another reason to compare him to Edward Hopper). I already mentioned the way a gaze through a window or a door is in fact a look into an inner reality or some aspect of the self. There is another quality to the door or window frames, however, which makes them emblematic of Carver's treatment of frames in general.

For Deleuze—who discusses the concept of frames in cinema—doors, windows, and other subframes inside the cinematic frame are equal to what he terms "geometric frames." The outlines of "geometric frames" are set by predetermined coordinates, and therefore are inflexible, unlike what he terms "physical-dynamical" frames which conform to their object elastically. There is another quality, however, to these rigid subframes that brings them nearer to frames in photography or in Flemish painting (which has often been compared to photography)—it is a frame in which the boundaries seem arbitrary: It cuts what seems to be its object, excludes part of it, and thus indicates, paradoxically, what lies beyond it, gesturing to the out-of-field or *hors-champ*. In that sense, the frame is rigid, but bound to be breached: It enforces a predetermined structure on its object, while at the same time confirms the object's existence beyond its limits. It is a frame that seems "unnatural," because it does not coincide with the familiar structure—or "frame"—which directs the viewer's set of expectations (this sense of the concept frame is often used in cognitive and phenomenological studies of art and literature). An arbitrary, seemingly artificial cutting highlights the act of framing and at the same time simulates a framing-free vision, where the boundaries are those of the field of vision.[17]

A literary analogy to this kind of arbitrary frame can be found in stories that appear to be "slices of life" rather than myth. They present a group of events that seem to be chosen accidentally in a story which begins and ends randomly. Indeed, Lotman's discussion of the concept of the frame involves the traditional distinction between a slice of life and myth.[18] For him, the issue of the frame, no matter the shape or form, is connected to a rule applying to all arts, which is that any work of art is a "finite model of an infinite universe," which undergoes a process of translation—a transformation. Being a model, the text both stands for part of reality and for all of its parts. Every work of art has a "story" aspect, as it reflects one episode of reality, and a mythic aspect, being a model of the entire universe. However, Lotman stresses that there is no such thing as a pure story, since the very process of selection models and mythologizes this particular slice of reality. Henceforth, the frame is connected to the mythic aspect of the text, which the story element subverts.

The vacillation between a slice of life and myth recurs in discussions of the short story. The genre is torn between these poles, since the palpability of its frame, the proximity of the beginning and the end, makes them co-present, as it were, in the mind of the reader, and sketches an imagined framed picture, as Poe suggested (especially if one takes his advice and reads the story "in one sitting"). Indeed, as Todorov has observed, the exits and entrance to a short story are too close to one another and allow the reader no time to forget fiction and—we may add—its dual relationship with reality: its aspiration both to be a miniature model of it and to represent one of its parts.[19] The frame is a reminder of the fact that the text has no escape from the mythic—no matter how episodic it may seem. In fact, in "slice of life" texts, in many instances, "framing is the event."[20]

Carver's corpus exemplifies this quality very well due to its focus on the everyday, for example, events which are not universally decisive or significant by the standards of a familiar plot. "Careful" is a good example for this argument, since it explores an event which undoubtedly has been experienced by many, but rarely, if ever, documented in literature: a person waking up in the morning to discover that his ear is clogged up with wax. Nevertheless, the ripping of this event from its everyday context results in defamiliarization, supported by the transforming power of the frame. By highlighting the insignificant and the unimportant, the frame removes it from the realm of the everyday (which, by definition, as indicated by Blanchot, is always latent, eluding meaning).[21] The sense of unreality or strangeness generated by Carver's stories, lies, inter alia, in the intensity that framing bestows on automatic actions and gestures which inherently lack any intensity. The movie director Robert Bresson exposed this paradox when he demanded his actors repeat everyday acts time and again, so that they would perform them mechanically, as if in life, during the shooting.[22] The effect of this device is confusing: While watching the gestures of Bresson's actors, framed by the cinematic frame, one experiences a de-automatization of the automatic; routine actions are permeated with intensity and not at all reminiscent of the absent-mindedness of everyday routine. This intensity might lead the viewer to recognize the singularity of the event as such, as intended by Shklovsky in his effect of defamiliarization (Russian Formalists were indeed much interested in frames).[23] At the same time, it calls for meaning and for the transformation of the event into an emblem or a symbol standing for a group of similar events. The intensity of the framed story thus poises it on the cusp between the random and the meaningful.[24] Carver's "Why Don't You Dance?" (discussed in chapter 3) aptly illustrates the frame's effect of defamiliarization, as well as the inevitable mythic-symbolic resonance it generates.[25] The central situation in which objects are removed from their usual context (i.e., the interior of a house) is in fact a replacement of a frame in the fictional world with a deictic narrative frame which isolates the event from its circumstances and confines it to a limited space-time slot. This intricate procedure not only results in a double defamiliarization of the situation but also in its transformation into a symbolic externalization of a psychic condition.

The event or the object of the text is thus experienced as something which is both itself and not itself (which is essentially what one experiences when encountering any artifice of hyperrealist art). Furthermore, the transformation inherent to an object's transposition (or in Lotman's terminology "translation") to the realm of art entails a transformation from motion to stasis, as the "slice of life" representation tends to tear an object violently from its dynamic context. This pertains to the rigor mortis attributed to the objects of photography, and the view of this art as a memento mori.

Indeed, much had been said (mostly in cinema studies) of the way a frame reifies or objectifies its living objects. This process is partly a result of the mythic aspect of art, which enforces a static, predetermined image onto a dynamic entity (note the way the frame in "A Man in a Case" made Byelikov one of the living dead). However, it is also a result of the frame's partial representation of its objects, detached from any continuity. With regard to this, Norman Bryson suggests that the typical frames of Western culture are the viewfinder, binoculars, and the telescope, which only enable a "tunnel vision" of the other, while ignoring the infinite whole of which the she/he/it is a part—a whole which Eastern art succeeds in expressing in defiance of the frame.[26] Through various frames, Carver expresses this partial and objectifying vision in stories rife with peepholes and voyeurs. Such is the look in "They're Not Your Husband," where a husband squeezes his wife into the narrow slot of male fantasy by forcing a slimming regime on her. This is what he sees when he adopts the unflattering viewpoint of strange men scrutinizing her body:

> The white skirt yanked against her hips and crawled up her legs. *What showed* was girdle, and it was pink, thighs that were rumpled and gray and a little hairy, and veins that spread in a berserk display. (*WICF*, 45, my emphasis)

As in hyperrealist art, this description blows details in "regular" vision out of proportion. It is impersonal both in terms of the viewer, who looks at his wife through a public eye, seeing "what showed," and in terms of the object, seen in an extremely partial vision, which erases her dynamic, multifaceted presence. The description is a radical manifestation of the danger of fragmental presentation, which "slice-of-life" stories tend toward. Returning to "Careful," Lloyd's discomfort in his narrow space and his rigor mortis may as well be an emblem of his condition inside the slice-of-life story—a space that grants him only a partial and static representation.

Yet the arbitrary frame, as well as its literary manifestation—for example, the slice-of-life story—has a double effect: Along with its fragmentation and the way it cuts off the object, it also presses the viewer/reader to the frame's margins. The frame thus expresses what has escaped from its boundaries; this part's very absence indicates its liberation from control which goes along with any act of centralization. This framing is also de-framing—to again use a term by Deleuze, who attributes to the most closed systems the power to include "lines of flights" which connect them to what lies beyond.[27]

Carver has many ways of reinforcing the de-framing effect. One of them is to insert details which are disturbingly out of place into stories which otherwise are lean and spare in details. Such is the case with the big man who stands on the porch in "Are You a Doctor?"; the fishing net protruding from a shelf as it sticks out from the story scheme in "Sixty Acres"; a man hanging on an electricity pole who is spotted in passing in "Boxes"; or the landlady lying on her back in "Careful." Note that here the use of the landlady example seems to contradict the previous analogy between her pose and Lloyd's. Indeed, the relevance of details is in the eye of the beholder or the reader, who can always ascribe some analogical-symbolic function to them, or at least a function of "reality effect." Nonetheless, on first reading, these details do seem out of place. They subvert the "unity of impression," demanding a broader explanatory context.[28]

Randolph Runyon's methods of interpretation are an indication of the effect of the out-of-place details. First, he provides an overall framework of interpretation, based on a psychoanalytical master story, by reading Carver's stories as dreams. As such, it is precisely their most detached details which matter, because they express unconscious desires and fears. At the same time, Runyon suggests, these details constitute an intertextual link to a wider literary context. Sometimes, the link is to stories by other writers (pointless information in "The Train" makes sense only if one considers a story by John Cheever to whom the story was dedicated; a minor anecdote in "Night School" refers to a story by William Styron; a digression in the fishing story "Nobody Said Anything" connects it to the story of Tobias). However, Runyon mainly points to links created *in* the collection of stories (the landlady lying supine in "Careful" is a "day residue" from the story "Vitamins," and this image reappears in the stories that follow; a wish expressed in "Intimacy" is fulfilled in "Menudo"; the hole in the window in "One More Thing" "is at the same time a breach in the wall that divides this story from its "neighbor" and so forth).[29] Similarly, the director Robert Altman, who adapted nine of Carver's stories for the screen in "Short Cuts," incorporated them to a one-frame story with a shared cinematic space, admitting that for him, they always form a one-piece work.[30] Critics often refer to "Carver Country," where his characters live in one lifelike space. I believe that even the inclination to read Carver autobiographically stems partly from the need to find a common space for details that seem to wander to the stories from real-life domains—their presumed original "frame." These reader responses are affected, naturally, by personal reading inclinations. Undoubtedly, they are encouraged by the fact that Carver tends to include similar motifs, situations, and characters (e.g., the "man in a case") in different stories, thus creating his own world. Still, these responses are also symptomatic of the fact that Carver stories, notwithstanding their existence in a claustrophobic, hermetic space, evoke a wider whole. The out-of-place details seem to call for expansion beyond the individual story in search of a wider frame (i.e., context, setting, or frame of reference). These are stories that have "opened on to a whole," to borrow Gilles Deleuze's formulation. Deleuze uses the "whole" and "open" terms in discussing movies in which the cinematic frame loosens its connection with adjacent frames and—more important—the links *in* the frame. It thus suggests a deeper connection with the open—the whole which for Deleuze is equivalent to time and thought, and the locus of movement and change.[31]

As much as Carver loosens inner connections, by interpolating details which tear open the fabric of the story, he loosens the story's frame in his treatment of openings and endings. His openings are often located after the fact, suggesting a prior dramatic occurrence to which the events in the story are a mere echo. His endings are open ended: Lacking closure, they do not exhaust the plot potential; the conflicts he presents are rarely resolved, and no thematic statement concludes the story. Most interesting are those cases in which the openness of the story, its spillage over the edges, is manifested in the ending's very content. This is the case in "Will You Please Be Quiet, Please?" whose first part introduces the static image of a woman, as she has become fixated in her husband's memory, freezing, as it were, his feelings for her. As the story unfolds, one sees there is in fact a deep crisis which imposes a change upon the husband, and the finale is sheer movement which seems to continue well beyond the story's limits:

> He held himself, *he later considered*, as long as he could. And then he turned to her. He turned and turned in what might have been a stupendous sleep, *and he was still turning*, marveling at the impossible changes he felt moving over him. (*WICF*, 182, my emphasis)

Even more interesting are endings in which there is a coexistence of closeness and openness, stasis and movement. The end of "Viewfinder," which abounds with interior and exterior spaces and all kinds of frames, has the memorable, mysterious throwing of a stone. The movement is meant to be preserved in a photo that will freeze it, while perhaps transferring it to a symbolic level.[32] Carver's placement of the image at the end, no doubt, enhances this stationary effect. At the same time, the stone seems to be thrown out of the photograph's frame in a gesture which suggests movement beyond the story's "frame."

Even endings which describe immobile objects sometimes conceal movement. "Are These Actual Miles?" ends with a description of a car that costs a couple the fidelity of the wife. The car is framed in the husband's memory, standing in the parking lot and "gleaming" in the sun. Still, this object's very essence is movement and it also gleams in the vibrant intensity of memory. Similarly, "The Bridle" ends with an almost technical description of a bridle—a motionless object left behind in an empty apartment, but it is an object which the story describes to the reader with the words: "When you felt it pull, you'd know it was time. You'd know you were going somewhere" (*Cathedral*, 208).

A story combining all kinds of frames which break on different levels is "The Calm." Richard Ford reveals that he had reservations about the story because while using a frame story, its interior story does not close. "Some sense of symmetry caused me to comment on it," Ford recalls, interpreting Carver's refusal to change the story as an indication of his deafness to criticism. For me, however, Carver's insistence on the original, more open structure is compatible with the rationale of the story, and particularly compatible with its ending, which expresses Carver's twofold approach toward the concept of the frame.

"The Calm" begins with the narrator's visit to the barbershop. During the visit, an unfamiliar client tells a dark hunting story which is interrupted midway by a confrontation with another client. The interior story remains unresolved, as well as the violence of the incident. The ending of the frame story is no less mysterious:

> The barber turned me in the chair to face the mirror. He put a hand to either side of my head. He positioned me a last time, and then he brought his head down next to mine. We looked into the mirror together, his hands still framing my head. I was looking at myself, and he was looking at me too. But if the barber saw something, he didn't offer comment.
>
> He ran his fingers through my hair. He did it slowly, as if thinking about something else. He ran his fingers through my hair. He did it tenderly, as a lover would.
>
> That was in Crescent City, California, up near the Oregon border. I left soon after. But today I was thinking of that place, of Crescent City, and of how I was trying out a new life there with my wife, and how, in the barber's chair that morning, I had made up my mind to go. I was thinking today about the calm I felt when I closed my eyes and let the barber's fingers move through my hair, the sweetness of those fingers, the hair already starting to grow. (*WICF*, 243–44)

A lyrical tone, uncommon in Carver's prose, colors this ending, yet the vision is unmistakably his: A sense of mystery wraps an everyday situation, which combines concentration with distraction—the stares are intense, yet while looking outside seem also to be turned inward. This everyday moment summons more of the encounters—or rather loops—of looks which concretize the self-and-other relationships in Carver's world: The other looks at you looking at him, and the look itself is the core rather than any ensuing realization. Here the look is accompanied by varied frames: the mirror's frame, the hand's frame circumscribing the face, and then there is the story's frame, against which the scene brushes by virtue of its very placement at the end.

Indeed, we are at the margins of "The Calm," and this concluding paragraph—as well as the title drawn from it—pulls the story to its margins in more than one way. The title focuses on the feeling of calm, which is absent from this rather disquieting story; and the voice of the narrator, hitherto just a witness, becomes overt when he speaks of his own life. The transition into the narration and the voice of an external narrator is, according to Uspensy, one of several devices meant to frame a story.[33] It facilitates the reader's exit from the domain of fiction, which has accommodated him for a while, by using an internal point of view. "The Calm" supplements this underscoring of a story's frame and the time of the narration through a shift of thematic center to the margins of the story. Suddenly, when the narrator "today" recalls his feeling of that moment in front of the mirror, the narration is revealed as retrospective. Hence, in addition to the frame of narrative and the actual frames described, memory itself can be seen at work in framing here. Regardless of what seems to be the center of the story so far—the incident at the barbershop—memory evokes one marginal moment and determines it to be the beginning of a change, of the decision to leave town. Does this decision have anything to do with a previous, intimidating incident, alluding perhaps to Nick Adams's decision to leave Summit at the end of "The Killers" (the story carries a strong allusion to Hemingway)? This is plausible. Still, clinging to the moment's immediate circumstances and a causal explanation would only reduce the rich elusive meaning of the scene and its deep underlying connection of form to content. The decision to leave town, which gestures, outward as it were, forms a part of an overall outward tug on all levels—outside of the "field" in which the scene is situated (*hors-champ*). This somehow hypnotic moment is one of stasis and rest, even as it is accompanied by all kinds of movements: a slight movement (the barber's hands move through the hair), an invisible movement (the hair already starting to grow), and a potential movement (the decision to leave). Different frames help to fixate the scene—in space, memory, and the story, thus enhancing its stationary elements. However, the moment latently entails change and movement which pull the story outside its limits, affecting the frame by rendering the marginal central and the everyday crucial.

Indeed, one of the side effects of the particular frame I have attempted to sketch here is the destabilization of the thematic center of gravity. In Chekhov's "A Man in a Case" the story's borders help to centralize the theme-portrait, since they accord with the "frames" of interpretation and understanding that the text encourages. They are therefore invisible and seem "natural." Carver's typical frame, on the other hand, sticks out and seems arbitrary and unnatural. Imposed on its subject like a narrow space, this frame deviates from familiar patterns of plot and theme set by reading habits. Paradoxically, by ignoring these accepted frames, it underlies the artificiality of fiction. However, as much as this frame is a reminder of the fictional status of characters, it suggests their basic freedom, their potential existence beyond the story's frame, and their evasion of control and centralization. It is therefore no accident that Carver rarely squeezes his characters into a fixed psychological diagnosis and prefers to characterize them through their gestures or current condition.

"Careful" concludes with Lloyd's control exercises, permeated with claustrophobic anxiety—far from the harmonious flow that ends "The Calm." Yet these two endings reveal, by their very polarity, the duality of Carver's frames or narrow spaces: While restricting the characters' movement, they also imply their continuity beyond the story's boundaries.

More "Men in Cases"

The narrow space, or case, as a metaphoric complement to the story's frame, both reflects and contrasts with the character it contains, and has additional functions. There are men in cases scattered throughout Carver's oeuvre, all of whom give diverse expression to the meaning of the case image. Some of these men, like Lloyd, are anxiety-stricken, other seek comfort and defense and find it in the case. In each of the three main collections of stories there is at least one "man in a case"—either as a central or a secondary character. I do not necessarily mean all those lonely figures, holed up in their houses, hiding from life's demands and horrors (in "Collectors" or "Viewfinder")—perhaps a reminder of the days when Carver had to hide from creditors and bad news.[34] Rather, these characters dwell in much smaller spaces—actual cases.

In "What's in Alaska?" and "What We Talk about When We Talk about Love," men in cases appear in minor anecdotes told by the characters. In the first story, one of the speakers mentions a prehistoric human being found in a block of ice in Alaska. In a story in which people mostly talk past each other, this image symbolizes the detachment and emotional frost in which they are caught. In "What We Talk about When We Talk about Love" (and in "Beginners"—its original version) this image is taken further. Two images are raised during the conversation in this story; combined, they illuminate the issue under discussion—love—somehow ironically. First, there is the image of a medieval knight, the emblem of courtly love. He is sealed within his armor, which was historically meant to protect him, but often proved the cause of death by suffocation, exhaustion, or hyperthermia. Along with the story of the knight, in the context of true love and the dangers of life, another image emerges. Mell, a physician, tells of an elderly couple injured in a car accident who had to be put in full body casts, from head to toe. The husband was depressed, Mell noticed, but the cause of his anguish was not so much the pain he was suffering but rather the fact that he was unable to look at his beloved wife through the peepholes that had been drilled in his cast. In a broader context, however, this image of true love ends up by questioning the notion of love itself. The mummy-lovers, lying side by side, unable to look at each other, remind one mostly of other couples in Carver stories (and this story is no exception), who lie side by side in rooms and beds, sealed away in the cover of their swathing of alienation and loneliness. In a story which, despite its name, has little love in it, this image does not unquestionably serve the idea of eternal love, while the knight in his prison-armor cracks, in turn, the ideal of courtly love.

For Runyon, seeking to find interconnections between stories, the peeping through the eyeholes reflects the way Carver's stories peep at each other, "half-aware of the nearly identical" neighboring story and "almost yearn to break out of their boundaries to make the connection."[35] However, one does not have to see these stories as pure allegory ("What We Talk about When We Talk about Love" also includes an image of a beekeeper's protective gear) to agree with Runyon that this dynamic—of a sealed, hermetic existence which at the same time allows leakage—works both thematically and structurally. This was already indicated by the analogy between Lloyd, the careful man, and the frames in the stories. Furthermore, in these last versions of the "man in a case" the opened-closed tension is tightly connected to the self-and-other relationship: The power of love to break one's boundaries is questioned along with the realization that even in the sealed armor of carefulness one is never fully protected from danger.

In the collection *Cathedral*, which includes "Careful," the image of the "man in a case" is further developed, moving from the episodic margins of the stories to their central characters. J. P., a patient in a rehabilitation center in "Where I'm Calling From," shares his life story with his friend, the narrator. He begins with a childhood event that made a big impression on him: He once fell into an empty well, where he was stuck for a while until his father came to his rescue, pulling him out with a rope. There is a clear connection between J. P.'s stay at the bottom of the well and his current locus, where, in the effort to give up drinking, he tries to rise from the lowest point of his life. Similarly, the child's call for help adds an intense emotional power to the story's title. Being stuck in the narrow space of the well, however, was not merely a frightful experience:

> But he told me that being at the bottom of that well had made a lasting impression. He'd sat there and looked up the well mouth. Way up at the top, he could see a circle of blue sky. Every once in a while a white cloud passed over. A flock of birds flew across, and it seemed to J. P. their wing beats set up this odd commotion. He heard other things. He heard tiny rustlings above him in the well, which made him wonder if things might fall down into his hair. He was thinking of insects. He heard wind blow over the well mouth, and that sound made an impression on him, too. In short, everything about his life was different for him at the bottom of that well. But nothing fell on

him and nothing closed off that little circle of blue. Then his dad came along with the rope, and it wasn't long before J. P. was back in the world he'd always lived in. (*WICF*, 281)

Lloyd's anxiety that he will wake up in the dark, the ceiling inches from his head, seems to be soothed here, in one of Carver's most beautiful and authentic stories. Nothing falls on the child J. P., and he can see this "little circle of blue"—a fragment of reality framed by the narrow space. As with other scraps of sights and sounds that J. P. experiences, this one is endowed with special intensity which makes the world inside completely different from the world outside. The well is a softened version of the rehabilitation center—another pocket of reality, removed from ordinary life, but where death is tangible and close (the story begins with a description of one of the patients in the halfway house having a stroke). The well story, on the other hand, with its folktale flavor, reveals the brighter side of the narrow space, its womb-like protective quality. What exactly is it that is being protected or preserved inside this case? This issue is addressed in "Preservation"—another story of a man buried in the bowels of the earth.

"Careful" revealed the depth of the anxiety that one could experience in such a case, but we only learn of the anxiety in "Preservation" from the frightened look in the eyes of this story's "man in a case." This man hardly talks, and his story is told from the outside, from the viewpoint of Sandy, his wife. Her husband, who is called "Sandy's husband" all through the story, was fired one day. In fact, this is not just another day: It is Valentine's Day, and the husband remembers to give his wife whisky and chocolate. However, this gesture marks the end of their active love relationship. Sandy's husband stops functioning both as a provider *and* as a lover. The very day when he gets fired is the day that he moves to "live on the sofa." Sandy feels that she still loves him, but is slightly repulsed, and finds it hard to believe that they ever made love on the sofa which now accommodates this sluggish man. The sofa isolates him, like the knight's armor and the plaster-cast suits detach the lovers, as Lloyd's clogged existence isolates him from his wife, and the way the coffin helps Byelikov escape the threat of marriage. Regarding the sofa, it is Carver's favorite piece of furniture. The sofa aptly expresses the inability to love by being both a site of quick sex and of impotency. Thus in "Where Is Everyone?" (the earlier, longer version of "Mr. Coffee and Mr. Fixit") a son sees his mother making love to a stranger on the sofa, and that very piece of furniture later becomes the site of his impotency. Failing to fulfill his duties as a husband and a father, he cuddles there (and later in his mother's bed) in an embryonic position and dives into a nightmarish sleep.

However, the name of the story implies that the sofa—the "case" in "Preservation"—serves mostly to "preserve" its tenant, which is also alluded to through the revelation that the husband was fired ("I was canned today," he says). The motif of preservation reappears in the story's *mise en abyme*—a picture from a book called "Mysteries of the Past" that Sandy's husband pretends to be reading, which shows the body of a prehistoric man dug up from under the earth.

> There she [Sandy] read about a man who had been discovered after spending two thousand years in a peat bog in the Netherlands. A photograph appeared on one page. The man's brow was furrowed, but there was a serene expression to his face. He wore a leather cap and lay on his side. The man's hands and feet had shriveled, but otherwise he didn't look so awful. (*Cathedral*, 36)

A serene expression on his face, the bog man (a common literary figure) "didn't look so awful." Again, it seems that the pocket of earth, snugly enclosing the dead man, had the power to protect and soothe. The analogy to this story's living dead—the unemployed husband—is clear:

> From where she stood in the kitchen, holding her purse, she could look into the living room and see the back of the sofa and the TV screen. Figures moved across the screen. Her husband's bare feet stuck out from one end of the sofa. At the other end, on a pillow which lay across the arm of the sofa, she could see the crown of his head. He didn't stir. He may or may not have been asleep, and he may or may not have heard her come in. But she decided it didn't make any difference one way or the other. (39)

> He adjusted the pillow under his head and put his hands behind his neck. Then he lay still. Pretty soon she saw his arms move down to his sides. (44)

The gaze at a person who betrays almost no sign of life, and a lit TV—are elements that bring to mind the description of the landlady in "Careful," perhaps asleep, possibly dead. It may also recall Lloyd at the end of the story—lying on his back, his hands at his sides. The moving figures on the television screen underscore the husband's stasis, while suggesting the intricate relationship of movement and framing. Indeed, in addition to the frame of the screen, Sandy's field of vision is also a frame which enhances the husband's stasis, both by enclosing him and by fragmenting his existence, focusing only on his head and feet.[36]

At the end of the story, this fragmentary vision is further and interestingly developed, but first, I would like to point to another analogy which illuminates the story. A coworker and friend, learning of Sandy's domestic situation, tells her about her uncle, who underwent a midlife crisis at forty, and suddenly paralyzed by the fear of death, took to his bed, where he still lay, twenty-three years later. Her husband, Sandy realizes, is only thirty-one. Still, she finds herself adding twenty-three years to his present age, imagining her life alongside the living dead until they are both in their fifties. The uncle's story reveals the same paradoxical response diagnosed in "Careful"—defending oneself from the fear of death by a dead position. Even more important, this anecdote emphasizes the time factor which reappears in the portrayals of the "men in cases" of this story: three months of living on the sofa (mentioned twice at the story's opening), two thousand years in the bowels of the earth, twenty-three years in bed.

Indeed, these "preserved" figures manifest, above all, a unique experience of time. Here, time is no longer expressed through movement and change (a sense Carver's characters are usually deprived of, as indicated in the first chapter), but rather through a static or seemingly static situation. It is experienced through the permanent and preserved and not through the transient and changing. In contrast to this stationary concept of time, the story presents elements of transition and loss, expressed both directly (through the loss of passion and love) and symbolically, through recurrent images of leakage. This motif seems to have leaked from "Careful" thanks to the episode of the broken refrigerator (the refrigerator in Sandy's house is broken on account of a Freon gas leak; water drips onto the floor from the defrosted meat; and Sandy recalls that a gas leakage in her father's car caused his death). In contrast to these images is a state of freezing and preservation. Flow and movement are suspended within the passage of time, both in the figures of dead living people (the husband and the uncle) and the dead who has been kept in a pseudo life-state (the bog man).

The tension between expressing time via the transient versus expressing it via the permanent culminates at the end of the story. Sandy responds to the refrigerator crisis with a burst of activity: She starts cooking the defrosted food, urging her husband to go to an auction and buy a new refrigerator. After his initial response, her husband sinks back into passivity. His behavior becomes even more automatic—a virtual walking dead man. The conversation between him and his wife dwindles: He mechanically repeats what she says or remains silent. His wife orders him to sit, but he just stands still near the table. The strangeness becomes more pervasive, although it is present from the beginning of the story, when Sandy (like Lloyd) realizes that they are leading a "weird" and unusual life, yet behaving "as if they were normal people" (37). This atmosphere, of something out of the ordinary, dominates the end of the story:

> It was then she saw puddles of water on the table. She heard water, too. It was dripping off the table and onto the linoleum. She looked down at her husband's bare feet. She stared at his feet next to the pool of water. *She knew she'd never again in her life see anything so unusual. But she didn't know what to make of it yet.* She thought she'd better put on some lipstick, get her coat, and go ahead to the auction. But

she couldn't take her eyes from her husband feet. She put her plate on the table and watched until the feet left the kitchen and went back into the living room. (46, my emphasis)

What is the effect of this fragmentary vision—a pool of water and her husband's feet—which causes Sandy to react in this way? What is so unusual about this sight—which is, again, a slice of life, which seems to be randomly chosen and framed, and yet is so full of meaning? Why does is seem to prevent the person who noticed it from taking any action? No doubt the vision illustrates the transitory and ephemeral, and the elements of motion and flow in the image (feet, water) underscore this. Sandy acknowledges the singularity of this moment here and then gone. Therefore it is indeed "unusual," regardless of its everyday nature. At the same time, this acknowledgment of the irreversible flow of time in which the present is forever lost, paradoxically allows her to experience it as something that will be preserved in memory, where perhaps it will acquire a meaning that eludes her now. This offhanded insight makes the experience part of a psychological and formal complex which I suggest calling, in the words of Gilles Deleuze, an "optic situation." Deleuze defines and thoroughly analyzes the optic situation in the second volume of his monumental study of cinema, *Cinema 2: The Time Image*. This concept, which illuminates "Preservation" and other stories, will be the focus of discussion in the next section. Eventually it will be used to tie together different features of the "man in a case" and to elucidate his complex role in Carver's oeuvre.

The Optic Situation

Before describing the optic situation in detail, first let me introduce Deleuze's study of cinema and its point of departure in a brief presentation that will also help me underpin and justify my use of this theory.

For Deleuze, the domain of philosophy is the creation of concepts. It is comprised of "images of thought," which are valid not because they are consistent with some kind of truth, but because they align with the process of thinking that generated them, with its "immanency." However, "images of thought" are not exclusive to philosophy, and transactions take place between varied arts and fields of knowledge. In accordance with this view, Deleuze does not impose a philosophic reading on cinematic pieces (or literary ones in other works), but rather formulates his concepts "alongside" them. He argues that cinema has mostly furnished "thought images" to the issues of time and movement, noting that the focus of philosophy on these issues has arisen simultaneously with the ascension of the silver screen. Moving from a typology of cinematic genres and a historical approach to the art of cinema, from philosophic discussion to analysis of specific pieces, Deleuze discusses these issues supported by the works of two major thinkers: Charles Peirce's semiotics and the philosophy of Henry Bergson. In fact, this book is not only a study of cinema, but also a systematic and outstanding reading of Bergson's philosophy, in which Deleuze offers four rounds of interpretation of Bergson's concepts of time and motion. In each of the chapters scattered throughout the book and subtitled "First/Second/Third/Fourth Interpretation of Bergson," Deleuze investigates the work of the French philosopher from a different angle, in the context of his own analysis of cinema.[37]

The structure of this two-volume study supports Deleuze's main argument. In its first part, *Cinema 1: The Movement Image*, Deleuze demonstrates the way cinema has succeeded in expressing movement specifically through montage and camera movement. It overcame the problem of representing movement by the mere juxtaposition of static and homogeneous segments—a problem which, according to Bergson, characterized Western thought since Zeno.[38] Deleuze further suggests that the process of transition from classic to modern postwar cinema is correlated—though in a much more accelerated manner—to the process undergone by philosophy in the time that elapsed from Greek philosophy to Kant. This progression resulted in perceiving time not through movement, but directly and purely, so that movement is no more a measure of time, but subjected to it. In cinema this process is expressed in the post–World War II shift from "movement image" to the "time image," and to movies which express time directly, unmediated by movement. The second volume, *Cinema 2: The Time Image*, is devoted to the results of this process.

It is important to note that we are not dealing here with a leap which connects two entirely different stages. As implied by the first volume, and as Deleuze explicitly says, the potential for a pure expression of time already existed in the movement image. However, it was developed and fully actualized in the second stage of cinema, and accelerated by the crisis of war. Only then did cinema—as all great art forms—reach its full potential. Therefore, Deleuze's study presents cinema as an art which expresses, in a concrete and intensified manner induced by a specific historical situation, thought processes parallel to philosophy. Deleuze's insights are therefore a philosopher's, not a cinema historian's, hence my basis for borrowing his concepts to discuss a literary—not cinematic—oeuvre, and one generated under different historical circumstances.[39]

Deleuze's first volume closes with the crisis following World War II, which produced situations that inhibited any description or response. In movies expressing this crisis, movement is discontinuous and aimless—rambling. Spaces are empty and fragmentary, and characters devoid of any context. Actions are performed absentmindedly and "float" in the situation in a nightmarish atmosphere. Hovering above the scene is the cliché—a present-day substitute for

Romanticism's Weltschmerz—equating outside and inside and tying everything together in a false union. This cluster of features is all part of what Deleuze terms "the crisis of the action image"—the "action image" being one aspect of the "movement image" which dominated cinema until then. While movement images were based on a tight connection between the characters' situation and their reaction to it, after the crisis in the wake of World War II, the link between perceiving and acting, situation and action-reaction, had been severed, and the action image collapsed. The first volume ends by posing a problem: How will cinema respond to the crisis of the action image, what new image will replace it, and how will it react to a world dominated by cliché without becoming one itself?

The second volume, focusing on the "time image," begins with a response to this problem. According to Deleuze, and inspired by André Bazin, the pioneers who introduced the new image belonged to Italian neorealism. Characters in these films were no longer portrayed in situations which Deleuze names, after Bergson, "sensory-motor situations." The sensed situations were no longer transformed into reaction by their extension to the outer world. Rather, there was a delay in the gap between perceiving a situation and reacting to it. Note that, according to Deleuze, the gap between a situation and a reaction already existed in the action image, whenever it involved subjectivity. Yet in the new image, this gap was filled. Now, the direct and immediate reaction was replaced by mental layers or "circuits" corresponding to different aspects of the object in reality, as the senses experience it. This circularity is accompanied by the circular return of perception to its subjective point of departure, which disrupts the linear progression of action: Rather than being transformed into a reaction in the objective world, perception lingers in reflection, turned back inward. Thus Deleuze says of the protagonist of Rossellini's *Europe 51*:

> *Her glances relinquish the practical function* of a mistress of a house who arranges things and beings, and *passes through every state of an internal vision*, affliction, compassion, love, happiness, acceptance . . . : she sees, she has learnt to see. (Cinema 2, 2; my emphases)

Neorealism thus created a cinema of the seer in lieu of the cinema of an *actant*—based on "optical and sound" situations rather than on "sensory-motor" ones; insight was born of sight, and sensory-motor connections were replaced by their "relation with time and thought," where time and thought are "visible and of sound" (17–18):

> If all the movement-images, perceptions, actions and affects underwent such an upheaval, was this not first of all because a new element burst on to the scene which was to prevent perception being extended

into action in order to put it in contact with thought, and gradually, was to subordinate the images to the demands of new signs which would take it beyond movement? (*Cinema 2*, 1)

In Italian neorealism, the transformation which Deleuze describes took the form of an encounter: transient, fragmentary and missed—an encounter between the eye (and the ear) and something "unbearable, too beautiful or too terrible" (20), that cannot be routed to active channels and absorbed into a response nor pragmatically justified to mitigate its effect:

> This is how, in ordinary or everyday situations, in the course of a series of gestures, which are insignificant but all the more obedient to simple sensory-motor schemata, what was suddenly been brought about is a *pure optical situation* to which the little maid [in Vitorio De Sica's *Umberto D*] has no response or reaction. (2, Deleuze's emphasis)

> It is a matter of something too powerful, or too unjust, but sometimes also too beautiful, and which henceforth outstrips our sensory-motor capacities. . . . It can be a limit situation . . . but also the most banal. (18)

As it gradually unfolds throughout the book, the seer's look—which is often a fragment: detached, seemingly insignificant and stripped of any function, while at the same time charged with such profound influence—is in fact a glimpse into time itself. This is time as Bergson sees it: a whole where present and past, the ephemeral and the preserved, the actualized and the virtual, are all bound up in one another—a "crystal," as Deleuze calls its extreme manifestation. Moreover, the concrete image of time is literal, resisting any metaphoric replacement, summoning a brutal and naked optic-sonoric encounter: "the thing in itself, literally, in its excess of horror or beauty, in its radical or unjustifiable character" (20).

Deleuze, however, simultaneously suggests that the sight is "readable" (*lisible*) as much as it is "visible," since it is subjected to thought functions and mental connections. In that sense, it "deletes," "replaces," and "displaces"(22) the object (or better—the object's objectivity) through its very description. This is, of course, a paradoxical suggestion that reveals Deleuze's efforts to soften the boundaries between objectivity and subjectivity, singularity and doubleness: the thing itself and its replacement with meaning—a tendency I will elaborate upon in the next chapter.

What are the conditions which allow or prompt the optic and sound situation? In terms of characters, the people most susceptible are those unable to function, or those who are helpless (e.g., children). In any case, in the optic situation, motor functions are dispensable and actions are futile. The situation is induced also by states of a break in perception: forgetfulness, stupor, and hallucination. In terms of its nature, the optic situation often emerges from an everyday situation. Everyday actions are carried out automatically and the links between reception-reaction (the sensory-motor scheme) are so mechanical, predetermined and resilient under scrutiny. It is precisely for that reason that everyday situations are so fragile and given to rupture at "the least disturbance of equilibrium between stimulus and response" (3). At the same time, crisis situations are also liable to become optic and sound situations. With regard to the body in this situation, it is no more the body which expresses the passage from present to future through its actions, but rather the body which expresses the past in its tiredness and the future in its passive waiting.

The environment which generates and accommodates the optic situation is an anonymous, fragmentary space which cannot be described. Deleuze names this space "any-space-whatever," pointing to its difference from the detailed, specific space which characterized the action image. Indeed, the deserted, shattered spaces which remained after World War II played a crucial part in the collapse of the movement image.

Deleuze deals with the cinema in specific historical circumstances. However, as I have attempted to demonstrate, his philosophical premises and method provide the opportunity to expand beyond this context and apply his insights to modern literature generally. The works of Joyce, Woolf, Faulkner, and Robbe-Grillet are rife with figures of viewers and voyeurs, and vision clashing with action and time becomes a major theme. Deleuze, who also diagnosed modern consciousness in his other books (for example, in his studies of Kafka and Proust), contributes to the understanding of this complex of vision-time-inertia.[40] He accurately describes its underlying processes, clarifies its mechanism, points to the interconnections between its elements, elucidates its logic, and supplies it with a philosophical infrastructure.

Although sometimes referred to as patently "neorealist," this epithet does not indicate any connection between Carver and Italian neorealism. Nonetheless, there is a striking similarity between the "new reality" of the postwar films and many of the situations depicted by Carver, who revived the American realistic short story in the nineteen sixties and seventies. The similarity lies in the concrete expression he gives to the optic situation's elements and causes, to the stories' events and characters, as well as their structure.

George Clarke has already described the way in which Carver's characters are often portrayed as being in a state of melancholic contemplation, suggesting the figures of Edward Hopper, who both look outside and are immersed in an inner reflection.[41] Indeed, Sandy in "Preservation" is typical in this regard: She is mesmerized by a fragment of visible reality, and acknowledges its power and impression on her memory without fathoming it. More than a few of Carver's characters are mysteriously and deeply affected by something they see or hear. Often banal, sometime menacing and occasionally beautiful, this sight or sound halts the regular course of life or sometimes ruptures it. Some of these encounters have already been mentioned: Claire in "So Much Water So Close to Home" who notices a fleeting, seemingly marginal detail, and is filled with unexpected compassion; Harry, looking at a mattress on the floor in "How About This?" is filled with fear; the protagonist of "Where Is Everyone?" who wakes up in horror to a roaring sound and white light; Jack in "What's in Alaska?" who is stupefied by the sight of a pair of eyes watching him. There are many other instances: Nancy, who lies in her bed, watching and listening, as the moon illuminates "The Smallest Things" in her yard; the narrator of "What We Talk about When We Talk about Love" who at the end of the (edited) story becomes aware of his heartbeat and the "human noise" in the room; Jack and Fran looking alternately at an ugly baby and a beautiful peacock in "Feathers"; and the characters in "Blackbird Pie" and "Call If You Need Me" who face a vision of horses in the fog. In these three last instances, people face great beauty which has a numbing effect, to the point of destruction. This prompted one of Carver's interviewers to comment that in his world "beauty affects the lower-middle class in a strange way" and poses the question to the author about whether they should "be kept out of art museums."[42]

While this intense state of looking often involves an inability to move or act, sometime the inertia is there to begin with. Thus, Sandy's unemployed husband sets the conditions for her to disconnect seeing from acting and to linger in the optic state, first by virtue of his extremely static existence and then in the visual, nonverbal message he transmits just by his standing still. Carver's "Mr. Coffee and Mr. Fixit" provides another example of the suspension of "sensor-motor links" by vision, which occurs on several levels in this story. Gordon Lish's editing of the story enhanced a strangeness that was already there in the earlier version ("Where Is Everyone?"), while the opening of both versions is pure Carver:

> *I've seen some things.* I was going over to my mother's to stay a few nights. But just as I got to the top of the stairs, I looked and she was on the sofa kissing a man. It was summer. The door was open. The TV was going. *That's one of the things I've seen.*
>
> My mother is sixty-five. She belongs to a singles club. Even so, it was hard. I stood with my hand on the railing and watched as the man kissed her. She was kissing him back, and the TV was going. (*WWTA*, 17, my emphases)

Again, this scene combines a state of seeing with varied frames: the frame of the door, the television screen's frame, and a textual frame created by the repeated platitude in the opening and conclusion of the first paragraph. In addition, vision is connected here to a visual culture that is overwhelmed by visual clichés, shown both in the presence of the TV, and in the nature of the description: a rather shabby version of the "primal scene" with more than a hint of soap opera. For the narrator, reminiscing about this state of seeing, the vision was only "one of the things I've seen," that is, one of many banal fragments of reality produced by his life story and his culture. Yet, at the same time, the sight is difficult and shocking, and it encapsulates his misery. The text specifically refers to the viewer's position—standing with his hand on the railing, a heightened state of stasis which led Runyon, in the spirit of Freud, to compare the impact of confronting one's mother's sexuality to the petrifying stare of the Medusa.[43]

In the shorter, later version of the story, the text further enhances the impression of stasis when it abandons the scene in the middle, wanders with a chain of associations, and returns a page and a half later with: "I left my mother with the man on the sofa." It thus put the seeing scene in a state of "pause," as if all this time the son was left standing motionless at his mother's door, his hand on the railing.

In this story too, the characters seem to cut loose of any network of activity and occupation. This holds true mostly for the story's "doubles": the wife's lover, Mr. Ross, an unemployed aerospace engineer, and the husband-narrator, who at the end of the longer version snuggles in his mother's bed, detaching himself from any activity. In addition, the story presents a range of out-of-work objects: a gun that never shoots, a television set with volume but no picture, and a bunch of "clunkers" or "antique cars" (like the refrigerator in "Preservation") which are no longer in use, and are piled up in the yard of Mr. Rose, aka Mr. Fixit.

The junkyard of Mr. Rose, the lame Mr. Fixit, seems to reflect the structure of this story: a pile of events, objects, and characters (the short, three-page version mentions ten, to which the longer version adds one). In a state of affairs designated as "crumbling situations" ("Where Is Everyone?" *Fires*, 175) the uselessness of characters and objects infiltrates the story's form, while resisting the creation of a functional interconnected chain of events subjected to plot progression. There are unclear time lapses—a "false continuity" to use Deleuze's expression (e.g., at what point in time should we locate the return of the wife, mentioned in the end?).[44] Told in retrospect, the narration nonetheless fails to help the reader in organizing the events: The links between the episodes—some of which seem utterly dispensable—are associative or lack any motivation (e.g., where did the episode of the father's death came from?). It is as if the narrator, who has retired from all activity in the "real world" of the story, also refuses to carry out his duty as a narrator and as an *actant* and to unfold the story properly by placing characters and events in a logical order. Instead, his moves in the time-space frame of both the text and the story are aimless, or a sort of Deleuzeian "rambling."

The loose, episodic structure led John Biguenet to use "Mr. Coffee," and especially the beginning of this story, in his assault on minimalist writing.[45] Biguenet likens the narrator to an alcohol-soaked type, who, drenched in self-pity, sits next to us at a bar counter and imposes his misfortunes on us with a tale that may hold some meaning and coherency for him, but for the chance listener can only remain a randomly chosen mix of anecdotes. This aesthetic claim against the incoherent structure is also an ethical indictment against the autism-narcissism of the protagonist-narrator, with regard to his communication with the other—the reader. Biguenet's accusation is consistent with that of other Carver critics who claim that his characters prefer self-pity over action. One such critic, for instance, wrote of the couple in "Preservation," saying: "So the refrigerator breaks—why don't they just call a repairman and get it fixed?" (A response, Carver remarked, which reflects an acute misunderstanding of the harsh blue-collar reality).[46]

These types of accusations against a passive character are not limited to believers in the capitalist way of life or in the soundness of the American dream. Similar claims have been voiced by Marxist critics against neorealist cinema and earlier by Georg Lukács against French "objectivism" and modernist literature.[47] For Lukács, ethical criteria are part and parcel of his aesthetic judgment. He denounces the stasis of characters in modernist and naturalist literature, both in terms of their behavior in the story and in terms of their literary function and their characterization in the text. At the first level, they are voyeurs refraining from participating in life, while at the second, they do not integrate into the story design and plot; their actions are no longer derived from their worldview or their spiritual life, nor from a well-defined personality. In both aspects of their existence—as human beings and as inactive literary *actants*—these passive characters help to underpin the current system, whether bourgeois or capitalist. While Biguenet argues that minimalist characters are narcissistic and solipsistic, Lukács argues that modernist characters are immersed in their subjectivity with no full awareness of reality. While Biguenet interprets the word "things" (as in Carver's "I've seen some things") as embodying the objectification of people and experience in minimalist literature, Lukács accuses modern description of equating man with the objects that surround him. While Biguenet portrays the minimalist narrator as deprived of authority and writing "under erasure," Lukács, in turn, describes the narrators of Zola, Joyce, or Dos Passos as those who have lost the capacity to observe and comprehend everything as the omniscient narrator did. Instead, these narrators grasp the interconnections only to the extent that the characters are familiar with them. They adhere to the present tense, and their view of reality does not allow a retrospective, broad vision which could endow events with their real meaning while tightening the connections between events and characters and their human nature.

Note that Lukács does not offer a simplified version of the *Poetics* of Aristotle, who subjected character and human nature to plot and action, by just expecting characters to act. He refers, for instance, to Goncharov's inactive and sedate Oblomov, who has a well-defined intellectual physiognomy, deep connections with other characters and a sound social context. He is therefore a dramatic-dynamic character and a social type, and cannot be compared to the isolated, objectified character of modernist literature who remains frozen in a story which is merely a pile of static situations, a sequence of unrelated and experimental fragments. Only action reveals man truly, as in the classic novel, where plot unfolds different aspects of the character, both as an individual and as a representative of an era and a society. In this dramatic novel the omniscient narrator and the broad perspective give major events their prominence, and characters are integrated into a dynamic, rich net of social interactions. Modern-modernist characters, on the other hand, float in the present tense, which is confined to the everyday, and equates major events with minor ones.

The claims against Carver are thus in the tradition of accusations against the static figure of the voyeur in modern and modernist literature: a character who comes hand in hand with a description detached from human action and situated in stories depicting a static situation in lieu of a plot, and with no narratorial authority to lend it meaning and substance. Like the artifacts surrounding these characters, they are isolated, detached, confined to their own time-space, within a story that bears no implications beyond their solipsistic experience.

However, as indicated by Deleuze, this slandered character—who is unable to react, whose actions "float," who is disconnected from situations, and whose links with both action in the world and plot of the story are so feeble—is precisely the one who succeeds in creating a unique experience while embodying it in his or her very presence. Underlying this experience is a vision which is disconnected from action and—much like the character responsible for it—is exempt of any traditional function. This vision, by its very disconnectedness, enables an access to time which is independent of movement. This vision, says Deleuze, is not intended for mere identification, unlike the typical vision of sensory-motor schema in which sensory experiences are routed to movement. No longer is the look capturing through a process of reduction and abstraction, the aspect of the object which is necessary for action and similar to other things, (that is the role cliché plays—Deleuze observes, following Bergson). Rather, the vision creates a description or an image which restores the object's lost, unnecessary parts, or exposes empty spaces in the image. Hence, by avoiding the illusion of wholeness, it reveals that which had not been represented. Avoiding the similarity principle, this image-description is lean and stripped of metaphoric richness (which, according to Deleuze, is a false one). It is merely a "slight fragment without importance," but this is precisely why this image "brings the thing each time to an essential singularity and describes the inexhaustible" (*Cinema 2*, 45). As such, it is much more "rich and typical": By its spareness and basic lack, it reveals the inadequacy of any representation. Pointing at its own insufficiency, it stimulates endless "circuits" of other descriptions in the effort to approach the object which is ever-changing, since it is an integral part of the subjective act of seeing in any given moment.

Deleuze thus presents the very same features of the static figure which Lukács denounced as the conditions for "vision" in the full sense of the word. According to Lukács, the modernist description fails to captures the "poetry of things," because it has no function and serves no human need or action, whereas for Deleuze, it succeeds in capturing the object's irreducible essence—both objective and subjective. Do Carver's descriptions fall in with this account? I began to address this question in the previous chapter and will return to it soon, but let me first bolster Deleuze's cinematic insights with some critical literary thinking from Formalist thought.

The distinction between vision and identification or recognition was made, in 1917, by Shklovsky in his influential essay "Art as Device," where he first coined the concept of *Defamiliarization* or *ostranenie* (остранение). Underlying his essay is the suggestion that everyday use of language is based on mental economy, and therefore employs symbols (in the algebraic, not the intricate, literary sense of the word). This use of language represents (and produces) a perception which captures what is similar to other objects in this particular object, while abstracting qualities and aspects which are unnecessary in practical, automatic functioning. The aim of literature, says Shklovsky, is to create defamiliarization of both reality and language by hampering this practical-economizing perception, which abstracts, deducts, and ignores dissimilarities. When successful, this sabotage results in a replacement of identification with seeing and vision (the religious connotations of this epiphanic experience are even stronger in Shklovsky's earlier essay "The Resurrection of the Word"). Vision is refreshed and objects are "defamiliarized," decontextualized, and liberated from the automatic mechanism of everyday perception and its cliché-ridden patterns. No longer are they identified "spatially, in the blink of an eye," which merely scrapes their surface, but rather are captured in their rich singularity and uniqueness. The reader thus becomes deeply involved in the process of creation, now focused on the process of perception rather than on the artifice itself.

> It [poetic language] is "artificially" created by an artist in such a way that the perceiver, *pausing* in his reading, *dwells* on the text. This is when the literary work attains its greatest and most long-lasting impact. The object is perceived *not spatially* but, as it were, *in its temporal continuity*. That is, because of this device, the object is brought into view. (My emphases)[48]

Both Deleuze and Shklovsky point to a process of hampering automatic identification, of sabotaging function-oriented, abstracting perception. Both are interested in the singularity of the thing itself versus the metaphor, the symbol, or the cliché. The similarity continues in the way both Deleuze and Shklovsky perceive the state of seeing or vision as a state of pause, dwelling, and temporality (according to Shklovsky, it is the state of the reader; according to Deleuze, of both character and viewer [*Cinema 2*, 19]). This pause does not infringe upon time, but rather creates a consciousness of time or even an access to pure time. Shklovsky describes an encounter between the time of perception-reading and the time of the object, detached as it is from the context of space and function, while for Deleuze, the time of inaction allows access to time itself, not subjected to movement, which is defined as a passage in time across space.

As discussed earlier, Carver's descriptions are closer to the definition of identification rather than to Shklovsky's or Deleuze's vision. Lukács, who focuses on Carver's predecessors, as well as other critics, who refer to neorealism and to Carver himself, indeed talk of these brands of writing in terms of glimpse versus vision.[49] However, as discussed before, Carver succeeds in using the cliché's tools—automatic identification, economy, and a flat, surface-scraping description—to express the "movement of the description" and the vibration of the subjective within the seemingly objective. Similarly, Carver manages to achieve a defamiliarization and fresh vision precisely via the channel this process seeks to avoid, namely by means of sights often marked by clichés, banality, and flatness. The unusual sight which Sandy knows she would never again see, these "unimportant fragments" of her husband's feet, the pool of water; the fragments which enter J. P.'s well—the circle of blue and rustlings seen and heard so differently; the sounds reaching Lloyd's clogged ear as if through a barrel or "copper pipe"; the tragic-comic cliché scene in "Mr. Coffee": All these sights and sounds, which entrap characters in a stasis while enhancing the experience of looking and hearing, are not defamiliarized at the level of language or style. Rather, they are rendered in ordinary, everyday language, sometimes colloquial but without diverting from standard language enough to bring to the fore language itself (Biguenet accuses minimalism of being "purged of any style").[50] In that sense, these images or descriptions do not disrupt the mechanism of standard perception, and sometimes (as in "Mr. Coffee and Mr. Fixit") they even underscore the reproducible and the cliché-ridden. Nevertheless, defamiliarization occurs effectively in all the ways described throughout this study, including the process of framing, discussed in this chapter. Furthermore, it is actualized in the very reality of the fictive world: in objects and characters whose loose connections to action and plot and fundamental uselessness all promote defamiliarization and embody it. By failing to be the conductors of action, by being dispensable and superfluous, these elements subvert abstraction, economy, and functionality. Their existence often derives from the everyday, even as it disturbs everyday functioning. Undergoing defamiliarization or experiencing it, these objects and people create the conditions for vision, and in their inertness they allow for an experience of pure time—the two basic elements defining the "optic situation."

Conclusion

How do we return now to the "man in a case"? What connects Lloyd, insulated in his small apartment, stiff in his imaginary, self-made coffin, to the optic situation of "Preservation," where a woman looks at her unemployed husband's feet? This is the time to tie together the various ideas raised in this chapter and tell the full story of the "man in a case," unfolded by Carver in several stories, each of which adds another dimension to his portrait.

The "man in a case" is cramped into an interior space, which suggests both claustrophobia and protection, a space embodying a physical and emotional rigor mortis, which at the same time allows an intense unusual experience. This experience brings to mind the effect of defamiliarization, while its intensity suggests the force imparted to everyday slices of life when demarcated by a story's frame. The different frames of the Carverian space—doors, windows, viewfinders, even his characters' field of vision—are likewise a reminder of the way a story frame closes in on its object. All these frames, embodied in the image of the closed space or case, demonstrate the potential to perceive or represent characters in a tunnel vision, as objects, to brutally uproot them from space-time continuum and deprive them of any dynamism by fragmentation, the frame being, as it were, their coffin. At the same time, Carver's frames also work at de-framing: his are not frames of the kind suggested by Poe—ones which create a "unity of impression" by isolating the event by the location of the short story (is there such a thing anyway?).[51] Rather, it is a frame which evokes what is out of the field, one which implies, in varied ways, the "open," that is, the dynamic continuity from which the character was detached. In this vicarious manner, the frame lends room for the movement it seems to prevent. Within the frame, the time and movement of the characters are expressed through their link to the ever-changing whole, rather than in their individual movement. Furthermore, this potential, pending movement which characterizes both the optic situation and the "man in a case" is connected to the openness of the text to the reader, another out-of-the-frame entity (to be discussed in the next chapter).

The "man in the case" shows this dynamic by his relationship both to the closed space and to the story's frame, but he illustrates it mainly in his approach to action. As much as he is secluded in space and cut off from personal interactions, he is a static figure, no longer an *actant* or a node in a web of interconnected actions. In the reality of the story, this man's deeds are marked by the "stationary movement" of the everyday, while in the text he is no longer a carrier of the plot's events.[52] However, this man's presence in the widening gap between situation-reaction engenders a state of sight-insight and an experience of time, which is no longer connected to space or movement. His stasis in both its manifestations—the confining space as well as the suspension of action—allows the "man in a case" to be a carrier of—or a crucial factor in—a unique and dynamic complex of vision-movement-time: Decontextualized, he is defined in terms of his existence in time and his link to an invisible whole. The more he is detached from space and loosened from action, the more intense this experience. Being practically a member of the living dead, the "man in a case" embodies the ephemeral and lost. The power of the case to preserve and protect is doubtful; time gnaws at everything and nothing is left but the fragments of sights, which, like this man, are detached, useless, and cannot be channeled into action. Yet precisely these "slices of life" reveal the capacity of the case to preserve, when it finally constitutes the space of memory.

This is how Carver describes the emergence of a story in his mind, where he always "sees" something:

> I start with an image, a cigarette being put out in a jar of mustard, for instance, or the remains, the wreckage, of a dinner left on the table. Pop cans in the fireplace, that sort of thing. And a feeling goes with that. And that feeling seems to transport me back to the particular time and place, and the ambience of the time.[53]

On another occasion, he acknowledged the resemblance of his stories and poems to pictures or snapshots because "there's a glimpse of something that stays fixed in your head."[54] The images that Carver chose (the remains of a dinner, cigarette butts, pop cans in the fireplace) faithfully illustrate the idea of "something that stayed." In that sense, they well represent a writer whose work may be seen as an endeavor to collect leftovers, scraps, and useless objects, shreds of life which have been unused for action, and become sunk in memory; a writer who is a collector of useless people who have dropped out of the functional world of action.[55]

Here is an observation made by Deleuze with reference to the marginal "useless" characters in the cinema of Werner Herzog:

> When Bruno asks the question: 'Where do objects go when they no longer have any use?' we might reply that they normally go in the dustbin, but that reply would be inadequate, since the question is metaphysical. Bergson asked the same question and replied metaphysically: that which has ceased to be useful simply begins to *be*. (Deleuze's emphasis)[56]

The useless, that which "was there" and "simply begins to be," is the focus of a brief essay by Roland Barthes. At the core of this substantial essay, one can sense the same longing for singularity, presence, and that which cannot be represented, so well expressed by Deleuze and Shklovsky. At the center of this essay is the concept of a superfluous, out-of-function detail, which is responsible for "the reality effect" of fiction.

The "reality effect" and the way Carver's world—with his unemployed people, his leftovers, and his unnecessary details—embodies both the complexity and attraction of this concept will be discussed in the next chapter.

Notes

1. Yoel Hoffman, *How Do You Do, Dolores?* (Jerusalem: Keter Publishing Ltd., 1995), 142 (in Hebrew).
2. Gentry and Stull, 50–51, 134.
3. "The Philosophy of Composition," in *Selected Writings of Edgar Allan Poe*, ed. Edward H. Davidson (Boston: Houghton Mifflin, 1956), 460.
4. See Halpert, 90.
5. Sherwood Anderson, "Loneliness," in *Winesburg Ohio* (New York: Modern Library, 1947), 199.
6. Runyon, 162.
7. See, for example, in the obituary of Carver by Peter Kemp, "The American Chekhov," *Sunday Times*, 7 August 1988, Book Section, 1–2.
8. Anton Chekhov, "The Man in a Case," in *The Wife and Other Stories*, trans. Constance Garrett (New York: Ecco Press, 1972), 249–68.
9. Nilli Mirsky, Epilogue to *A Boring Tale* by Anton Chekhov (Tel Aviv: Am Oved, 1996), 99 (in Hebrew).
10. Frank O'Connor stated this view of the short story as the genre of man in his isolation in *The Lonely Voice: Study of the Short Story* (London: Macmillan, 1965), 19. On Carver's appreciation of O'Connor, see Gentry and Stull, 17, 213.
11. Tony Tanner, *City of Words: American Fiction: 1950–1970* (New York: Harper and Row, 1971), 15–19. The descriptions which Tanner collected from American literature for illustrating his argument are images of rigidity and fluidity so common in "Careful," and the image of armor, to be analyzed later.
12. Gentry and Stull, 127.
13. Mikhail Bakhtin, *Problems of Dostoevsky's Poetics*, trans. Caryl Emerson (Minneapolis: University of Minnesota Press, 1984), 52.
14. Lotman, 209–17. Boris Uspensky, *A Poetics of Composition: The Structure of the Artistic Text and Typology of Compositional Forms*, trans. Valentina Zavarin and Susan Wittig (Berkeley: University of California Press, 1973), 137–51. On the importance of the selection process in making the frame the most important factor in endowing fictional reality with meaning, see Brooke-Rose, 295.
15. Gentry and Stull, 155.

16. Brooke-Rose defines a frame where "the signified is itself framed (or not) by other 'signifiers'"(164). She draws her examples from James in *The Turn of the Screw* and from the fiction of Robbe-Grillet, whose frames she names "enlarged inset" (295).

17. This analysis is a synthesis of three thinkers' conceptions of the frame: Gilles Deleuze, Svetlana Alpers, and J. A. Ward. Deleuze (*Cinema 1*, 12–18) speaks of the geometric frame in terms of its incompatibility with the object; Alpers offers a description of a frame (that of northern painting) in which the arbitrary cut simulates "regular" vision (although for her the image of the window embodies that of the southern tradition of painting); J. A., Ward, on the other hand, relates the arbitrary cut to the window image, suggesting that the window and other subframes in Edward Hopper's paintings draw sight to the margins. See his *American Silences: The Realism of James Agee, Walker Evans, and Edward Hopper* (Baton Rouge: Louisiana State University Press, 1985), 176–77. Similarly, Roland Barthes uses the image of the window frame in *S/Z*: "It could be said that the speaker, before describing, stands at the window, not so much to see, but to establish what he sees by its frame: the window frame creates the scene. To describe is thus to place the empty frame which the realistic author always carries with him . . . before a collection or continuum of objects which cannot be put into words without this obsessive operation." See *S/Z*, trans. Richard Miller (New York: Hill and Wang, 1974), 54–55. See also Barthes's discussion of the tableaux in the works of Diderot, Brecht, and Eisenstein (in *Image, Music, Text: Essays Selected and Translated by Stephen Heath* (New York: Hill and Wang, 1977), 69–78.

18. Lotman, 209–17.

19. Tzvetan Todorov, *The Poetics of Prose*, trans. Richard Howard (Oxford: Basil Blackwell, 1977), 107.

20. This is Russell's observation with reference to the hyperrealist cinema of Chantal Akerman and the structural films in the sixties and seventies. Both cases involve a framing of an everyday slice of life: banal, mundane, and seemingly chosen at random. See Catherine Russell, *Experimental Ethnography: The Work of Film in the Age of Video* (Durham: Duke University Press, 1999), mostly on page 165.

21. Blanchot, "Everyday Speech," 12–20.

22. Robert Bresson, *Notes on the Cinematographer*, trans. Jonathan Griffin (London: Quartet Books, 1986), 59–60. Through this technique, Bresson's strived to recover "the automatism of real life" and to derive from his actors (or "models") "the unknown and the virgin" (ibid.)

23. See Gerald L. Bruns, "Toward a Random Theory of Prose," in Victor Shklovsky, *Theory of Prose*, trans. Benjamin Sher (Elmwood Park, IL: Dalkey Archive Press, 1991), ix–xiv. Fredric Jameson, in his critical reading of texts by Russian formalism (especially Shklovsky's and Eikenbaum's), points to the relation between the frame and defamiliarization while discussing Shklovsky's link to short story theory and to Edgar Allan Poe's concept of frame. See Fredric Jameson, *The Prison House of Language* (Princeton: Princeton University Press, 1972), 59–75.

24. See Margulies, especially in her concluding chapter, "It Is Time." Margulies believes that extended duration—analyzed here in the first chapter—contributes to the oscillation between the literal and the metaphorical.

25. Of the mythic aspect of Carver's stories, especially "Why Don't You Dance?" see Charles E. May, *The Short Story: A Reality of Artifice* (New York: Prentice-Hall, 1995), 26, 93–94.

26. Norman Bryson, "The Gaze in the Expanded Field," in Foster, *Vision and Visuality*, 87–108. Bryson compares Sartre's and Lacan's conceptions of "the gaze" and "the frame" to those of the Japanese philosopher Kitaro Nishida and his disciple Keiji Nishitani. Bryson shows how the frame in the East (e.g., in fifteenth-century Chinese ink paintings) gives room to random forces uncontrolled by the subject.

27. The term "de-framing" (*décadrage*), originally coined by Bonitzer, is used by Deleuze in *Cinema 1*, 15; and in a slightly different sense in "Percept, Affect, and Concept," in Gilles Deleuze and Félix Guattari, *What is Philosophy?* trans. Hugh Tomlinson and Graham Burchell (New York: Columbia University Press, 1991), 187.

28. On the way multiple details stimulate the reader to seek a frame of interpretation, see Frank Kermode's third chapter ("Man in the Macintosh, Boy in the Shirt"), in *Genesis of Secrecy: On the Interpretation of Narrative* (Cambridge: Harvard University Press, 1979), 49–73.

29. Runyon, 173, 32–34, 26–28, 162, 191, 135.

30. Altman, 7. His idea is comparable to that of Lainsbury, whose study of Carver is based on the view of the stories as a composite novel which shapes the Carverian "chronotope."

31. *Cinema 1*, 17–18. While discussing the out-of-field, Deleuze distinguishes between a relative out-of-field, for example, the connection of a system to a wider one (e.g., the relation between a cinematic frame and other frames) and an absolute out-of-field which is the "thread" that crosses each and every system, allowing it to connect with other systems ad infinitum. This thread connects any single frame to the whole or to the "open," which Deleuze defines as the locus of qualitative change where movement is more than mere translation of parts (ibid., 8–11). The concept of the "whole" or the "open" is the focus of Deleuze's earlier 1966 book, *Le Bergsonisme*, where he unfolds its different meanings.

32. Uspensky presents some examples of endings by Gogol and Chinese theater, where time freezes and characters are positioned in "tableaus vivant." For him, this ending constitutes a shift from "action into image" and from "living people" to "puppets" (150).

33. Uspensky, 146–51. The previously mentioned "Little Things" employs this framing device in its conclusion, when it shifts to an external, narratorial point of view.

34. See in Richard Day's introduction to Carver's play "Carnations" (Day, iv).

35. Runyon, 133.

36. On this effect see Clarke, 116.

37. On the concepts of "immanency" and "thought images" and the interactions between philosophy and the cinema, see the introduction by Hugh Tomlinson and Barbara Habberjam to Deleuze's *Cinema 1*, xi–xiv. Deleuze addresses these issues in *Negotiations*, 46–61, and in Gilles Deleuze and Claire Parnet, *Dialogues*, trans. Hugh Tomlinson and Barbara Habberjam (New York: Columbia University Press, 1987), 4. A good analysis of the "thought image" (as opposed to the dogmatic image which is based on identification) can be found in the editor's introduction to *Deleuze: A Critical Reader*, ed. Paul Patton (Cambridge, MA: Blackwell, 1996), 1–17.

My analysis of Deleuze's "optic situation" is based on both *Cinema 1* and *Cinema 2*. I will refer to a page number only when quoting.

38. See a concise description of Henry Bergson's view in his "Croissance de la vérité. Mouvement retrograderétrograde du vrai," in *Le pensée et le mouvant: essays et conferences* (Paris: Librarie Félix Alcan, 1934), 7–13. The "cinematographic illusion" was denounced as an expression of a false spatial concept of movement in Henry Bergson [1911], *Creative Evolution*, trans. Arthur Mitchell (New York: Modern Library, 1944), especially in pages 323–33. However, according to Deleuze (in *Cinema 1*, 1–3), Bergson criticized cinema but also foreshadowed the "movement image" of cinema in his earlier book *Matter and Memory*.

39. See Tomlinson and Habberjam, introduction to *Cinema 1* by Deleuze.

40. On Deleuze's closeness to modernist literature, see John Marks' introduction to Ian Buchanan and John Marks, ed., *Deleuze and Literature* (Edinburgh: Edinburgh University Press, 2000), 1–13. These traits of modern prose are described by Spiegel in his discussion of Joyce (53–89), by Ann Banfield in her discussion of Woolf (in *The Phantom Table*, throughout the book), and by Robbe-Grillet in his discussion of modern literature (*For a New Novel*, 24, 143–56).

41. On the resemblance of Carver's characters to those of Hopper and Segal, whose figures are frozen in a moment in time, see Clarke, 118. Hopper's paintings often present a figure looking out from a window or a door at a space invisible to the viewer. The effect is a blurring between inside and outside and between visible reality and a projected wish (common also in cinema); see Rolf Günter Renner, *Edward Hopper 1882–1967: Transformation of the Real* (Köln: Benedikt Taschen, 1993), 71. Renner speaks of Hopper's wish to make his images undergo a process of "decay" that will transform them from images of reality to mental images (the word "decay" no doubt implies time's work in this process). This is another feature he shares with Carver, and it is connected to the qualities of Carver's vision described in the fourth chapter.

42. John Elton's interview of Carver in 1986, in Gentry and Stull, 166.

43. Runyon, 93–94.

44. *Cinema 2*, 16.

45. John Biguenet, "Notes of a Disaffected Reader: The Origins of Minimalism," *Mississippi Review* 40–41 (1985): 40–45.

46. See Gentry and Stull, 79, 112. The critic is Anatol Boyard.

47. The negative reaction to neorealism is mentioned by Deleuze in *Cinema 2*, 19. George Lukács' view as summarized here is based on his essays "Narrate or Describe?" and "The Intellectual Physiognomy in Characterization," in *Writer and Critic and Other Essays*, 110–88.

48. Shklovsky, 12.

49. Karlsson, 149.

50. Biguenet, 44.

51. The break in the frame, the realization that it is never closed, is not exclusive to Deleuze. This was also noted by Derrida who, in his essay "Paregon," deconstructs the concept of the frame as an epitome of the autonomy of art. See Jacques Derrida, *The Truth in Painting*, trans. Geoff Bennington and Ian McLeod (Chicago: University of Chicago Press, 1987), 15–47.

52. Blanchot, "Everyday Speech," 15.

53. Gentry and Stull, 154. Similarly, Runyon maintains that the image of the remains is crucial to Carver. For him, however, they are remains of other stories and not, as I suggested here, detached details which, not used for action, enable vision and an access to time independent of movement.

54. Gentry and Stull, 223.

55. Regarding the work of memory, see Deleuze on the recollection-image in *Cinema 2*, 47–55. Carver describes his work of collecting moments that have randomly sunk into memory in Gentry and Stull, 95.

56. Deleuze, *Cinema 1*, 185. Bruno, like other marginal characters in Werner Herzog cinema, is a man who is "incapable of being used" (184).

CHAPTER 6

Singularity or Doubleness

EFFET DE RÉEL OR SYMBOL?— TOWARD CONCLUSION

A reader moved by stories like "Cathedral" or "A Small, Good Thing" will find it hard to agree with the characterization of Carver's world as lacking emotional depth or values. The label "minimalist" would then seem inadequate, all the more so because of its negative connotations. A memorable response to the debate on whether Carver is a minimalist is posed by William Kittredge in Halpert's *An Oral Biography*.[1] For him, Kittredge insists, Ray was definitely not an emotional minimalist, since he deals with "major emotions"—a view which emphasizes the emotional effect of his works on the reader.

One of Carver's more moving pieces, which clearly involves major emotions, is not a story or a poem but a nonfiction piece—an autobiographical essay called "My Father's Life," which was published in *Fires*. The force of this essay is no doubt linked to its confessional and personal nature. These features of the essay—its emotional effect and its nonfiction nature (as much as an autobiography can still be considered nonfiction)—are interconnected and inform the issues it raises.

A discussion of this text raises some difficulties. First, there is the fear that analytical tools might be inadequate for such a direct and personal piece, that abstraction might sterilize it and miss its main point. Then there is the consideration of whether an autobiographical text may be treated as a fictional text and serve as a key to Carver's oeuvre. However, these difficulties touch the very core of this essay, and are directly connected to, and should be part of, a discussion of this piece and ensuing issues. The father and the son theme leads to a questioning of "real" facts, their status and their emotional impact. In fact, the main argument of this chapter is that the tension which underlies the relationship of the son (Carver) and his father also informs the attempt to link oneself to mere facts and extract meaning from them—an attempt which is the real focus of this chapter.

"My Father's Life" and "The Father"

The essay "My Father's Life" includes a poem, which was also published separately. The poem, "Photograph of My Father in his Twenty-Second Year," is based on a photograph that Carver received from his mother. He used to look at it carefully from time to time "trying to figure out some things about my dad, and maybe myself in the process" (*Fires*, 20), but his father "just kept moving further and further away from me and back into time." Over the course of time, the photograph was lost. "It was then," Carver adds, "that I tried to recall it, and at the same time make an attempt to say something about my dad, and how I thought that in some important ways we might be alike." The poem was born of his will to remember, and stands in place of the lost photograph, accompanied by the need to understand himself and his father and to fathom the similarity between them. The circumstances and reasons for writing the poem also apply to the essay as a whole. The opening—factual and laconic as one would expect from Carver, especially in autobiographical writing—suggests the strong link between his father's identity and his own:

> My dad's name was Clevie Raymond Carver. His family called him Raymond and friends called him C.R. I was named Raymond Clevie Carver, Jr. I hated the "Junior" part. When I was little, my dad called me Frog, which was okay. But later, like everybody else in the family, he began calling me Junior. He went on calling me this until I was thirteen or fourteen and announced that I wouldn't answer to that name any longer. So he began calling me Doc. From then until his death, on June 17, 1967, he called me Doc, or else Son. (13)

There is no need to wonder, especially in an autobiographical piece, why the son preferred one name over another, and why he declared his independence by refusing to answer to the name "Junior." Still, the names are significant in the sense that each stands for another facet of the son's identity, as it is shaped in relation to his father's: an identity which is almost like his father's, with a slight difference (Raymond Carver Junior); an identity which is derived from his difference from his father, the resented appendage to his father's name (Junior); an identity shaped by his relationship with his father, as embodied in the nickname he gives his son ("Doc"); and a somewhat impersonal identity—of the "son" as such.

However, the nature of the son's relation to his father—the similarity and the difference, their individual contact versus their roles as father and son—is not only the essay's pivotal subject and a recurring theme in Carver's stories. It is also a key to Carver's intricate approach to the question of meaning. The father-son relationship concretizes it and may even be its source. A disquieting incident caused by the identity of names points to the direction this issue will take:

> When he died, my mother telephoned my wife with the news. I was away from my family at the time, between lives, trying to enroll in the School of Library Science at the University of Iowa. When my wife answered the phone, my mother blurted out, "Raymond's dead!" For a moment, my wife thought my mother was telling her that I was dead. Then my mother made it clear which Raymond she was talking about and my wife said, "Thank God. I thought you meant my Raymond." (ibid.)

The proper name "alone and in itself says death," even "while the bearer of it is still living," says Derrida in his obituary to Roland Barthes.[2] Here this insight has an interesting manifestation: For a short while, the shared name of the father and the son indeed signifies death. The misunderstanding is soon clarified, but not before it has made its impact. The symbolic resonance of this anecdote suggests that the difference from his father is crucial for the son's existence—without it he is considered dead. Still, the essay revolves around the principle of similarity and analogy, rather than around dissimilarity and difference. The son learns of his father's death when he is "between lives," and the life story of the father as told here begins when he is also "between lives"—when he is about to move from Arkansas to Washington, get married, and start a family. Some stages in the father's life and wandering are parallel to stages in his son's life of wandering. In a photograph from the son's infancy, the baby's bonnet is on crooked, and the father's hat is pushed back on his forehead. Sometimes there is an inverse analogy, as when the lower and higher points in their life collide: The son becomes a father during his father's illness, and his father is hospitalized where his grandson was born. When the son tells his father that he has became a grandfather, the latter mutters, "I feel like a grandfather." Still, this event is exceptional. As a whole, there is a straightforward analogy: The failures of the father are reflected in the son's life—in his alcoholism, his struggle to make ends meet, and his weakness of character.

The son's similarity to his father is mainly negative, and the anecdotes from the father's life which the son extracts from his mother, or from his own memory, consist mainly of the father's failures. Carver's stories carry many instances of analogies of failure. Hamilton from "Bicycles, Muscles, Cigarettes" gets involved in a fight when he tries to resolve an argument that his son gets caught up in. He overcomes his rival, yet regrets that his son has had to witness this surge of violence, and recalls a fistfight *his* father was involved in. Suddenly, this becomes the only memory he has of his father: "Hamilton had loved his father and could recall many things about him. But now he recalled his father's one fistfight as if it were all there was to the man" (*WICF*, 31). In "Sacks" a father and a son meet briefly at a terminal. The son is in the midst of a marital crisis, and the father in turn relates the collapse of his marriage to the son's mother. The present he brought for the son's family, a sack of candy, is forgotten. The negative similarity between father and son leaves no room for give and take. Likewise, in "My Father's Life," Carver, Jr., finds it hard to thank his father since, like his father, he "can't hold his liquor either."

As a counterpart to the figure of the father, whose failure the son witnesses (among these is also the father of "The Third Thing that Killed My Father Off"), there is the hated and violent son, with whom the relationship is slightly Oedipal.[3] In "The Compartment," Meyers decides, impulsively, to miss his appointment with his son, whom he has not seen for years, when he recalls him as the boy who "had devoured his youth" and "turned the young girl he had courted and wed into a nervous, alcoholic woman" (*Cathedral*, 54). In this story, as in others ("Where Is Everyone?", "Elephant"), there is also a reference to a violent encounter with the son, and this hostility is reflected in Carver's nonfiction writing as well. In the collection of poems *A New Path to the Waterfall*, there is a shockingly harsh poem dedicated to a son, in which the father-speaker admits that he often wished him dead. In his essay "Fires," Carver confesses that with the exception of some moments of joy, raising his children was a constant source of misery; it was the constraints of their very being that shaped his work more than any specific influence. It is only in Carver's late work, in a story like "Elephant," that the generations reconcile, as the father appears in a moving dream, and—in an analogy to the son who is burdened with his family's demands—carries him on his back like an "elephant."

Disillusion, hostility, an unbridgeable chasm, and negative similarity between fathers and sons—the stories of Carver, as well as his life, are populated by men who fail to meet their responsibilities: fathers who disappoint their families, sons who fail as fathers, and they all pass on a legacy of defeat.[4] Carver continues Hemingway in his preoccupation with American manhood, widening the cracks in his master's representation into a real fissure.

In light of this brief review of the representations of fathers and sons in Carver's oeuvre, it is necessary to ask: Is it only the father's failures that make the similarity in names so lethal in "My Father's Life" ("Raymond's dead")? The finale of the essay, which tells of the father's funeral, points to a new direction in understanding the issue of similarity, and conjoined with another story, helps shed light on this question.

> I thought I'd remember everything that was said and done that day and maybe find a way to tell it sometime. But I didn't. I forgot it all, or nearly. What I do remember is that I heard our name used a lot that afternoon, my dad's name and mine. But I knew they were talk-

ing about my dad. *Raymond*, these people kept saying in their beautiful voices out of my childhood, *Raymond*. (21, Carver's emphasis)

The voices calling the father's name are among the sparse memories Carver has of the funeral. Other than the voices, there are only a few episodes and a marginal detail which has sunk into memory (a bonnet worn by an annoying woman). These are the voices of memory in two senses: They encompass the memory left from the funeral, and they are also the "beautiful voices out of my childhood," that is, voices that evoke voices from the past and merge with them. However, this momentary overcoming of forgetfulness—which hangs over the entire essay (the narrator admits that he has forgotten much and keeps repeating the words "I remember" and "I recall")—and the very possibility of remembering and establishing a continuity with the past, entail an awareness of separateness. Carver's ability to talk about "our name," even as he acknowledges the name of the father as separate from his own ("I knew they were talking about my dad"), paves the way to the connection with the past. Interestingly enough, it is not sight that facilitates this connection. In his photograph, the father keeps moving "further" and "back into time," and finally the photograph is lost. Sight is replaced by voice: the voice of the poet who evokes the photograph and brings back the figure of the father, and the "beautiful voices" from his childhood calling his name. The immediacy of sight is replaced by the sound which, despite—and maybe because of—an element of intermediacy, allows the contact that sight fails to supply.

In a sense, the ending of the essay is dominated by connection: the emotion which finds expression in tears; the fact that Carver turns to his wife for consolation; the way he connects with his father's family. The main connection is with memory that evokes the voices of childhood. This connection, however, is accompanied by the sense of separateness, as circumstances compel Carver to acknowledge the difference between him and his father. Thus, the end of the essay moderates the dominance of similarity, which proved to be "lethal." The link with the past, which allows a continuity of personality, comes hand in hand with an acknowledgment of the difference within similarity. Only thus—as the end suggests, both in tone and content—an option of life opens up before Raymond Jr., who at the moment is "between lives."

To counter "My Father's Life," there is "The Father"—one of Carver's more enigmatic stories—possibly influenced by William Carlos Williams.[5] The story opens with a tableau, a frozen image, which depicts the women of a family, a mother, a grandmother, and three little sisters, as they stand around a baby lying in a basket decorated and painted in blue. The father sits in the kitchen, and can hear the chattering of the women, asking questions that the occasion calls for: Whom does the baby love? Whom does the baby look like? As is common in this kind of talk, the speakers suggest a similarity between the baby and different family members. However, and typical of Carver, the banal conversation echoes menace and uncertainty: No one knows who the baby looks like. Finally, one of the girls suggests that he looks like Daddy. Does the baby really look like the father? It is hard to know, since while looking at the father they encounter another problem:

> "But who does Daddy look like?" Phyllis asked.
> "Who does Daddy look like?" Alice repeated, and they all at once looked through to the kitchen where the father was sitting at the table with his back to them.
> "Why, nobody!" Phyllis said and began to cry a little.
> "Hush," the grandmother said and looked away and then back at the baby.
> "Daddy doesn't look like anybody!" Alice said.
> "But he has to look like somebody," Phyllis said, wiping her eyes with one of the ribbons. And all of them except the grandmother looked at the father, sitting at the table.
> He had turned around in his chair and his face was white and without expression. (*WYPB*, 42)

Why does the father look like nobody? Why does he sit alone, detached from the rest of the family? What is the meaning of the father's reaction? While "My Father's Life" is dominated by resemblance and analogy, "The Father" is dominated by difference and dissimilarity. The son does not look like anybody, and if he looks like "Daddy," the father, in turn, does not look like anybody.

Unlike the relationship with the mother, uncertainty underlies the relationship of any son with his father. The similarity to the father is not a condition for continuity, yet it serves as a sign and a proof of it. Why does the grandmother try to point to a resemblance of the child to the grandfather—perhaps the father's father? Why does she hush the speakers when they say that the father resembles no one, and refuse to look at him? We could easily assume a hidden drama in the background of this story, with dark family secrets that this scene reveals. However, rather than a possible sensation, what makes this story so intriguing is the way in which the doubt, inherent in the relationship between fathers and sons, concretizes the issue of continuity. The father's white and expressionless face, where identity seems to be totally obliterated, suggests that here, as in "My Father's Life," death is always present. Yet whereas in "My Father's Life," it was the similarity and sameness which threatens the son ("Raymond's dead"), in "The Father," the threat lies in total dissimilarity, where there is no hint of affinity, and the very continuity between generations is uncertain. The death-like expression on the father's face makes this threat tangible.

Both poles on the similarity-difference axis—the pole of total sameness and that of total difference—lead to petrification and death. One pole is of total stasis, allowing no change, a sequence with no progression (it is only the difference of Raymond from his father which allows him to go on living). At the other pole, similarity has been totally erased and there is a gap in the assumed continuity between generations. This gap is also threatening, since the link to the father, which is expressed in similarity, is the condition for the son's existence. Only at the end of "My Father's Life" is there a degree of equilibrium between sameness and difference, repetition and change, unity and disparity. This balance allows for a link between the generations and some continuity, even as it preserves movement and progression.

Singularity or Doubleness?

We have seen two texts, two radical variations of the relationship between father and son and its underlying tensions. However, Carver's personal interest in the man who was his father and their deep similarity goes well beyond the father-son theme. The two father stories are merely a point of departure, through which I wish to outline a tension that manifests itself in other stories, on different levels, and in different kinds of continuities. In fact, the continuity between the generations is but one aspect—albeit essential and important—of the issue of continuity as such. It illustrates the oscillation that any sort of continuity entails between the petrifying homogeneity of sameness and isolating difference, both threatening movement and progression.

The issue of continuity has been present in this study from its very beginning, in different guises and senses. In the first chapter, focusing on the "fractioning" of movement, I have tried to show how Carver challenges the possibility of representing movement by presenting a sequence of actions as a series of static segments. Applying the concept of movement to the level of meaning, Carver's dialogues were characterized as "static." The continuity of meaning between speakers was revealed to be uncertain due to both over-similarity (the uniformity of cliché, the hollow echoing of one word) and over-difference (the splitting of the word between different meanings in different contexts). In chapter 3, the voice of Carver's narrator was described as embodying the experience of a character who occupies an "unoccupied perspective," a singular, isolated shell of existence, detached from the continuity of a remembering and signifying consciousness. Carver's "eye of the camera" and his typical way of looking were characterized in chapter 4 as capturing a fragment that sticks out from the space, disrupting its continuity and coherency. In chapter 5, we became acquainted with the counterpart of this detached detail—Carver's "man in the case," with his tenuous links to action, plot, and function.

Somewhat artificially, this review stresses the pole of singularity and disparity, which the dissimilarity of the father and son in "The Father" symbolizes. However, the collapse into sameness, as embodied in the incident of the son who almost "died" with his father, is no less central to Carver. Its most obvious manifestation is the dominance of cliché in different aspects of the characters' lives, as well as their representation: The platitudes, the flat descriptions, the soap-opera scenes—all impose unity and conformity on experience and personality, allowing for no dynamism and progress. The work of the cliché in hollowing any inner, particular essence echoes the concept of character described in chapter 3. The impersonal voice of the narrator, like his characters, suggested a deictic sense of self, a slot of time and space devoid of individual consciousness. However, as much as this slot is singular and isolated, in the sense that it allows for no continuous subject, it is also interchangeable with other subjects. This pull toward sameness suggests the existence of a double.

According to William Kittredge, in his library Carver kept a textbook from his college days, all marked up and scribbled, with all sorts of doppelgänger stories—a fact that suggests his interest in the concept of the double.[6] Critics keep referring to doubles and doubleness in his works. For Randolph Runyon, who focuses on the connection between stories, the doubles theme has a tight connection to the issue of continuity. According to Runyon, each of the collections has a "fold" in its middle, which divides the book into two halves. We often find the counterpart of a motive, character, or any other element in the other side of the book (which would have been merged with it had we folded the book). Like others, Runyon points to the existence of inexplicable details in the stories, yet in his readings he shows how these acquire meaning when transplanted into a new context. The repetition of details opens up the seemingly hermetic stories to each other. A link is created both between stories in succession and between corresponding stories on the "other side" of the book, and they become "interchangeable." This symmetry, which Runyon points to, can also be found in the content of the stories. Thus, in his interpretation of "Mr. Coffee and Mr. Fixit," Runyon sees the lover of the narrator's wife as the husband's "double."[7]

"Mr. Coffee," which has already been discussed in the previous chapter, calls for a discussion in this context as well. The husband and the lover are doubles not only because of their striking similarity (both are alcoholics, losers, and lack any dexterity), but also because of their parallel places in the relationship—on the wife's two "sides." The characters thus become, like the stories, interchangeable—"symmetric partners" or "rivals," to use a term by Barthes, to whom rivalry is a "question of place."[8] Furthermore, the story as a whole, and on all levels, is a radical example of a "hollow" doubleness. Both versions contain clichés and banal scenes, which replicate patterns from popular or popularized culture. The characters and events are interconnected by flat analogies (all the characters drink and are considered "losers," both the mother and the wife are "putting out"). The father's appearance in the story—another drunk and loser—is also telling. The narrator, whose life story seems to be derived from the author's biography, as told in "My Father's Life," recalls how his father went back to bed one morning, after drinking a quart of Four Roses, and was found dead by his mother. As if Carver were trying to dramatize this episode from his life ("Raymond's dead"), the son also enters his mother's bed (in the story's longer version), and withdraws from life while duplicating his father's death scene.

"Mr. Coffee" is thus situated at the pole of over-similarity, as symbolized in "My Father's Life." Critics point to various manifestations of doubleness, repetition, and symmetry. This inclination seems to contradict Carver's presentation of mere facts devoid of "the double, the mirror-image, the value-added of significance."[9] Indeed, there often seems to be no obvious connection, by analogy and repetition, among characters, events, and other elements of the story, or an overtly symbolic resonance (all of which encourage signification). This current of singularity is therefore considered the stories' "surface," for example, the first impression readers get before symbolism strikes them.

The dual impression of the lifelike presentation of singular facts versus a sense of symbolism and meaningfulness is resolved by critics in different ways. According to Marc Chénetier, Carver resists metaphor because it formulates, in a positive way, the unformulated.[10] However, overall situations are often constructed metaphorically, and "one gets a clear sense of allegorical treatment." Claire Fabre-Clark suggests that despite the text's literalness, a metaphoric net is woven through the use of clichés.[11] For Daniel Lehman, the sense of meaningless reality, on account of which Carver is given the label "postmodernist," comes from the characters who lack insight, while what he calls the text's "rhetoric" allows for a symbolic reading, and is meaning-friendly.[12] It is therefore more effective when the characters suggest no psychological depth, as in Carver's early prose, whereas in his later stories, with their fuller characters, the symbolism becomes superfluous, artificial, and loses much of its power. A similar approach, with a stake in the existence of a signifying process despite its being way over the head of the bewildered characters, is that of Arthur F. Bethea.[13] He thus makes a well-founded case against the postmodernist view of Carver. Arias-Misson finds a middle ground between doubleness and singularity, by his view of Carver's metaphor as avoiding psychological or dramatic elucidation; yet providing "a passage though an apocalyptic moment, an unsuspected transcendence of the text."[14] Likewise, Kirk Nesset contends that although Carver uses metaphor, he does not exhaust it, because it suggests stability, unity of vision, and awareness, which his world denies.[15]

For Moshe Ron, the sense of arbitrariness, the piling up of heterogeneous, singular details, belong to Carver's so-called "minimalism," which coexists with a symbolic-modernist inclination, creating a hybridism of "symbolic minimalism."[16] In many of the stories Ron discerns a state of reflection: From an initial position of suspicion and alienation, one character meets another who turns out to be a kind of mirror image, either desired ("Fat") or denied ("Viewfinder," "Why Don't You Dance?"). Carver's first three collections outline a progression from stories where the core of the story is the encounter itself, to stories where the gaze at another character, not always accompanied by an overt, verbalized insight, has evolved into a gesture of identification and even contact. On another level, the body, being a concrete, accurately described object pertaining to the story's reality, and therefore a metonymy, is also, according to Ron, a metaphor of subjectivity. Objects too, he insists, have a symbolic resonance. In the later stories, Carver turns to Christian symbolism (like the cathedral or the bread in "A Small, Good Thing"). However, his force lies in "homemade" symbols, such as the ashtray in "A Serious Talk"—an everyday object which succeeds in capturing the essence of the relationship of a couple who have crossed the border beyond which love fever becomes a consuming fire. Ron stresses, however, that despite the dominancy of doubleness in Carver's work—the figure of the double, the metaphor, and the symbol—this aspect never undoes the metonymic design of his stories.

According to Roman Jakobson, metonymy is what distinguishes realistic prose from poetry, because it is based on reality-like contiguity rather than the principle of similarity; yet he suggests that even in prose, metaphor is derived from metonymic connections.[17] Applying this insight to our point of departure, it seems that the search for similarity and analogy between the generations (if we ignore its underlying genetic assumptions) is a symbolic confirmation of the presence of metaphor in any metonymic sequence—in life as in literature.

Indeed, there is no need to decide which of the two poles dominates Carver's world: metonymy or metaphor, the casual object or the symbol, the dissociated "man in a case" or the double with its analogical links, minimalism or symbolism. It seems that these oppositions coexist. Nevertheless, it is appropriate to continue exploring the meaning of Carver's attraction to the poles of difference and sameness, singularity and doubleness, and mainly the poles of contingency and meaning that the above critical responses expressed in different ways. To address this, let us return to the counterpart of the useless "man in a case," that is—the useless detail, which already made its appearance, in different guises, in this study—in the redundancy of dialogue, via the glimpse or the sidelong look, and as the "useless" object.

"The Reality Effect" and the *Punctum*

I find that one of the images that typifies Carver, and his American essence, is the yard sale, which opens "Why Don't You Dance?" and also appears in one of his poems. Naturally, it is connected to the capitalist way of life, with its unrestrained acquisition and waste, and endless production of objects which sooner or later will become useless, turning into junk. Thus, "Are These Actual Miles?" describes the price which the culture of acquisition charges for the luxuries it offers. In this story, a couple's buying fever drives them to bankruptcy, and they are forced to sell their car, which costs them their marriage. Along with "Neighbors," this story has the longest lists of furniture and accessories in Carver's work. Indeed, like his dialogues, which give the impression of at once having "too much" and "too little," his descriptions of material reality strike the reader as both lacking (in context, motivation, and background) and abundant in what seem to be unnecessary details.

These details—even when representing the abundance of capitalist society—have no function in the fictional world as in other levels of the stories. First, as already shown, the stock-taking rendition of numerous objects does not promote the visualization of a fictional space and sometimes even inhibits it. Second, their function in the text, if we perceive it as a structured, meaning-oriented system, remains unclear, as reflected in readers' responses. The sense of symbolism is accompanied by a bewilderment or doubt of the role of some objects in the stories. Thus, Chénetier denies the symbolism of these accessories and sees them as "unexplained and disquieting symptoms," while Karlsson sees them as "physically present tokens of silence and secretiveness," of "absence," which surrounds the characters who cannot express their feelings.[18] According to Carver, these objects do have a role, though not necessarily as symbols. He contends that they should not be inert, and should be presented with some weight which will connect them to the lives around them:

> I see these objects as playing a role in the stories; they're not "characters" in the sense that the people are, but *they are there* and I want my readers to be aware that *they're there*, to know that this ashtray *is here*, that the TV *is there*. (My emphases)[19]

Carver's feeling that the reader should be aware that things are "there" or "here" is, in my view, his own perception, as a creative artist, of the concept coined by Roland Barthes as the "reality effect," in his famous article ("L'effet de reel," 1968). This fascinating, brief essay puts in a nutshell an entire literary perspective. In reading it, I will attempt to track the development of the notion of the "reality effect" in Barthes's writing, and point to its parallels in the writing of other thinkers. This is necessary to deepen and underpin our understanding of the descriptive detail in Carver's oeuvre. It calls for a fairly long theoretical digression which will unravel a thread of thought by which different, contradictory senses of this detail have been developed. The descriptive detail will thus be presented as encapsulating Carver's complex approach to the issue of meaning, as previously outlined, allegorically, by the father-son relationship.

"The Reality Effect" opens with an object which, thanks to Barthes, was saved from oblivion as well as superfluous redundancy.[20] This is the barometer in the description of Madame Aubain in Flaubert's "A Simple Soul." As with other details mentioned by Barthes, this detail is redundant in the sense that it does not serve any role in the structure of the text. It does not even fulfill indirect functions, such as filling out characterization or promoting an atmosphere, usually achieved by the cumulative effect of such secondary elements (*catalysts*). By the standards of structuralist analysis, this is a "sensational" detail, for it challenges the structure's aspiration to hold together and be applied to *all* the ingredients of a story. The useless detail is a small-scale manifestation of the disturbing nature of description as such. Unlike narrative, which is built upon junctures of alternatives, determined by the overall purpose and future of the system, the structure of description is additive. It lacks the narrative's striving for unity by binding together different elements. A pure description has no purpose, in terms of action or communication, and it even hinders the significance, the coherency, and the intelligibility of the text, as it does not serve to render a closed system which operates organically.[21] In other words, the descriptive detail undermines the story's purpose and directionality and sabotages its thematic unity.

In a brief review of the history of description, Barthes distinguishes the details in traditional descriptions, which in the spirit of classical rhetoric were aesthetic and decorative, from details in modern literature, which, inspired by historical, "objective" writing, are designed to promote realism. In the new type of fiction, the detail divested itself of its aesthetic function, and its nonfunctional function became a token of its "having been there" (*avoir été là*) and to create a "reality effect." Paradoxically, although it has slipped in from the "reality" that the text represents, it ends up undermining the text's pretension to represent reality. This detail, says Barthes, dissolves the sign, for it skips directly from signifier to referent. The signified—the mental concept of the referent and its purpose in the text—is cast away, and so is the form of the signified, which is the narrative structure itself. This transformation in the nature of the descriptive detail prompted a new kind of verisimilitude, which challenges representation no less than modern pieces that push away the referent-object-real and remain in the realm of signifiers.

It is not easy to follow the argumentation of Barthes's essay. Especially elusive is the historical description in which he points to the changes that description has undergone since the days of classical rhetoric through to its challenge to the conventions of representation. However, the main obstacle to accepting Barthes's argument is that he does not give an explanation of his choice of the barometer as *the* unnecessary detail in Flaubert's description of the house. This choice seems to be subjective, and Barthes offers no clear criterion for his choice of the details which have no function in the text's design. Is it really impossible to find a symbolic (or any other) function to Flaubert's barometer? Where is the line beyond which a detail stops being functional in the text's closed system and becomes a vestige of "reality"? Does Barthes really have such a narrow concept of function, or perhaps the very concept of a "reality effect" questions this function-oriented, closed concept of a text? Here, too, the difficulties make this essay so intriguing and point to the future direction of Barthes's thinking. In the essay, Barthes refers to the way a description or a descriptive detail can be permeated with the "radiance of desire" (an aspect described as the rhetorical figure of *hypotyposis*). Surprisingly, Barthes will find this subjective, unrealistic quality in a medium tightly connected to the rise of realism, which he discusses in his final book. In *Camera Lucida* (*La chambre claire*), the detail becomes the core of subjectivity, not necessarily that of the creator, but rather that of the reader, the viewer, the subject of the piece, or even the subjectivity of the work of art itself.

Barthes's last book, in which he discussed the medium of photography, was published in 1980. There the detail appears in the guise and the name of the *punctum*, and through this detail Barthes reveals his attraction to everything that cannot be integrated into signifying systems, that which escapes the set meanings of the culture and its myths. This attraction, which Barthes betrayed even in his earliest structuralist days, is what draws him to the body, the sensual pleasure of reading, or to types of writing and culture focused on the surface of things on the one hand, or, on the other hand, on mere signs (e.g., the *noveau roman*, Japanese culture, and haiku).[22] Around the time that "The Reality Effect" was written, Barthes's article "The Third Meaning," defines a level of meaning, which he calls the "obtuse meaning" (*obtus*) versus the "overt meaning" (*obvie*). This is a kind of meaning that escapes the different systems that inform any work of art (the author's psychology, his corpus, his culture, his individual style, medium, etc.), and produce various kinds of symbolism. Unlike other meanings, the obtuse meaning reflects the work's artificiality without loosening the connection to the referent, and has an added emotional value. Later in his writing, Barthes would link this level of meaning to Kristeva's concept of the "semiotic"—the realm of preverbal perceptions and senses—and the carnivalesque: the "sensational" and subversive aspect of literature.[23]

Ten years later, when Barthes discusses photography, he identifies two elements which are possible reactions to a photograph. The *studium* is the obvious reaction, dictated by the knowledge and codes of culture that one internalizes. This reaction can stem from a photograph which lends itself easily to a unifying reading. The second element in viewing a photograph is Barthes's *punctum*, which "crosses" the field, the *studium*, and undermines its unity. It disturbs and dishevels it, and is parallel, to a degree, to the "obtuse meaning."[24] This is a personal reaction, he argues, which only few photographs give rise to, and it happens when a detail shoots out from a photograph and "pierces," "punctures," or "wounds" the viewer in a way that exceeds any cultural reaction. With the metaphors of puncturing or wounding, the concept of *punctum* still remains somehow enigmatic. In fact, Barthes avoids conceptualizing it entirely. However, one can still infer that it is singular, limited to a point, and escapes any signifying system. These features also characterized the reality effect, yet in the *punctum* Barthes stresses an emotional reaction to a detail and the way it is entirely dependent on the subjectivity of a particular viewer. The *punctum* is inside the photograph, and at the same time it is the viewer who "adds" it. Barthes mentions details which have "punctured" him: a necklace on a black woman's neck, the Danton collar of a boy from a New Jersey institution, the crossed arms of a boy in a sailor suit. Still, he does not imply that these would puncture or wound any viewer but him (for Barthes, the wound repeatedly signifies subjectivity).[25] Giving an example of a detail or a *punctum* is "to *give myself up*," he admits and opens an opportunity for a range of psychoanalytical interoperations of the "partial objects" that have affected him simply by "being there."[26]

However, the *punctum*, Barthes insists, is not only the detail. It has another meaning which tightens and deepens its connection with the literary "reality effect." The *punctum* is not only a form (detail versus field), but also "intensity." In that sense, says Barthes, it is equal to time, which becomes materialized whenever our indifference to the element of truth in the photograph is replaced by a deep acknowledgment that "this has been" (*ça-a-été*). This sudden acknowledgment touches on the essence of photography. This is a medium which is able, thanks to a chemical reaction, to bring into the present something of the referent itself. It is precisely photography, which brought about the revolution of mechanical reproduction, that made possible the contact with the singular—the particular referent that "has been there"—and not only with the signified, for example, its abstract, a-temporal concept. This realistic argument is part of Barthes's conception of the photograph as a "message without a code," and he adheres to it in defiance of the semiotic approaches that view it as naïve.[27]

According to Barthes, the photograph's power lies in giving proof to time rather than to the existence of the object. The *punctum* presents the viewer with an alogical, nongrammatical combination, a superimposition of present and past—"this," which is a deictic pertaining to the moment of utterance, combined with the "has been" (of the past).[28] Thus the *punctum* embodies the element of presence and "truth" in photography, which the reality effect and literary realism generally strive to simulate. At the same time, the *punctum* goes beyond a particular photograph and its contexts, imbued as it is with absence and with the power of expansion. The presence of something that is dead and gone, the contact with the thing itself, is entirely dependent on the subject's experience, on viewing it from across the divide of another time and "adding" the *punctum*. This breeds a multifaceted tension. The *punctum* arises from the "reality" of the photograph, rather than from an intentional act, and is therefore random, with no dimension of construction and formulation, yet it takes a hold in the viewer's consciousness, which validates it, and where it unfolds. The *punctum* is a point, isolated in the cultural field of the photograph, yet it has a potential of openness and expansion. In terms of Barthes's method and style, the *punctum* echoes the deep tension he expresses in the beginning of *Camera Lucida*. This consists of the aspiration to breach the closed, dogmatic systems of understanding and an inclination toward expressive language, which clashes with his commitment to analytical language.

Indeed, even more than in the subtle construction of critical insights and concepts, the uniqueness of this book lies in its structure and personal nature, which is tightly bound up with Barthes's conception of photography. The search for the essence of photography is concurrent with the search for a photograph of the writer's mother, who recently died. Through the photograph, he hopes to grasp the "quality" of her personality, which could only be furnished by her living presence. Eventually, Barthes will find such a photograph—"the winter garden"—around which his insights into photography in general will evolve. This photograph does not resemble his mother, but "is" his mother—a particular mother and not *the* mother as such. Love allows this encounter with that which lies beyond images, as well as death.[29] The shiver Barthes experiences when he looks at the picture of this child, his mother, who will eventually grow up and die, is part of the madness that underlies photography. Only through this medium, the presence and existence of something which "has been" becomes an unshakable fact. This happens through the viewer's affect, which guarantees, according to Barthes, the truth of the photograph. It introduces the viewer to an other who died, but is still present, a kind of living dead, who lived in the past, but is present in the viewer's present and embodies his future death. The result is an almost unbearable, maddening compassion aroused by the encounter with the depth of the other's subjectivity, with this part of him or her which is inaccessible to others—death. This encounter forces the viewer to confront his own contingency and death, death as such, the deaths of those he loves, the many deaths that will be experienced before his or her own death. (The book was published few days after Roland Barthes's own death.)

Barthes's *punctum*—the singular, subjective, inaccessible element—has no place in the systems of signs and meanings, yet it nevertheless permits the contact between subjects. It gradually becomes equal to death. This intertwinement of three elements—the referent, the total other, and death—is the center of Derrida's essay written after Barthes passed away: "The Deaths of Roland Barthes." Derrida reads the earlier Barthes (*Writing Degree Zero*) and his last book (*Camera Lucida*). Over the course of these readings, he processes his own mourning, and addresses the otherness and death of Barthes, both as a person and as a creative writer. He acknowledges that Barthes's death made him more "other" and at the same time more liable to be appropriated by the self of the person who mourns him. He questions the very possibility of an encounter with the other as such, and all the more so—with the dead other. Should we reach out to him through our living and talking self or by annihilating it, through a silence that simulates death? Should the will to express the other's singular presence force us to give up on language and its intersubjective aspirations? Aren't we going to "wound" the other in each of these possible ways?

Derrida approaches these questions (though he hardly answers them) in the spirit of deconstruction, when he demonstrates how Barthes blurs the boundaries between various sets of binarisms, even those he had defined. Thus, Derrida suggests, the *punctum* and the *studium* are not as opposed as they appear, but they relate to each other in a "metonymic composition" or a sort of musical "counterpoint."[30] The *studium*, the cultural field in which the photograph is situated, steals into the *punctum*. The *punctum* is the "other" inside the *studium*—it "punctuates" the field and gives it rhythm. Yet without the *studium*, Barthes would not have been able to articulate this point of singularity. Derrida thus questions the singularity of that which claims to be beyond culture and language, but does not deny it all together. He insists on the element of repetition and plurality (hence the plural in the title: "The *Deaths* of Roland Barthes"), and points to its necessary expansion beyond itself.

If Barthes writes, as he says, only about his own particular mother and her one-time, singular essence rather than about the Mother (who belongs to the cultural *studium*), why are we so moved by the search for her picture? Indeed, Barthes explicitly argues that the *punctum* is metonymic, added by the viewers, expanded by them, and in the process, replaced with something else. Following this, Derrida keeps stressing that the *punctum* "gives itself away" to metonymy, and through it he succeeds in connecting its two senses: the *punctum* as the detail that "wounds" the subject, and the *punctum* as intensity, as the "this has been" of a photograph—the *punctum* as time. The detail that sticks out from the photograph never escapes metonymy, while time *is* metonymy itself:

> For is not Time the ultimate resource for the substitution of one absolute instant for another, for the replacement of the irreplaceable, the replacement of this unique referent by another which is yet another instant, completely other and yet the same? Is not Time the form and punctual force of all metonymy *in its last instance?* (Derrida's emphases)[31]

Here Derrida executes a double move. He binds together the two senses of the *punctum* through metonymy. At the same time, he connects and softens the boundary between the *studium*, as the cultural, general, intersubjective field, and the *punctum* as the singular and subjective. The *punctum* is after all metonymic. By constituting a part of a whole or by replacing one name for another, it never stays within its own boundaries and this grants it the power of expansion, and allows, in Derrida's words, for a "passage." The passage is between times (facing a photograph of a young man condemned to death, Barthes simultaneously experiences his time, the time of the photograph, and the time of the future death of the man in the picture, which has already occurred). This is a passage between self and other—a passage between the time of the person condemned to death in a photo from 1865 to the child-mother in "The Winter Garden" and to the future death of the viewer, Roland Barthes. (Should we add that the future death of Derrida lurks here too?) Thus, it is the singular element in the photograph, the *punctum*, that allows a passage—tentative, elusive, doubtful, yet still a passage. The otherness of the other allows for contact with one's own other—one's own death, and vice versa. The heterogenic element, which disturbs the unity of the photograph, and represents a unique, isolated essence, ends up bridging the gap between various subjects and othernesses and (using Barthes's term) "crosses" them.

There is a striking similarity between Barthes's discussion of the *punctum*—with its various meanings—and the way two thinkers, already discussed here, described a visual encounter with a fragment. These are Lacan (discussed in the "Vision" chapter) and Deleuze (discussed with reference to the "man in a case"). Barthes explicitly refers to Lacan in *Camera Lucida*, and he might have been influenced by him in "The Reality Effect." Deleuze's study of the cinema was written after the death of Barthes and the publication of *Camera Lucida*, and it does not mention Barthes. Yet Robbe-Grillet's theory of description, which deeply influenced Barthes's poetic vision, has an important part in Deleuze's writing too. The connection might be conscious or unconscious. Either way, there are some striking points of contact.

ESCAPING STRUCTURE AND SUBVERTING REPRESENTATION

In Lacan, the encounter with a fragment, which has no place in the structure, takes the form of a brief look at the fragment of the "real," which eludes any symbolic net. It seems unreal because it escapes our concept of reality, which is always mediated by the symbolic, and challenges the kind of representation that claims dominance in the field of vision.[32] For Deleuze, the "optic situation" introduces the viewer to a fragment which does not fit into clichés of representation that tend to erase unnecessary parts in the image by outlining the similar and suppressing the singular. Likewise, Barthes's reality effect has no function in the unifying structure of narrative. The importance of the fragment in subverting representation illustrates Robert Bresson's argument that "fragmentation is indispensable if one does not want to fall into representation."[33]

OBJECTIVITY-SUBJECTIVITY

The fragment is complex: It is the thing itself and yet realized only in an encounter with a subject. For Lacan, the encounter with the real is an encounter with subjective residues and traumas that have undergone no process of symbolization. (The psychoanalytical Freudian readings of *Camera Lucida* are based on this concept.) For Deleuze, being partial and insufficient, the fragment drives the viewer to endless "circuits" of description," where there is no distinction between the object and its subjective perception, nor between reality and imagination. This is another way in which the detail challenges representation and its underlying separation between subject and object.

THE SECOND MEANING OF THE PUNCTUM—TIME

For Lacan, the encounter with the real (for example in Holbein's "The Ambassadors") introduces the viewer to his or her own contingency and death. For Lacan, time is synonymous with the ephemeral, with loss and contingency. For Deleuze, the experience of time is the core of the "optic situation." The glimpse into the fragment is a glimpse into time itself—a whole where there is a coexistence of present and past, presence and memory, the time of the viewer and the time of the viewed. This is, in fact, the only concept of time to allow Barthes's phrase "this has been," which combines presence and past, to exist.

A DUAL APPROACH TO MEANING

For Barthes, a photograph, and the *punctum* as its essence, is flat, "platitudinous in the true sense of the word," yet it is an image which—in Blanchot's words—summons up "the depth of any possible meaning."[34] In Lacan, the "real" is both the core of the meaningless and a condition for symbolization. It "opens up the abyss of the search for a meaning"—to use Žižek's interpretation.[35] In his Lacanian readings of popular culture and cinema, Žižek showed how the contingent, out-of-place, meaningless detail, which sticks out from the frame, renders everything meaningful and starts a "movement of interpretation."

Derrida elaborates on this complexity: He concretizes the double nature of the detail, in terms of meaning and intersubjectivity, by linking it to the self-other relationship. Being metonymic and constituting a "bit" of the thing itself, the detail serves as mediator and allows for a passage to various kinds of otherness: the other's otherness, the self's otherness, death's otherness, the past's otherness, and the otherness of the work of art with reference to its reader or viewer.

Passages

This discussion also calls for a passage, or even better, two passages: first a passage from photography to literature—from the *punctum* back to the reality effect—and then a passage from theory to Carver's stories.

Reaching for the essence of his mother, Barthes also reaches for the essence of photography. In fact, the search for a unique essence and presence, free of the mediation of signs and of culture, drives the book as a whole. According to semiotic approaches, which Barthes helped develop, photography is coded as any product of culture. Thus, Umberto Eco finds no less than ten codes which mediate between the photograph and the viewer.[36] Nevertheless, Barthes insists that a photograph does preserve a remnant of the referent, a contingent element which does not fit into any set of codes.

However, if this is photography's defining element, how can it be applied to literature? Unlike photography, Barthes reminds us, writing and language are always fictional, and entail a process of codification. The reality effect is therefore always an "effect"—a false impression of reality in a text where the opposition between reality and meaning is but an illusion. The text might try to emulate the randomness of reality, yet it is always subjected to literature's processes of construction and signification.

Still, Barthes also reminds us that the rise of realism, and the descriptive reality and its reality effect, were part of a universal effort to validate the real, pertaining to the rise of "objective" history and the invention of photography. As part of this global process, the role of the reality effect should then be defined more modestly. It is not what makes the referent present, but part of the longing for what Derrida calls "the great enigma of the Referent."[37] Both Roland Barthes and Walter Benjamin address this longing when they describe the state of photography in the age of mechanical reproduction. This is an age when there is a challenge to the status of the referent, caused both by technology and by the awareness of the cultural construction of any approach to "reality." However, the passion to reach the referent keeps growing. Derrida modifies Barthes's approach by insisting that the referent is never there, even in a photograph. It is suspended, partly on account of the metonymic nature of the *punctum*, which calls for its replacement by another meaning. Like any process of representation, it is given to repetition and reproduction. Nevertheless, the referent is present in the intentional gesture toward it—the "reference." This is the reason for the importance of the affect—the emotional response to a photograph—in the definition of photography. This is why the remnant of the referent, which "remains" in a photograph, the "bit" (as Derrida calls it) that "comes from the other," is also and mainly "a bit of me."[38] By substituting the referent with the reference and stressing intentionality, Derrida is now able to apply the photographic *punctum* to all systems of signs:

> By taking a thousand differential precautions, one must be able to speak of a *punctum* in all signs (and the repetition and iterability structures it already), in any discourse, whether it be literary or not. Provided that we do not hold to some naïve and 'realist' referentialism, the relation to some unique and irreplaceable referent *interests* us and animates our most sound and studied readings: what happened one time only, while dividing itself already, in order to take aim, in front of the lens of the *Phaedo* or *Finnegans Wake*, the *Discourse of Method* or Hegel's *Logic*, John's *Apocalypse* or *Coup de dés*. The photographic apparatus reminds us of this irreducible referential by means of a very powerful telescoping.[39] (Derrida's emphases)

When Derrida refers to photography as a reminder of the "irreducible referential," which allows one to speak of the *punctum* in all signs, he provides us with the necessary passageway between photography and literature. It is therefore timely to move from literature in general to the particularity of Carver stories. In the previous chapters we have seen various ways in which the detail-*punctum* in Carver's literary texts sometime refuses to become integrated in different systems of the text, and thus makes its impact on the reader. However, Carver has provided us with a better way to examine his approach to the unnecessary detail by himself choosing to tell its story in one of his latter pieces. It is no accident that this story combines two elements that photography reminds us come hand in hand—the referent and death.

"Errand"

The death is Anton Chekhov's, in "Errand"—the last story in the collection Carver published before his death. Other stories and poems by Carver have been published posthumously, and it seems that Carver was not fully aware of his own illness when he wrote "Errand." Nevertheless, it is hard not to see this story as his last, and difficult not to assume that the author had some kind of premonition about his own death. It is certainly tempting to think of the connections between these two writers and their deaths.

The first part of the story strikes one as an exercise in intertextuality—one of several Carver made toward the end of his life.[40] It is based on, and sometimes even quotes, the biography of Chekhov by Henry Troyat. The very choice of passages from this book is telling, since it reveals the way in which Carver felt connected to Chekhov. Thus, for instance, he refers to the Russian author's credo: the commitment to having no credo or solid worldview, and limiting oneself to describing how characters "love, marry, give birth, die, and how they speak" (*WICF*, 514). The story opens dramatically and abruptly with a one-word fragment:

> Chekhov. On the evening of March 22, 1897, he went to dinner in Moscow with his friend and confidant Alexei Suvorin. (*WICF*, 512)

The name "Chekhov" constitutes a separate unit, and only the next sentence develops it. This beginning indicates the nature of this story, which is in fact an improvisation on a familiar theme. The familiarity of this subject matter is also evident in the description of Chekhov on the night he met Suvorin:

> Chekhov was impeccably dressed, as always—a dark suit and waistcoat, his usual pince-nez. He looked that night very much as he looks in the photographs taken of him during this period. (ibid.)

The implied reader of the story is expected to be familiar with Chekhov and his public character, with the figure that the photographs show, perhaps even the one on the cover of the biography by Troyat. This familiar image dominates the first part of the story, and influences its tone, which differs from Carver's typical style. As always, it is simple and direct, slightly ironic and distinctly self-conscious about the pretense of dealing with "true" events (thus when the narrator comments that "everyone kept a journal or a diary in those days" [514] or that Chekhov's doctor "left the room and, for that matter, history" [521]). Nonetheless, it lacks the usual poignancy of his writing in rendering scenes bursting with emotions with a unique combination of terseness and intensity. Carver admitted that he used the biography to overcome the enormous difficulty he felt when approaching the material of this story, and the traces of this effort are evident in this part of the text.[41] The historical and biographical data accumulate, yet the events seem distant, and so is Chekhov's character. It remains a public figure, the man from the photographs, the character from Henry Troyat's biography, who supplied Carver with scenes and facts from the life and death of the author he admired.

Things change from the moment of Chekhov's death. Carver picks out an anecdote from Troyat, an action which is said to be "so entirely appropriate it seems inevitable" (519). Prior to Chekhov's death, his physician, Doctor Schowöhrer, ordered champagne to be delivered to his patient's hotel room in Germany. Chekhov, his wife, Olga, and the doctor drank the champagne, and right after, Chekhov stopped breathing. In the original biography Troyat adorned the death scene, and Olga's sitting by her dead husband, with some descriptive details:

> A large, black-winged moth had flown in through the window and was banging wildly against the lamp. The muffled sound soon grew maddeningly distracting. Dr. Schwöhrer withdrew after a few words of consolation. All at once there was a joyous explosion: the cork had popped out of the champagne bottle and foam was fizzing out after it. The moth found its way out of the window and disappeared into the sultry night. Silence returned. When day broke at last, Olga was still sitting and staring into her husband's face. It was peaceful, smiling, knowing. "There were no human voices, no everyday sounds," she wrote. "There was beauty, peace and the grandeur of death."[42]

At first glance, it seems that the biographer used a butterfly and the cork of champagne in order to spice up the facts, or perhaps mitigate the pathos in the "beauty, peace and the grandeur of death." However, according to Olga in her memoir, the cork from the champagne bottle is not Troyat's invention, but rather "had been there" at the moment of Chekhov's death.[43] In any event, this detail, as well as the episode of the champagne as a whole, seems to have captured Carver's imagination, and he uses it as an opening to the world of Chekhov, whose life story he read enthusiastically, trying to imagine everything that was left untold. If we prefer to see this detail as a "reality effect" (that it was included not because it was really "there," but because the *impression* of having being there that it creates), Carver's use of it is particularly sophisticated: This detail becomes the very locus in the story where the real sets off the fiction and the random draws to it the meaning of the text.

After improvising on Chekhov's "true" biography, the story enters the gap between the facts—between the time Olga sat silently near the dead man and the transportation of the body to Moscow in the morning. Carver adds a fictional episode told from the point of view of a young servant who enters the room to take away the bottle and glasses and to announce that breakfast will be served in the garden. The servant stands with a vase of flowers in his hand. Olga, "the woman," absorbed in her pain, stares distracted at the floor. The servant notices the cork of champagne on the floor, but the vase is in his hands and the fear of intruding makes him hesitate to pick it up. He waits, glimpses the dead body in the next room, when Olga suddenly turns to him. She asks him to go to the mortician, but the request has a strange character. Instead of simply giving orders, the woman begins a story, which she delivers in an improbable manner. Are these the words that a strange woman would use when speaking to a servant? Metaphor and literal meaning intermingle. Olga asks the servant to conduct his errand in dignity, as if he were holding a vase of roses to be delivered to a very important man (and the servant does hold such a vase), and then warns him not to drop the vase (which was only an image she used). Gradually, the hypothetical becomes concrete—first by the use of conditional ("This mortician would be in his forties. . . . Probably he would be wearing an apron. The mortician would hear him out" [525]), and then in the use of the present tense ("The mortician takes the vase of roses . . . the mortician's eyebrows rise just a little" [526]). For a moment, the present tense makes the reader believe that the scenario has been actualized. However, in the next passage we are still with Olga in the hotel room, and the servant has not yet set out on his errand.

In fact, Olga's orders repeat and enact Carver's own use of the facts from the biography: She puts into words a possible reality which could well have taken place, or is about to happen.[44] This potential reality glides into the reality of the text, rendering imagination into (textual) reality. And the permutations of imagination, reality, and fiction play through to the end of the story. The champagne cork, taken from the reality of the biography, is now at the foreground of Carver's fictional supplement. The woman finished her instructions. "Do you understand what I'm saying?" she asks. "Will you go?"

> But at that moment the young man was thinking of the cork still resting near the toe of his shoe. To retrieve it he would have to bend over, still gripping the vase. He would do this. He leaned over. Without looking down, he reached out and closed it into his hand. (526)

Carver's sympathies naturally gravitate to this simple, anonymous young man ("his name hasn't survived," he notes, "and it's likely he perished in the Great

War" [523]). Instead of making history, this man is busy doing his modest duty and putting things in order. In that sense, he belongs to the sphere in which other of Carver's (and Chekhov's) characters move. These characters take—in Chekhov's words—their author "from the sofa to the junk room and back" (514). Their actions are the everyday "errands" rather that the major events that history books record. It is no accident that the previous story in Carver's final collection, "Blackbird Pie," ends with a farewell to history in favor of autobiography, which is defined as "a poor man's history" (*WICF*, 511). This, and other alternate ways of writing, redeem the simple man from oblivion, and allow those who come after to rebuild his life from the clues and silences he left behind.

Nevertheless, it is Chekhov who was Carver's hero. The photograph that he mentions at the beginning of the story hung over his desk. Why does he then choose to remove the author from the main part of this story, where his voice and his peculiar way of looking reemerge? Why has Chekhov been replaced by an anonymous servant? Is it just for the sake of irony? And, for that matter, was Chekhov really present in the first part of the story? Rather, it seems that the detached tone, which lacks Carver's typical immediacy, and the voice that he borrowed from the biographer to render facts from the past, provide some indication of Carver's distance from his favorite writer. This distance is both a product of time (compare Carver's feelings toward his father's picture) and of the fact that the figure in the photograph only "looks like" Chekhov's public image, a character in the official biography (the kind of likeness that did not satisfy Barthes when he looked for a photograph of his mother). However moving the anecdotes chosen from the biography might be, Chekhov still remains trapped in his image, and his presence is still inaccessible. He remains a dead man, belonging to the past.

This is not the case with the champagne cork and the servant who holds it in his fist. By putting these marginal details on center stage, they now have a function; they become a factor in the plot or symbols of the text; they acquire meaning and partake of its overall thematics. In fact, this happens every time a detail moves into the focus of the reader's mind. Therein lies the complexity of the term "reality effect," which this story reveals. Yet, whatever the function one ascribes to the detail, it still embodies the aspiration to make the past present, not through memory, but as presence.[45] As Barthes suggests, the signified of the unnecessary detail is not its particular content, but its aspect of "being there"—the very existence of this detail in a certain moment. Rather than being analogous to reality, based on similarity, it aspires to bring in a "bit" of it.

The reality effect embodies the text's desire for a referent; and the detail which creates it is the locus of the reader's desire for presence, as well as his or her own individual presence. Thus, when Carver borrows from Troyat the detail of the champagne cork and invests it with its own subjectivity and imaginative power, he enlarges it and makes it a metonymy of this distant situation. This metonymy—as suggested by Derrida—allows for the tentative contact with another time, which becomes simultaneous with one's own time. Through this metonymy, the detail succeeds, despite its singularity (and through it), in creating an intersubjective link, cutting across different times and subjects. It is only through this detail that Carver (a reader of Troyat and the author of "Errand") is able to connect with his admired author—across time, across the barrier of Chekhov's otherness and death. For the reader (of "Errand" and other stories) this isolated, meaning-resistant detail becomes a point of contact which combines the time of the reader, the time of the story (of Chekhov's death), and the time of writing (right before Carver's own death).

"Errand" is atypical of Carver—in terms of tone, technique, and themes. His use of the unnecessary detail is also unique, for it moves from the margins to the center of the story and thus ceases to be superfluous. However, by being an exception, this detail and this story shed light on Carver's work as a whole. The story reenacts the work of the detail and the way it becomes a meeting point. The reader's subjectivity—which his or her response to one particular detail reveals—opens up to the subjectivity of the work of art, as the unnecessary details indicate that this work exists (or strives to exist) outside the systems of representation and signification.

Conclusion

I began this chapter with Carver's connection to his father, and concluded with the connection to an admired figure. Both echo the connection of the reader to the text—and the continuity of meaning between them. I began with an autobiographical essay and meandered toward a fictional story about a historical figure and true events. The emotional response to a confessional-personal essay has led to the reader's response of "being there" in a fictional, pseudo-biographical text. What is it that links together the elements of the father-son connection, the reality-fiction of the text, the contact between reader and text and the meaning this connection produces?

Let us return to the father's photograph in "My Father's Life." The son looks at it, but the father only moves further "back into time." After a while, in the effort to connect to the dead father, he writes a poem, in which he evokes looking at the photograph. Indeed, the picture itself was lost, and all that is left is its memory (in a sense, as suggested by Barthes, one always looks at a photograph *in absentia*, with one's eyes closed). The poem begins with an indication of the time of the father's death—October—and this is only one of the times that the photograph and the poem encapsulate: the time of the photograph, when the father was twenty-two, the time of his future death, the time of looking, and the time of writing. After quoting the poem, the writer notes:

> The poem is true in its particulars, except that my dad died in June and not in October . . . I wanted a word with more than one syllable to it to make it linger a little. But more than that, I wanted a month appropriate to what I felt at the time I wrote the poem, a month of short days and failing light, smoke in the air, things perishing. June was summer nights and days, graduations, my wedding anniversary, the birthday of one of my children. June wasn't a month your father died in. (*Fires*, 21)

"The date" (says Derrida) "accentuates the contingency or insignificance of the interruption. Like an accident and like death, it seems to be imposed from the outside."[46] When Carver changes the date of his father's dying, and confuses the time of death with the time of writing, he lets *his* sense of reality change the insignificant facts. He deliberately slips into the pathetic fallacy, drawing an analogy between the inside and the outside. For the sake of meaning, he encroaches on the fictional.

This is a clear example of Barthes's "mythical" opposition between the true to life and the intelligible, where the "real" is assumed to be contingent and meaning-resistant.[47] The gesture of changing the date, the true-to-life detail, reveals Carver's need to find meaning in real facts. Indeed, the search for meaning is the principle that informs this essay and allows the reader to approach it almost as a fictional, constructed text. This principle draws from the son's need to understand his father, himself, and their connection. It is manifested in the steps one takes in any effort to signify: tracing repetitions and analogies, looking for similarity, and establishing a personal link. And it requires a balance between two poles: that of over-similarity (as manifested in "My Father's Life") and that of total difference (as in "The Father").

Thus, the connection to the father concretizes an experience that Carver's oeuvre embodies on all its levels: a longing for continuity and connection, where one is torn between too much meaning (over-similarity, clichés, doubles, a world which keep reflecting the self, yet has no room for an individual self) and the lack of meaning—a pile of heterogenic, contingent, external facts, with no interconnections, nor link to the self's experience. Facing that, a Carver reader, in the search for various kinds of links—in the text and outside it, drawn from the culture or from personal experience—is also doomed to be torn between the poles of the significant and the random. Yet this opposition is not clear-cut, and these poles do not exclude each other. While in Carver's poem about his father the random was removed in favor of the meaningful, in his fiction they live side by side in tense coexistence.

And that which embodies this coexistence of the random and the meaningful, and the oscillation between them, is the detail that produces the reality effect. It is an external, "objective" detail which happens to be "there," in the space of fiction, becoming present again in the ever-changing "now" of the text. This isolated element, with its resistance to meaning, draws the reader's subjectivity into the text, and in a random world it constitutes an opening to "the depth of any possible meaning."

Notes

1. Halpert, 152.
2. Jacques Derrida, "The Deaths of Roland Barthes," in *Philosophy and Non Philosophy Since Merleau-Ponty*, ed. Hugh S. Silverman (New York: Routledge, 1988), 259.
3. As Runyon shows in his interpretation of stories such as "The Compartment" and "A Small, Good Thing" (Runyon, 144–51).
4. See Gentry and Stull, 165, on the difficulty of Carver's male figures in meeting their responsibilities. On sons and fathers in Carver, see Lainsbury, 100–41.
5. Gentry and Stull, 222.
6. Halpert, 147–48.
7. Runyon, 1–10, 90–99.
8. Barthes, *A Lover's Discourse*, 65.
9. Brooke-Rose, 5, following Clément Rosset.
10. Chénetier, "Living On/Off," 181–86.
11. Fabre-Clark, 177–79.
12. Daniel Lehman, "Raymond Carver's Management of Symbol," *Journal of the Short Story in English* 17 (1991): 43–57. See also his more recent article "Symbolic Significance in the Stories of Raymond Carver," *Journal of the Short Story in English* 46 (2006): 75–88.
13. Bethea, *Technique*, 41–50. Decker also connects Carver with modernism's artistic vision in Decker, 46–47.
14. Arias-Misson, 628.
15. Nesset, 47.
16. Ron's approach, as summarized here, is based on his epilogue to Raymond Carver, *Last Stories* (in Hebrew). It is also based on several lectures he gave at the Hebrew University and on Israeli radio and television from 1993 to 2002.
17. Jakobson, "Two Aspects of Language and Two Types of Aphasic Disturbance," *Language in Literature*, 114. See also "Linguistic and Poetics," *Language in Literature*, 81 ff.
18. Chénetier, "Living On/Off, 174; Karlsson, 147.
19. Gentry and Stull, 107.
20. "The Reality Effect," *French Literary Theory Today: A Reader*, ed. Tzvetan Todorov (Cambridge: Cambridge University Press, 1982), 11–17.

21. On the blockage of meaning by description, see also Genette, "Flaubert," 182–210. Cf. Genette's discussion of description and the reality effect in "Frontiers of Narrative," *Figures of Literary Discourse*, trans. Alan Sheridan (New York: Columbia University Press, 1982), 133–37, and in *Narrative Discourse Revisited*, 47–49, where he sees the reality effect as one of the text's functions.

22. See Jonathan Culler, *Roland Barthes* (New York: Oxford University Press, 1983), 95–97, 120. For Culler, Barthes's attraction to that which eludes codes and cultural myths, such as the body, the referent, or "meaningless" literature, constitutes another myth, and thus becomes "nature." This is why Culler is critical of Barthes's uncommitted and "lazy" later writing, including *Camera Lucida*. See also Alpers, 235, no. 11.

23. "The Third Meaning," in *Image, Music, Text*, 52–68. For the connection between the third meaning and the *punctum* see Margaret Iversen, "What is a Photograph?" *Art History* 17:3 (1994): 450–64, and Victor Burgin, "Re-Reading *Camera Lucida*," in *The End of Art Theory: Criticism and Postmodernity* (London: Macmillan, 1986), 71–92.

24. Margaret Iversen, who offers a psychoanalytical reading of *Camera Lucida*, points to the similarity between the *punctum* and the obtuse meaning. However, the obtuseness suggests that unlike the *punctum*'s poignancy, the third meaning blunts the acknowledgment of loss and avoids reenacting the trauma.

25. See, for example, Barthes, *A Lover's Discourse*: "Where there is a wound, there is a subject" (189).

26. Roland Barthes, *Camera Lucida: Reflections on Photography*, trans. Richard Howard (New York: Hill and Wang, 1981), 43 (Barthes's emphasis). For a psychoanalytical reading of *Camera Lucida*, see Burgin and Iversen. Both insist on an intersubjective aspect to Barthes's assumed subjective reaction. For Iversen, Barthes's "beautiful story" of his mother is in fact an interpretation of Lacan's *Four Fundamental Concepts of Psychoanalysis* (Iversen, 450).

27. Barthes formulated this view in an earlier essay: "The Photographic Message" in *Image-Music-Text*, 15–31.

28. According to Banfield, free indirect discourse embodies an alogical situation in language. See Banfield's "L'imparfait," 76–77.

29. As Culler observes, the elements of love and death bring Barthes back to the universal meanings which he renounced. See Culler, *Barthes*, 97.

30. The word "counterpoint" comes from the Latin *punctom contra punctum* (note against note).

31. Derrida, "*Barthes*," 288.

32. For a similar description of the "absurdity" in the fragment of the real, which has no place in the interpretive grid, see Robbe-Grillet, 19. On a representation which ignores the real, see Iversen on Lacan, in Iversen, 457.

33. Bresson, 121. The full quotation is: "See beings as things in their separate parts. Render them independent in order to give them a new dependence. Displaying everything condemns cinema to cliché, obliged it to display things as everyone is in the habit of seeing them. Failing which, they would appear false or sham."

34. Barthes, *Camera Lucida*, 106.

35. Žižek, 91. Cf. Hamon, who sees the detail—both the reality effect and the *punctum*—as turning to the reader/viewer's subjectivity by the very hermeneutic effort it stimulates. See Philippe Hamon, "Thème et effet de réel," *Poétique* 64 (1985): 495–503.

36. Umberto Eco, "Critique of the Image," in *Thinking Photography*, ed. Victor Burgin (London: Macmillan Press, 1982), 32–38.

37. Derrida, *Barthes*, 280.

38. Ibid., 282.

39. Ibid., 290.

40. See Tess Gallagher, "Introduction to *A New Path to the Waterfall*," in Carver, *All of Us*, 315.

41. Carver, "On Errand," in *Call If You Need Me*, 197–98.

42. Henry Troyat, *Chekhov*, trans. Michael Henry Heim (New York: E.P. Dutton, 1986), 333.

43. Olga Knipper-Tchehov, "A Few Words about Tchehov," in *The Letters of Anton Pavlovitch Tchehov to Olga Leonardova Knipper*, trans. Constance Garnett (New York: Benjamin Bloom, 1966), 14–15.

44. For a similar approach to this shift of tenses in Olga's speech, see Martin Scofield's reading of "Errand" in "Story and History in Raymond Carver," *Critique* 40:3 (1999): 277–78. See also Verley, who meticulously analyzes the stages and devices that form the move in "Errand" from the "seemingly objective biographical data to the totally fictional narrative."

45. Barthes insists that the photograph does not bring back the past through memory, but rather testifies of his existence as a present in the past. Cf. Deleuze in his discussion of the virtual image of memory, which is preserved in time, as present in the past.

46. Derrida, 291.

47. Barthes, "The Reality Effect," 14.

Conclusion

It has become clear, even more so today than in Carver's lifetime, that the current "visual turn" has entirely changed the stories we tell about ourselves and the way we tell them. Along with introducing new images and concerns to our mental territories, this turn has at the same time deeply influenced the way vision, time, truth, and subjectivity are conceived.

Consequently, "camera aesthetics" not only defines Carver's poetics but is inextricably bound up with the very existence of the men and women who populate his world. Applying visual terms to Carver's writing—thinking of him as a writer who has refined and enriched the eye-of-the-camera technique in fiction—provides a new theoretical frame of reference in which we can now place the experiences and life stories we glimpsed through his prose. This photographic angle both confirms the form and content interconnection and demonstrates how a visual discourse can enhance the reading of fiction by providing a set of metaphors as well as an Archimedean point outside literature itself.

In the eye-of-the-camera aesthetic, as was analyzed here, duration is a set of fragments undermining the sense of continuity of time and meaning; the narrator is an empty, contingent perspective; literary space is disintegrated, with redundant "real" details which paradoxically undermine the sense of the real; and the frame is an arbitrary, petrifying space. These features, taken together, contribute to the rigor mortis effect of the snapshot-story, offering as it does an unmediated encounter with death. Carver's visual poetics thus incarnates the condition of his characters, who experience detachment, lack of meaning, being subdued by contingency and loss, and who struggle to express themselves in a world of cliché and reproduction.

The state of affairs I have just described leaves little room for hope, and indeed reinforces Carver's image as the architect of "Hopelessville." The same story, however, can be told differently in a more dynamic way, which will reflect more accurately, I believe, not only the essence of Carver's work, but the dynamics of this very study. The beginning of this story is in the first option of photography in "Viewfinder," where movement is represented in a sequence of static fragments. The end is the other possibility—of the man who throws a rock, yelling "now!" and wishes his movement to be captured in a single shot. Accordingly, the beginning of this journey (and the first three chapters) are marked by the fractioning of movement; time fragmented to motion shots; dialogue punctuated by silences. We found there an unbridgeable gap between speakers; the self ripped of context; a present already colored by forgetfulness; memory speckled with lacunae; and a "cellular," imprisoned existence of the kind John Tagg[1] attributed to the objects of photography. However, at the end (and in the third part of this study), the "man in a case," the short story's slice of life and the reality effect succeed—like the man who throws a stone outside the photograph's margins—in breaking through boundaries by their very call to the open. The more arbitrary and violent the boundaries, the more resonant the call.

What is it that ties together beginning and end? What is it that enables the passage between the sequence of static fragments and the movement which shatters the photograph's frame? The answer is exactly what makes Carver's work so unique (and was first formulated in chapter 4): It is an art where (like photography at its best) the outward look is ultimately an inward one. The gaps in the sequence become nodes of the interweaving of the outside with the inside, opening new, unexpected channels of communication. The absence of sight in looking, the unseen outside the field of vision, express the character's consciousness, and at the same time make room for the Other—the reader's—consciousness and for "the movement of the description" in the pending "now" of reading. Indeed, as Deleuze makes clear, sometimes it is necessary to loosen connections within an image, to suppress depth, in order to allow for the deeper connection to the open—to time and thought.

This unique expression of subjectivity, and the way Carver allows this encounter between consciousnesses to take place in a seemingly neutral space, is what makes his work so complex, yielding varied, even contradictory, responses and interpretations.

"The people I'm writing about often have difficulty communicating head-on," Carver said in an interview, "but things *do* get done, things *do* get said in the stories. Sometimes, the meanings are a little askew, but things do transpire."[2] Carver seems to use a determined yet reserved tone suited to the nature of the connections, movements, and "passages" that occasionally occur in his stories. These connections—between events, speakers, self and other, reader and text—are subordinated to the constraints of cliché, accompanied by the awareness of one's own singular yet replaceable existence and one's own death. The contact they suggest is forever tentative and consumed by doubt—doubt of the possibility and meaning of such contact, doubt of the possibility of any meaning. Yet, these qualities—opposed as they are to the unambiguousness of cliché—have a crucial role in the creation of this rich image, in which—to adopt Bachelard's view[3]—lies the power of literature. This image, which Carver molds from a flat, dull world, resonates in our—the readers'—mind as it moves inward from the surface, taps into great depths, and stirs our innermost sense of being.

Notes

1. John Tagg, *The Burden of Representation: Essays on Phototraphies and Histories* (Minneapolis, MN: University of Minneapolis Press, 1988), 76.

2. Gentry and Stull, 208, Carver's emphases.

3. Gaston Bachelard, *The Poetics of Space*, trans. Maria Jolas (Boston: Beacon Press, 1964).

References

Works by Raymond Carver

"View Finder." *Iowa Review* 9:1 (1978): 5–50.
Will You Please Be Quiet, Please? New York: Vintage, 1992.
What We Talk about When We Talk about Love. New York: Vintage, 1992.
Cathedral. New York: Vintage, 1984.
Where I'm Calling From: Stories. New York: Vintage, 1989.
Fires: Essays, Poem, Stories. New York: Vintage Books, 1989.
All of Us: The Collected Poems. New York: Vintage, 1996.
Call If You Need Me: The Uncollected Fiction and Other Prose. Edited by William L. Stull. New York: Vintage, 2001.
Collected Stories. Edited by William L. Stull and Maureen P. Carroll. New York: The Library of America, 2009.
"Beginners." *The New Yorker*, 24 December 2007. www.newyorker.com/reporting/2007/12/24/071224fa_fact (accessed January 30, 2008).
"Letters to an Editor." *The New Yorker*, 24 December 2007. www.newyorker.com/reporting/2007/12/24/071224fa_fact (accessed January 30, 2008).

Secondary Works

Adelman, Bob. *Carver Country: The World of Raymond Carver.* New York: Arcade Publishing, 1990.
Alpers, Svetlana. *The Art of Describing: Dutch Art in the Seventeenth Century.* Chicago: Chicago University Press, 1985.
Altman, Robert. Introduction to *Short Cuts: Selected Stories by Raymond Carver*, 7–10. New York: Vintage Books, 1993.
Arias-Misson, Alain. "Absent Talkers." *Partisan Review* 49:4 (1982): 625–28.

Bachelard, Gaston. *The Poetics of Space*. Translated by Maria Jolas. Boston: Beacon Press, 1964.

———. *Water and Dreams: An Essay on the Imagination of Matter*. Translated by Edith R. Farrell. Dallas, TX: Dallas Institute for Humanities and Culture, 1983.

Bakhtin, Mikhail. *Problems of Dostoevsky's Poetics*. Translated by Caryl Emerson. Minneapolis: University of Minnesota Press, 1984.

Bal, Mieke. "Introduction: Visual Poetics." *Style* 22:2 (1988): 177–78.

———. *The Mottled Screen: Reading Proust Visually*. Translated by Anna-Louise Milne. Stanford, CA: Stanford University Press, 1997.

———. *Narratology: Introduction to the Theory of Narrative*. Toronto: University of Toronto Press, 1997.

———. "Poetics, Today." *Poetics Today* 21:3 (2000): 479–502.

Banfield, Ann. "Describing the Unobserved: Events Grouped Around an Empty Centre." In *The Linguistics of Writing: Arguments between Language and Literature*, edited by Fabb Nigel and others, 265–87. Manchester: Manchester University Press, 1987.

———. *Unspeakable Sentences: Narration and Representation in the Language of Fiction*. London: Routledge & Kegan Paul, 1987.

———. "L'imparfait de l'objectif: The Imperfect of the Object Glass," *Camera Obscura* 24:3 (1990): 64–87.

———. "The Name of the Subject: The 'il'?" *Yale French Studies* 93 (1998): 133–74.

———. *The Phantom Table: Woolf, Fry, Russell and the Epistemology of Modernism*. Cambridge: Cambridge University Press, 2000.

Barth, John. "A Few Words About Minimalism." *New York Times Book Review*, 28 December 1986, 1–2, 25.

Barthes, Roland. *Le degré zero de l'écriture*. Paris: Editions du deuil, 1953.

———. *Writing Degree Zero*. Translated by Annette Lavers and Colin Smith. New York: Hill and Wang, 1967.

———. "L'effet de réel," *Communications* 11 (1968): 84–89.

———. *Critical Essays*. Translated by Richard Howard. Evanston, IL: Northwestern University Press, 1972.

———. *S/Z*. Translated by Richard Miller. New York: Hill and Wang, 1974.

———. *A Lover's Discourse: Fragments*. Translated by Richard Howard. New York: Hill and Wang, 1978.

———. *Image, Music, Text*. Translated by Stephen Heath. London: Collins/Fontana, 1979.

———. *Camera Lucida: Reflections on Photography*. Translated by Richard Howard. New York: Hill and Wang, 1981.

———. "The Reality Effect." In *French Literary Theory Today: A Reader*, edited by Tzvetan Todorv, 11–17. Cambridge: Cambridge University Press, 1982.

———. "La chambre claire: Note sur la photographie" (1980) in *Oeuvres complètes*, tome III, 1111–2000. Paris: Seuil, 1995.

Baudelaire, Charles. "The Modern Public and Photography," (1862). In *Classic Essays on Photography*, edited by Alan Trachtenberg, 83–90. New Haven: Leete's Island Books, 1980.

Bedell, Jack B. and Norman German. "Echoes of Slammed Doors: Resonant Closure in Raymond Carver's Fiction." *Short Story* 8:2 (2000): 87–93.

Benjamin, Walter. "The Work of Art in the Age of Mechanical Reproduction." Translated by Harry Zohn. In *Illuminations*, edited by Hanna Arendt, 217–51. New York: Schocken Books, 1968.

———. "A Short History of Photography." In *Classic Essays on Photography*, edited by Alan Trachtenberg, 199–216. New Haven: Leete's Island Books, 1980.

Benveniste, Emile. *Problems in General Linguistics*. Translated by Mary Elizabeth Meek. Miami: University of Miami Press, 1971.

Bergson, Henry. *Le pensée et le mouvant: essays et conferences*. Paris: Librarie Félix Alcan, 1934.

———. *Creative Evolution* (1911). Translated by Arthur Mitchell. New York: The Modern Library, 1944.

Bethea, Arthur F. *Technique and Sensibility in the Fiction and Poetry of Raymond Carver*. New York: Routledge, 2001.

———. "Raymond Carver's Inheritance from Ernest Hemingway's Literary Technique." *Hemingway Review* 26:2 (2007): 89–104.

Biguenet, John. "Notes of a Disaffected Reader: The Origins of Minimalism." *Mississippi Review* 40–41 (1985): 40–45.

Blanchot, Maurice. *The Space of Literature*. Translated by Ann Smock. Lincoln: University of Nebraska, 1982.

———. "Everyday Speech," *Yale French Studies* 73 (1987): 12–20.

———. *The Infinite Conversations*. Translated by Susan Hanson. Minneapolis: University of Minnesota Press, 1993.

Boxer, David and Cassandra Phillips. "'Will You Please Be Quiet, Please?': Voyeurism, Dissociation, and the Art of Raymond Carver." *The Iowa Review* 10:1 (1979): 75–90.

Bramlett, Frank and David Raabe. "Redefining Intimacy: Carver and Conversation." *Narrative* 12:2 (2004): 178–94.

Bresson, Robert. *Notes on the Cinematographer*. Translated by Jonathan Griffin. London: Quartet Books, 1986.

Brooke-Rose, Christine. *The Rhetoric of the Unreal: Studies in Narrative and Structure, Especially of the Fantastic*. Cambridge: Cambridge University Press, 1981.

Brooks, Peter. *Reading for the Plot: Design and Intention in Narrative*. New York, Knopf, 1984.

Bryson, Norman. "The Gaze in the Expanded Field." In *Vision and Visuality*, edited by Hal Foster, 87–108. Seattle: Ray Press, 1988.

Buchanan, Ian and John Marks, eds. *Deleuze and Literature*. Edinburgh: Edinburgh University Press, 2000.

Burgin, Victor. *The End of Art Theory: Criticism and Postmodernity*. London: Macmillan, 1986.

Casey, Edward S. "Literary Description and Phenomenological Method." *Yale French Studies* 61 (1981): 176–201.

Chamberlain, Lori. "Magicking the Real: Paradoxes of Postmodern Writing." In *Postmodern Fiction: A Bio-Bibliographical Guide*, edited by Larry McCaffery, 5–12. New York: Greenwood Press, 1986.

Charney, Leo. "In a Moment: Film and the Philosophy of Modernity." In *Cinema and the Invention of Modern Life*, edited by Leo Charney and Vanessa R. Schwartz, 279–94. Berkeley: University of California Press, 1995.

Chekhov, Anton. "The Man in a Case." In *The Wife and Other Stories*, translated by Constance Garrett, 249–68. New York: The Ecco Press, 1972.

Chénetier, Marc. "Living On/Off the 'Reserve': Performance, Interrogation, and Negativity in the Works of Raymond Carver." In *Critical Angles: European Views of Contemporary American Literature*, edited by Marc Chénetier, 164–90. Carbondale: Southern Illinois University Press, 1986.

———. *Beyond Suspicion: New American Fiction Since 1960*. Translated by Elizabeth A. Houlding. Philadelphia: University of Pennsylvania Press, 1996.

Clarke, Graham. "Investing the Glimpse: Raymond Carver and the Syntax of Silence." In *The New American Writing: Essays on American Literature since 1970*, edited by Graham Clarke, 99–122. London: Vision Press, 1990.

Cohn, Dorrit. "K. Enters The Castle: On the Change of Person in Kafka's Manuscript." *Euphorion* 62:1 (1968): 38–45.

———. *Transparent Minds: Narrative Modes for Presenting Consciousness in Fiction*. Princeton, NJ: Princeton University Press, 1978.

Culler, Jonathan. *Flaubert: The Uses of Uncertainty*. Ithaca, NY: Cornell University Press, 1974.

———. *Structuralist Poetics*. London: Routledge, 1975.

———. *Roland Barthes*. New York: Oxford University Press, 1983.

Day, Richard Cortez. Introduction to *Carnations: A Play in One Act by Raymond Carver*, edited by William L. Stull, i–iv. Vinebury, CA: Engdahl Typography, 1992.

Decker, Christof. "Faces in the Mirror: Raymond Carver and the Intricacies of Looking." *Amerikastudien* 49:1 (2004): 35–49.

Deleuze, Gilles. *Cinema 1: The Movement-Image*. Translated by Hugh Tomlinson and Barbara Habberjam. Minneapolis: University of Minnesota Press, 1986.

———. *Cinema 2: The Time-Image*. Translated by Hugh Tomlinson and Robert Galeta. Minneapolis: University of Minnesota Press, 1989.

———. *Negotiations: 1972–1990*. Translated by Martin Joughin. New York: Columbia University Press, 1990.

———. *Bergsonism*. Translated by Hugh Tomlinson and Barbara Habberjam. New York: Zone Books, 1991.

Deleuze, Gilles and Félix Guattari. *What is Philosophy?* Translated by Hugh Tomlinson and Graham Burchell. New York: Columbia University Press, 1991.

Deleuze, Gilles and Claire Parnet. *Dialogues*. Translated by Hugh Tomlinson and Barbara Habberjam. New York: Columbia University Press, 1987.

Derrida, Jacques. "Les morts de Roland Barthes." *Poétique* 47 (September 1981): 269–92. "The Deaths of Roland Barthes." In *Philosophy and Non Philosophy since Merleau-Ponty*, ed. Hugh S. Silverman, 259–96. New York and London: Routledge, 1988.

Duve, Thiery de. "Time Exposure and Snapshot: The Photograph as Paradox," October 5 (1978): 113–25.

Eco, Umberto. "Critique of the Image." In *Thinking Photography*, edited by Victor Burgin, 32–38. London: Macmillan Press, 1982.

Emerson, Ralph Waldo. *Essays: First Series.* New York: AMM Press, 1968.
Esrock, Ellen. *The Reader's Eye: Visual Imaging as Reader Response.* Baltimore: Johns Hopkins University Press, 1994.
Fabre-Clark, Claire. "The Poetics of the Banal in Elephant and Other Stories." In *New Paths to Raymond Carver: Critical Essays on his Life, Fiction and Poetry,* edited by Sandra Lee Kleppe and Robert Miltner, 173–86. Columbia: University of South Carolina Press, 2008.
Facknitz, Marc A. R. "'The Calm,' 'A Small, Good Thing' and 'Cathedral': Raymond Carver and the Rediscovery of Human Worth." *Studies in Short Fiction* 23:3 (1986): 287–96.
Felman, Shoshana. "Turning the Screw of Interpretation." In *Literature and Psychoanalysis: The Questions of Reading: Otherwise.* Edited by Shoshana Felman, 94–207. Baltimore: Johns Hopkins University Press, 1982.
Flaubert, Gustav. *The Letters of Gustav Flaubert 1857–1880.* Translated by Francis Steegmuller. Cambridge, MA: Belknap Press of Harvard University Press, 1982.
———. "A Simple Heart." In *Three Tales,* translated by Robert Baldick, 17–56. London: Penguin, 1987.
Fludernik, Monica. *Towards a "Natural" Narratology.* New York: Routledge, 1996.
Ford, Richard. Introduction to *The Granta Book of the Short Story,* edited by Richard Ford, vii–xxii. London: Granta, 1993.
———. "Good Raymond," *New Yorker,* 5 October 1998.
Foucault, Michael. "What is an Author?" In *The Foucault Reader,* edited by Paul Rainbow, translated by Josué Harari, 10–21. New York: Pantheon, 1984.
Genette, Gérard. *Narrative Discourse.* Translated by Jane E. Lewin. Ithaca, NY: Cornell University Press, 1980.
———. "Frontiers of Narrative," "Flaubert's Silence." In *Figures of Literary Discourse,* translated by Alan Sheridan, 122–44, 183–201. New York: Columbia University Press, 1982.
———. *Narrative Discourse Revisited.* Translated by Jane E. Lewin. Ithaca: Cornell University Press, 1988.
Gentry, Marshall Bruce and William Stull, eds. *Conversation with Raymond Carver.* Jackson and London: University Press of Mississippi, 1990.
Grana, Cesar. *Modernity and Its Discontents: French Society and the French Man of Letters in the Nineteenth Century.* New York: Harper and Row, 1967.
Hagstrum, Jean H. *The Sister Arts: The Tradition of Literary Pictorialism and English Poetry from Dryden to Gray.* Chicago: University of Chicago Press, 1987.
Haig, Stirling. *Flaubert and the Gift of Speech: Dialogue and Discourse in Four "Modern" Novels.* Cambridge: Cambridge University Press, 1986.
Halpert, Sam. *Raymond Carver: An Oral Biography.* Iowa City: University of Iowa Press, 1995.
Hamon, Philippe. "Rhetorical Status of the Descriptive." *Yale French Studies* 61 (1981): 1–26.
———. "Thème et effet de reel." *Poetique* 64 (1985): 495–503.
Head, Dominic. *The Modernist Short Story: A Study in Theory and Practice.* Cambridge: Cambridge University Press, 1992.

Hemingway, Ernest. "Hills Like White Elephants." In *The Short Stories*, 371–76. New York: The Modern Library, 1938.

Henning, Barbara. "Minimalism and the American Dream: 'Shiloh' by Bobbie Ann Mason and 'Preservation' by Raymond Carver." *Modern Fiction Studies* 35:3 (1989): 689–97.

Herzinger, Kim A. "Introduction: On the New Fiction." *Mississippi Review* 40–41 (1985): 7–22.

Irigaray, Luce. *The Sex Which Is Not One*. Translated by Catherine Porter and Carolyn Burk. Ithaca, NY: Cornell University Press, 1985.

Iversen, Margaret. "What is a Photograph." *Art History* 17:3 (1994): 450–64.

Jakobson, Roman. "Linguistics and Poetics." In *Language in Literature*, edited by Krystyna Pomorska and Stephen Rudy, 62–94. Cambridge, MA: Belknap Press, 1987.

James, Henry. "The Art of Fiction." In *The Art of Fiction and Other Essays*, 3–23. New York: Oxford University Press, 1948.

Jameson, Fredric. *The Prison House of Language*. Princeton, NJ: Princeton University Press, 1972.

Janouch, Gustav. *Conversations with Kafka*. Translated by Goronwy Rees. London: Derek Verschoyle, 1953.

Jay, Martin. "Scopic Regimes of Modernity." In *Vision and Visuality*, edited by Hal Foster, 3–28. Seattle: Ray Press, 1988.

———. *Downcast Eyes: The Denigration of Vision in Twentieth-Century French Thought*. Berkeley: University of California Press, 1994.

———. "Vision in Context: Reflections and Refractions." In *Vision in Context: Historical and Contemporary Perspectives on Sight*, edited by Teresa Brennan and Martin Jay, 3–12. New York: Routledge, 1994.

———. "Photo-unrealism: The Contribution of the Camera to the Crisis of Ocularcentrism." In *Vision and Textuality*, edited by Stephen Melville and Bill Readings, 344–60. Durham, NC: Duke University Press, 1995.

Jefferson, Ann. *Nathalie Sarraute, Fiction and Theory: Questions of Difference*. Cambridge: Cambridge University Press, 2000.

Karlsson, Ann-Marie. "The Hyperrealistic Short Story: A Postmodern Twilight Zone." In *Criticism in the Twilight Zone: Postmodern Perspectives on Literature and Politics*, edited by Danuta Zadworna-Fjellestad and Lennart Björk, 144–53. Stockholm: Almqvist and Wiksell International, 1990.

Kemp, Peter. "The American Chekhov," *Sunday Times*, 7 August 1988, G.1–2.

Kermode, Frank. *The Genesis of Secrecy: On the Interpretation of Narrative*. Cambridge: Harvard University Press, 1979.

———. "'No Tricks.' Review of Call If You Need Me: The Uncollected Fiction and Prose by Raymond Carver." *London Review of Books*, 19 October 2000. www.lrb.co.uk/v22/n20/kerm01_.html (accessed January 30, 2008).

Kleppe, Sandra Lee. "Women and Violence in the Stories of Raymond Carver." *Journal of the Short Story in English* 46 (2006). http://jsse.revues.org/index497.html (accessed January 30, 2010).

Knipper-Tchehov, Olga. "A Few Words about Tchehov." In *The Letters of Anton Pavlovitch Tchehov to Olga Leonardova Knipper*, edited by Constance Garnett, 3–15. New York: Benjamin Bloom, 1966.

Krauss, Rosalind E. "The Blink of an Eye." In *The States of Theory: History Art and Critical Discourse*, edited by David Carroll, 175–99. New York: Columbia University Press, 1990.

———. *The Optical Unconscious*. Cambridge, MA: MIT Press, 1993.

Lacan, Jacques. *Four Fundamental Concepts of Psycho-Analysis*. Translated by Alan Sheridan. London: Hogarth Press, 1997.

Lainsbury, G. P. *The Carver Chronotope: Inside the Life-world of Raymond Carver's Fiction*. New York: Routledge, 2004.

LeClair, Thomas. "Fiction Chronicle–June 1981." *Contemporary Literature* 23:1 (1982): 83–91.

Lehman, Daniel W. "Raymond Carver's Management of Symbol." *Journal of the Short Story in English* 17 (1991): 43–57.

———. "Symbolic Significance in the Stories of Raymond Carver." *Journal of the Short Story in English* 46 (2006): 75–88.

Lessing, G. E. *Laocoön: An Essay on the Limits of Painting and Poetry*. Translated by Edward Allen McCormick. New York: The Bobbs-Merrill Company, 1962.

Lindey, Christine. *Superrealist Painting and Sculpture*. New York: William Morrow and Co., 1980.

Lotman, Jurij. *The Structure of the Artistic Text*. Translated by Gail Lenhoff and Ronald Vromm. Ann Arbor: University of Michigan Press, 1977.

Lukács, George. *Writer and Critic: and Other Essays*. Edited and translated by Arthur D. Kahn. New York: Grosset and Dunlap, 1970.

Madison, Bill. "Less Is Less: The Dwindling of American Short Story." *Harper's* (April 1986): 64–69.

Magrino, William L. "American Voyeurism." In *New Paths to Raymond Carver: Critical Essays on his Life, Fiction and Poetry*, edited by Sandra Lee Kleppe and Robert Miltner, 75–91. Columbia: University of South Carolina Press, 2008.

Malamet, Elliott. "Raymond Carver and the Fear of Narration." *Journal of the Short Story in English* 17 (1991): 59–72.

Margulies, Ivone. *Nothing Happens: Chantal Akerman's Hyperrealist Everyday*. Durham, NC: Duke University Press, 1996.

Mathis, Gilles, ed. *Le Cliché*. Toulouse: Presses Universitaires du Mirail, 1998.

Max, D. T. "The Carver Chronicles." *New York Times*, 9 August 1998. www.nytimes.com/1998/08/09/magazine/the-carver-chronicles.html?pagewanted=1 (accessed January 29, 2010).

May, Charles E. *The Short Story: A Reality of Artifice*. New York: Prentice-Hall, 1995.

McCaffery, Larry, ed. *Postmodern Fiction: A Bio-Bibliographical Guide*, xi–xxviii. New York: Greenwood Press, 1986.

McGrath, Charles. "Whose Words: I, Editor Author." *New York Times*, 28 October 2007. www.nytimes.com/2007/10/28/weekinreview/28mcgrath.html?_r=2&emc=eta1&oref=slogin&oref=slogin (accessed January 30, 2008).

McInerney, Jay. "Raymond Carver: A Still, Small Voice." *New York Times Book Review*, 6 August 1989. http://query.nytimes.com/gst/fullpage.html?res=950DE6DD1530F935A3575BC0A96F948260&sec=&spon=&pagewanted=2 (accessed January 30, 2008).

McSweeney, Kerry. *The Realist Short Story of the Powerful Glimpse: Chekhov to Carver*. Columbia: University of South Carolina Press, 2007.

Merleau-Ponty, Maurice. *Sense and Non-Sense*. Translated by Hubert L. Dreyfus and Patricia Allen Dreyfus. Evanston, IL: Northwestern University Press, 1964.

Meyer, Adam. *Raymond Carver*. New York: Twayne Publishers, 1995.

Mirsky, Nilli. Epilogue to *A Boring Tale* by Anton Chekhov, 95–100. Tel Aviv: Am Oved, 1996 (in Hebrew).

Mitchell, W. J. T. "Spatial Form in Literature: Towards a General Theory." *Critical Inquiry* 6:3 (1980): 539–67.

———. *Iconology: Image, Text, Ideology*. Chicago: University of Chicago Press, 1986.

———. "The Pictorial Turn." In *Picture Theory: Essays in Verbal and Visual Representation*, edited by W. J. T. Mitchell, 11–35. Chicago: University of Chicago Press, 1995.

Mullen, Bill. "A Subtle Spectacle: Televisual Culture in the Short Stories of Raymond Carver." *Critique* 39:2 (1998): 99–114.

Nesset, Kirk. *The Stories of Raymond Carver: A Critical Study*. Athens: Ohio University Press, 1995.

O'Connor, Frank. *The Lonely Voice: Study of the Short Story*. London: Macmillan, 1965.

Patton, Paul, ed. *Deleuze: A Critical Reader*. Cambridge, MA: Blackwell, 1996.

Pickering, Jean. "Time and the Short Story." In *Re-Reading the Short Story*, edited by Clare Hanson, 45–54. London: Macmillan Press, 1989.

Poe, Edgar Allan. "Nathaniel Hawthorne's Twice-Told Tales," in *The Complete Works of Edgar Allan Poe*, edited by James Harrison, vol. XI, 104–13. New York: George D. Sproul, 1902.

———. "The Philosophy of Composition," in *Selected Writings of Edgar Allan Poe*, edited by Edward H. Davidson, 452–63. Boston: Houghton Mifflin, 1956.

Proust, Marcel. *A la recherche du temps perdu*, vols. I, VIII. Paris: Gallimard, 1954.

———. *Swan's Way*. Translated by C.K. Scott Moncrieff. London: Penguin Books, 1957.

Rabb, Jane M., ed. *Short Story and Photography 1880s–1980s: A Critical Anthology*. Albuquerque: University of New Mexico Press, 1998.

Reed, Graham F. *Obsessional Experience and Compulsive Behavior: A Cognitive-Structural Approach*. Orlando, FL: Academic Press, 1985.

Renner, Rolf Günter. *Edward Hopper 1882–1967: Transformation of the Real*. Köln: Benedikt Taschen, 1993.

Rich, Motoko. "The Real Carver: Expansive or Minimal?" *New York Times*, 17 October 2007. www.nytimes.com/2007/10/17/books/17carver.html (accessed January 30, 2008).

Rimmon-Kenan, Shlomith. *Narrative Fiction*. London: Routledge, 2002.

Robbe-Grillet, Alain. *For a New Novel: Essays in Fiction*. Translated by Richard Boward. New York: Grove Press, 1965.

Rohmer, Eric. *The Test for Beauty*. Translated by Carol Volk. Cambridge: Cambridge University Press, 1989.

Ron, Moshe. Epilogue to *Last Stories* by Raymond Carver, 181–95. Tel Aviv: Hakibbuthz Hameuchad, 1998 (in Hebrew).

———. Epilogue to *Uncanny Portraits*, ed. Moshe Ron, 267–333. Tel Aviv: Hakibbutz Hamehuchad, 2001 (in Hebrew).

Runyon, Randolph Paul. *Reading Raymond Carver*. Syracuse: Syracuse University Press, 1992.

Russel, Catherine. *Experimental Ethnography: The Work of Film in the Age of Video*. Durham, NC: Duke University Press, 1999.

Saltzman, Arthur M. *Understanding Raymond Carver*. Columbia: University of South Carolina Press, 1988.

Sarraute, Nathalie. *Tropisims and the Age of Suspicion*. Translated by Maria Jolas. London: John Calder, 1963.

Sawyer, David. "'Yet Why Not Say What Happened?' Boundaries of the Self in Raymond Carver's Fiction and Robert Altman's Short Cuts." In *Blurred Boundaries: Critical Essays on American Literature, Language and Culture*, edited by Klaus H. Schmidt and David Sawyer, 195–219. Frankfurt: Peter Lang, 1996.

Scarry, Elaine. *Dreaming by the Book*. New York: Farrar, Straus & Giroux, 1999.

Scofield, Martin. "Negative Pastoral: The Art of Raymond Carver's Stories." *Cambridge Quarterly* 22:3 (1994): 243–62.

———. "Story and History in Raymond Carver." *Critique* 40:3 (1999): 266–80.

Scott, A. O. "Looking for Raymond Carver." *New York Review of Books*, 12 August 1999, 52–59.

Shaw, Valérie. *The Short Story*. London: Longman, 1985.

Shklovsky, Victor. "Art as Device" (1925). In *Theory of Prose*, translated by Benjamin Sher, 1–14. Elmwood Park: Dalkey Archive Press, 1991.

Sontag, Susan. *On Photography*. New York: Farrar, Straus & Giroux, 1973.

Spiegel, Alan. *Fiction and the Camera Eye: Visual Consciousness in Film and the Modern Novel*. Charlottesville: University Press of Virginia, 1978.

Steiner, Wendy. *The Colors of Rhetoric*. Chicago: University of Chicago Press, 1982.

Stern, Joseph Peter. *On Realism*. London: Routledge & Kegan Paul, 1973.

Stoppard, Tom. "Reflections on Ernest Hemingway." In *Ernest Hemingway: The Writer in Context*, 19–27. Madison: University of Wisconsin Press, 1984.

Stull, William L. "Beyond Hopelessville: Another Side of Raymond Carver." *Philological Quarterly* 64:1 (1985): 1–15.

———. "Raymond Carver Remembered: Three Early Stories." *Studies in Short Fiction* 25:4 (1988): 461–77.

Stull, William L. and Maureen Carroll. *Remembering Ray: A Composite Biography of Raymond Carver*. Santa Barbara: Capra Press, 1993.

Tagg, John. *The Burden of Representation: Essays on Phototraphies and Histories*. Minneapolis, MN: University of Minneapolis Press, 1988.

Tanner, Tony. *City of Words: American Fiction: 1950–1970.* New York: Harper and Row, 1971.

Terrell, Carroll F. *A Companion to the Cantos of Ezra Pound.* Berkeley: University of California Press, 1980.

Time-Life Library of Photography. *The Art of Photography*, edited by the editors of Time-Life. New York: Time-Life Books, 1971.

Verley, Claudine. "'Errand,' or Raymond Carver's Realism in a Champagne Cork." *Journal of the Short Story in English* 46 (2006). http://jsse.revues.org/index502.html (accessed January 27, 2010).

Uspensky, Boris. *A Poetics of Composition: The Structure of the Artistic Text and Typology of Compositional Forms.* Translated by Valentina Zavarin and Susan Wittig. Berkeley: University of California Press, 1973.

Ward, J. A. *American Silences: The Realism of James Agee, Walker Evans, and Edward Hopper.* Baton Rouge: Louisiana State University Press, 1985.

Wolff, Tobias. Introduction to *The Vintage Book of Contemporary American Short Stories*, xi–xvi. New York: Vintage Books, 1994.

Wood, Sarah. "Optic Nerve." *Oxford Literary Review* 26 (2004): 139–53.

Wyschogrod, Edith. "Doing before Hearing: On the Primacy of Touch." In *Textes pour Emmanuel Levinas.* Edited by François Laruelle, 179–202. Paris: Editions Jean-Michel Place, 1980.

Žižek, Slavoj. *Looking Awry: An Introduction to Jacques Lacan through Popular Culture.* Cambridge: MIT Press, 1995.

Zoran, Gabriel. *Text, World, Space.* Tel Aviv: Tel Aviv University–Hakibbutz Hamehuchad, 1997 (in Hebrew).

Index

Ackerman, Chantal, 38, 14
"After the Denim." *See* Carver, Raymond, stories
alcohol/alcoholism, 10, 26, 33, 90, 107, 109, 112, 123, 134, 147, 148, 153
Altman, Robert, 67n25, 118
American dream, xii, xvi, 134
"Are These Actual Miles?" *See* Carver, Raymond, stories
"Are You a Doctor?" *See* Carver, Raymond, stories
Arias-Misson, Alain, 70, 153
Aristotle, 24, 135
Auerbach, Erich, xix

Bachelard, Gaston, 79, 177
Bakhtin, Mikhail, 57, 113
Bal, Mieke, xxiii, 5, 10–11
Banfield, Ann, xxii, xxiv, 55–57, 60
Barthelme, Donald, xv
Barthes, Roland, xxii, xxv, 8, 53, 56–57, 60, 65, 73, 78, 90, 140, 147, 152, 155–64, 168, 169, 170; *Camera Lucida*, 56, 157–60, 161, 162; *punctum*, 155, 157–64; "The Reality Effect," 78, 140, 155–57; "Rhetoric of the Image," 19n15; *studium*, 158, 160, 161; "The Third Meaning," 157
Bazin, André, 129

Beginners. *See* Carver, Raymond, collections
behaviorism, in literature, xiv, xvi, 21–24, 37, 62, 71; in psychology, 64–65
Benjamin, Walter, 19n16, 88, 164
Bergson, Henry, 16, 42n25, 128–30, 135, 139, 143n38
Bethea, Arthur F., 41n9, 153
"Bicycles, Muscles, Cigarettes." *See* Carver, Raymond, stories
Biguenet, John, 134, 137
"Blackbird Pie." *See* Carver, Raymond, stories
Blanchot, Maurice, xvii, 57, 60, 63, 116, 163
blue-collar people, xii, 5, 34, 111, 134, 155
Boxer, David, 26, 51, 53, 59. *See also* Phillips, Cassandra
"Boxes." *See* Carver, Raymond, stories
Bresson, Robert, 116, 162
"The Bridle." *See* Carver, Raymond, stories
Brooke-Rose, Christine, 36
Bryson, Norman, 1

"Call If You Need Me." *See* Carver, Raymond, stories
"The Calm." *See* Carver, Raymond, stories

Camus, Albert, 48, 53
capitalist way of life, 111, 134, 155
"Careful." *See* Carver, Raymond, stories
Carver, Maryann, xx, 47, 63–64, 66n7
Carver, Raymond: personal life of, xiii–xxi, 18n11, 45, 47, 55, 63–64, 66n7, 122, 145–51, 169–70; reception of, xii, xiv, 134–35; theory, approach to, xi–xii, xxii
Carver, Raymond, collections: *Beginners*, xx, 6, 122; *Cathedral*, 12, 90, 106, 123; *Fires*, 145; *A New Path to the Waterfall*, 148; *What We Talk about When We Talk about Love*, xv, xx, 6, 32, 53, 123; *Will You Please Be Quiet, Please?* 51, 61, 69
Carver, Raymond, essays: "Fires," 148; "My Father's Life," 146–51, 169–70; "On Writing," 84, 92
Carver, Raymond, poems: "Company," 107; "Distress Sale," 67n18; "Fear," 112; "Luck," 107, 112; "Photograph of My Father in his Twenty-Second Year," 146, 169–70; "The Other Life," 107
Carver, Raymond, stories: "After the Denim," 28, 75; "Are These Actual Miles?" xii, 10, 119, 155; "Are You a Doctor?" 26, 118; "Bicycles, Muscles, Cigarettes," 147; "Blackbird Pie," xiv, 132, 168; "Boxes," 52, 118; "The Bridle," 119; "Call If You Need Me," 132; "The Calm," 120–22; "Careful," 8, 9, 83, 50, 75, 87, 106–10, 116, 117–18, 122–26; "Cathedral," 9, 12, 72, 90–98, 145; "Collectors," 27, 31, 50, 61, 122; "The Compartment," 83, 148; "Elephant," 52, 148; "Errand," xxvi, 8, 110, 165–69; "Fat," 18n5, 26, 63, 83, 114, 154; "The Father," 149–52, 170; "Feathers," 12–15, 132; "Fever," 15; "Furious Seasons," xv, 74, 80; "Gazebo," 35, 40; "The Hair," 16; "How About This?" 85; "I Could See the Smallest Things," 135; "The Idea," 59, 71; "Intimacy," xx, 15, 35, 42n28, 47–50, 52, 53, 63–65, 118; "Jerry and Molly and Sam," 83; "Little Things," 8, 105–6; "Menudo," 15, 35, 50, 118; "Mr. Coffee and Mr. Fixit," 108, 124, 132–34, 137, 152–53; "Neighbors," 9, 58–59, 72, 76, 155; "Night School," 28, 76, 118; "Nobody Said Anything," 18n5, 118; "One More Thing," 118; "Popular Mechanics," 8, 105–6; "Preservation," 8, 28, 33, 40, 124–27, 131, 133, 134, 138; "Put Yourself in My Shoes," 37, 51, 61–63, 65, 76, 77; "Sacks," 148; "Signals," 11, 25, 28, 87; "Sixty Acres," 15–16, 87, 118; "A Serious Talk," 18n5, 26, 88, 154; "A Small, Good Thing," 34, 58, 72, 145, 154; "So Much Water So Close to Home," 65, 69–77, 79, 80, 82, 83, 85, 88–89, 132; "The Student's Wife," 75; "The Third Thing that Killed My Father Off," 148; "They're Not Your Husband," 59, 71, 117; "The Train," 9, 118; "Viewfinder," xviii, 3–8, 11, 12, 17, 29–32, 50, 52, 54, 57, 61, 76, 88, 119, 122, 154, 176; "Vitamins," 40, 118; "Will You Please Be Quiet, Please?" 10, 15, 26, 83, 84, 119; "What Is It?" xii; "What We Talk About When We Talk About Love," 26, 40, 122–23, 132; "What's in Alaska?" xviii, 26–29, 32, 33, 36, 51, 84, 87, 122, 132; "Where I'm Calling From," 10, 11, 123–24; "Where Is Everyone?" 84, 124, 132, 133, 148; "Whoever Was Using This Bed," 16, 50, 58–59; "Why Don't You Dance?" 15, 53–55, 57–59, 60, 63, 64, 116, 154, 155
Cathedral. *See* Carver, Raymond, collections
"Cathedral." *See* Carver, Raymond, stories

INDEX

change, representation of, 12–17, 70, 121, 126, 151
Charney, Leo, 17
Chekhov, Anton, xi, xxii, 8, 16, 110, 165–66, 168; "A Man in a Case," 110–14
Chénetier, Marc, xiii, 16, 43n48, 55, 153, 155
Clarke, Graham, 131
cliché, xvii, xxiv; in speech, 34–36, 39–40, 41; in representation, 95, 128–29, 135–37, 151, 152, 175–77. *See also* Deleuze, Gilles
closure. *See* endings
Cohn, Dorrit, 52
"Collectors." *See* Carver, Raymond, stories
communication, xii, xviii–xix, xiv, xxviin19, 28, 32–34, 37, 39–41, 59, 107, 134, 156, 176. *See also* miscommunication
"Company." *See* Carver, Raymond, poems
"The Compartment." *See* Carver, Raymond, stories
Compton-Burnett, Ivi, 21, 22
consciousness, representation of, xii, xiv–xv, xxiv, 25, 52, 55–65, 72, 78–79, 82, 98, 151, 152, 176
covert narrator. *See* scene; neutral narrator

Davidson, Bruce, 88
death, 57–60, 63, 65, 71, 124–26, 175–76; of Chekhov, 8, 165–66, 169; of the father, 146–47, 150–51, 153, 170; and frame, 105, 110–13; in Lacna, 87, 162; and photography, xvii, 16, 57, 60, 159–61. *See also* rigor mortis
Decker, Christof, xxviin19, 98n2, 171n13
deconstruction, 160. *See also* Derrida, Jacques
defamiliarization, xxiv, 10, 38, 54, 81, 87, 116, 136–38. *See also* Shklovsky, Victor

deixis/deictic, 31, 55–57, 65, 116, 152, 159
Deleuze, Gilles, xix, xxii, xxiv, 52, 57, 88, 127–37, 176; cliché in, 39, 128–29, 135, 137; frame in, 115–17, 119; optic situation in, 127–37, 139, 140, 161, 162
Derrida, Jacques, 43n47, 84, 143n51, 147; on Barthes, 160–61, 163–64, 169, 170
description, xxii, xxiii, xxiv, 71, 72, 76–82, 92–94, 96, 97–98, 130, 134–35, 137, 156–57, 161, 162; movement of the, 80–82, 97–98, 176. *See also* Robbe-Grillet, Alain
diegesis, xiv, 92. *See also* telling
direct discourse, 25, 38–39, 48–49
"Distress Sale." *See* Carver, Raymond, poems
Dos Passos, John, 134
doubling, 152–54
Duve, Thiery de, 16–17

Eco, Umberto, 163
"Elephant." *See* Carver, Raymond, stories
Emerson, Ralph Waldo, 93
endings (of stories), xvii, xxviin22, 105, 119–21
"Errand." *See* Carver, Raymond, stories
Esrock, Ellen, xxiii
Evans, Walker, 99n17
everyday, the, xvii, 8, 83, 86, 116, 120–21, 127, 131, 135, 136, 138, 139, 154, 168; language, 21, 34, 81, 83, 95, 136, 137
experimentalism, in literature, xii, xv, xxvin15, 6, 80; in cinema and theatre, 38
eye-of-the-camera technique, xiv, xv, xvi, xxii, 9, 53, 56, 61, 65, 175

Fabre-Clark, Claire, 34, 153
"Fat." *See* Carver, Raymond, stories
"The Father." *See* Carver, Raymond, stories

father-son relationship, xiv, 145–51, 169–70
Faulkner, William, xv, 74, 86, 131
"Fear." See Carver, Raymond, poems
"Feathers." See Carver, Raymond, stories
Felman, Shoshana, 63
"Fever." See Carver, Raymond, stories
Fires. See Carver, Raymond, collections
"Fires." See Carver, Raymond, essay
flatness xvii, 77, 95, 137, 152, 163, 177
Flaubert, Gustav, xxii, 77, 80, 82, 96; "A Simple Heart," 77–79
focalization, xxiii. See also point of view
Ford, Richard, xii–xiii, 59, 63–64, 120
formalism, Russian, xxv, 116, 136. See also Shklovsky, Victor
fragment, 27, 75, 82, 91, 124, 130–31, 135, 137, 151, 161–62
fragmentation, xix, 7, 28–29, 34, 77–84, 117, 138, 162
frame, xxiv, 49, 63, 105–6, 108–9, 112–22, 125, 132–33, 138, 176
Frank, Robert, 87
free indirect discourse, 48–49, 55–56
Freud, Sigmund, 83, 133, 162
Friedlander, Lee, 88
"Furious Seasons." See Carver, Raymond, stories

Gallagher, Tess, xxviiin32, 18n11
"Gazebo." See Carver, Raymond, stories
Genette, Gérard, 39, 52, 79
Godard, Jean-Luc, 38

Halpert, Sam, 47
"The Hair." See Carver, Raymond, stories
Hemingway, Ernest, xiv, xv, xvi, xxii, 5, 9, 22, 28, 37, 38, 53, 69, 110, 121, 148; "Cat in the Rain," 25; "Hills Like White Elephants," 22–25
Herzinger, Kim, xii
Herzog, Werner, 139
Homer, 93
"How About This?" See Carver, Raymond, stories

hyperrealism, xiv, xv, 17, 36, 54; in painting, xvi, 17, 36, 54, 116, 117. See also photorealism

"I Could See the Smallest Things." See Carver, Raymond, stories
"The Idea." See Carver, Raymond, stories
indirect discourse, 48
Ingarden, Roman, xix
intentional fallacy, xx
"Intimacy." See Carver, Raymond, stories
Irigaray, Luce, 96
Iser, Wolfgang, xix

Jakobson, Roman, 28
James, Henry, 86
Jay, Martin, xv–xvi
"Jerry and Molly and Sam." See Carver, Raymond, stories
Joyce, James, 18n8, 131, 134

Kafka, Franz, 96, 97, 131
Kittredge, William, xxvn5, 145, 152
Knipper-Chekhov, Olga, 166–67. See also Chekhov, Anton
Kristeva, Julia, 157

Lacan, Jacques, xxii, xiv, 57, 83–84, 87, 161–63
Lainsbury, G. P., xxvn5, 142n30
Lehman, Daniel, 153
Lessing, Gotthold Ephraim, xxiii, 77, 93, 96
liminality, 56, 60, 108
Lish, Gordon, xx, xxi, xviiin32, 6–7, 30, 132
litotes, 54
"Little Things." See Carver, Raymond, stories
Lotman, Jurij, 113–14, 115, 116
"Luck." See Carver, Raymond, poems
Lukács, George, 77, 96, 134–37

Marey, Étienne-Jules, 88
Mars-Jones, Adam, 59

Marxist criticism, 134. *See also* Lukács, George
McCaffery, Larry, 25, 54
McInerney, Jay, xi
"Menudo." *See* Carver, Raymond, stories
Merleau-Ponty, Maurice, 64–65, 101n59
metaphor, xv, 72, 78, 80, 93–94, 130, 134, 135, 137, 153–54
metonymy, 154, 160–61, 169
mimesis, xiv, 5, 17, 23, 26, 92, 94, 97. *See also* showing
minimalism, xii, xiv, 6, 137, 154
Mirsky, Nilli, 111
miscommunication, xviii, xxiv, 17, 32, 40, 39. *See also* communication
Mitchell, W. J. T., xxii, xxviiin36
modernism, xv, xxiv, 86, 134–36
"Mr. Coffee and Mr. Fixit." *See* Carver, Raymond, stories
Muybridge, Edward, 4, 7, 8, 16, 88
"My Father's Life." *See* Carver, Raymond, essay

narratlolgy, xiii, xxii, xxviii, 52, 72
naturalist writing, 134
"Neighbors." *See* Carver, Raymond, stories
A New Path to the Waterfall. See Carver, Raymond, collections
neo-realism, Italian, 129–30, 131, 137
Nesset, Kirk, 153–54
neutral narrator, 50–53, 54
New Criticism, 47
"Night School." *See* Carver, Raymond, stories
"Nobody Said Anything." *See* Carver, Raymond, stories
nouveau roman, 11, 38. *See also* Robbe-Grillet, Alain

O'Connor, Flannery, xi, 12
O'Connor, Frank, 111
"One More Thing." *See* Carver, Raymond, stories

"On Writing." *See* Carver, Raymond, essay
openings (of stories), 55, 105, 119, 133
optic situation. *See* Deleuze, Gilles
other/otherness, xviii, xxi, xxii, 88–89, 98, 120, 134, 159–64, 169, 176; self as, 51–53, 57, 59, 61, 63–64
"The Other Life." *See* Carver, Raymond, poems

paralipsis, 52. *See also* Genette, Gérard
past tense, 73, 74
pathetic fallacy, 170
Perry, Menahem, xix
Peirce, Charles, 128
Phillips, Cassandra 26, 51, 53, 59. *See also* Boxer, David
"Photograph of My Father in His Twenty-Second Year." *See* Carver, Raymond, poems
photography, reception of xvii, 95, 117
photorealism, xvi, 16. *See also* hyperrealism
Poe, Edgar Allan, 16, 106, 109, 111, 115, 138
point of view, xiv, xxiii, 50, 54, 59, 60, 71, 77, 105, 108, 121, 169. *See also* focalization
"Popular Mechanics." *See* Carver, Raymond, stories
postmodernism, xiv, 153
Pound, Ezra, xvin12, 78
present tense, 72–74, 76, 80, 81, 134, 135, 167
"Preservation." *See* Carver, Raymond, stories
Proust, Marcel, xxiii, 11, 79, 91, 98, 131
Punctum. See Barthes, Roland
"Put Yourself in My Shoes." *See* Carver, Raymond, stories

reader response, xviii, xix, xxii, 7–8, 32, 37, 40, 77, 96–98, 168–69
real, the, 16–17, 36, 38, 54, 58, 170, 176; in Lacan, 84, 87, 100n32, 162–63

realism, xii, xiii–xv, 38, 41, 156–57, 159, 163–64
reality effect, 78, 82, 118, 140, 155–62, 166, 168, 176. *See also* Barthes, Roland
rigor mortis, xiv, 54, 112, 117, 138, 175. *See also* stasis
Rivette, Jacque, 38
Robbe-Grillet, Alain, xxii–xxiii, 53, 73, 80–82, 93–94, 95, 96–97, 131
Rohmer, Éric, 24–25, 38
Ron, Moshe, 59, 67n15, 154
Runyon, Randolph Paul, xiii, 83, 108, 118, 123, 133, 152

"Sacks." *See* Carver, Raymond, stories
Sarraute, Nattalie, 21, 22–23, 25, 29, 33, 37, 39, 41, 48, 52
Sartre, Jean-Paul, 70, 142n26
Scarry, Elaine, xxii, 86, 98
scene, xiv, xv, xxiv, 5–8, 10, 12, 25, 29, 48. *See also* showing
scopic regime, xxii, 101n59
Scofield, Martin, xxviin23, 55, 173n44
Segal, George, xvii, 143n41
"A Serious Talk." *See* Carver, Raymond, stories
Shklovsky, Victor, 81, 85, 116, 136–37, 140; *See also* defamiliarization
short story, xi, xvi, 84, 85–86, 110, 111, 113, 115–16; as a picture, xvi, 113, 138; menace in, 84
showing, xiv, xviii, 5, 6, 17, 23, 52, 63. *See also* mimesis
sight, xviii, 72–77, 82, 89–92, 96–97, 132, 139, 149; absence of, xviii, 70, 82, 85, 89, 91, 96–98, 176; in Deleuze, 129–31; in Lacan, 83; in Robbe-Grillet, 97
"Signals." *See* Carver, Raymond, stories
"Sixty Acres." *See* Carver, Raymond, stories
"A Small, Good Thing." *See* Carver, Raymond, stories

soap opera, 35, 133
"So Much Water So Close to Home." *See* Carver, Raymond, stories
space, representation of. *See* description
spatiality, in literature, xvi. *See also* description
stasis xvi, xvii, xviii, xxiii, 54, 117, 119, 121, 133–34, 137, 139, 151; in characterization, 113; in dialogue, 29, 32; in photography, xvii, 16, 117; in short story, xvii, 175; of body, 54, 112, 117, 138. *See also* rigor mortis
Sternberg, Meir, xix
structuralism, 47
"The Student's Wife." *See* Carver, Raymond, stories
studium. *See* Barthes, Roland
Stull, William, xxvn5, 16, 28n25, 36

Tagg, John, 176
Tanner, Tony, 112
television, 13, 35, 92, 94, 96, 107–8, 125, 132, 133, 155
telling, xiv. *See also* diegesis
"The Third Thing that Killed My Father Off." *See* Carver, Raymond, stories
"They're Not Your Husband." *See* Carver, Raymond, stories
Tolstoy, Leo, 62
"The Train." *See* Carver, Raymond, stories

unemployment, 125, 132–33, 140
unoccupied perspective. *See* Banfield, Ann
Uspensy, Boris, 113–14

Verley, Claudine, xiv, 173n44
Vietnam War, xvi
"Viewfinder." *See* Carver, Raymond, stories
visualization, 9, 71, 81, 82, 86, 92, 94, 98, 113, 155
"Vitamins." *See* Carver, Raymond, stories
voyeurism, 51, 92, 135

"What Is It?" *See* Carver, Raymond, stories
What We Talk about When We Talk about Love. *See* Carver, Raymond, collections
"What We Talk about When We Talk about Love." *See* Carver, Raymond, stories
"What's In Alaska?" *See* Carver, Raymond, stories
"Where I'm Calling From." *See* Carver, Raymond, stories
"Where Is Everyone?" *See* Carver, Raymond, stories
"Whoever Was Using This Bed." *See* Carver, Raymond, stories

"Why Don't You Dance?" *See* Carver, Raymond, stories
Williams, Carlos William, xv, 110, 149
Will You Please Be Quiet, Please?. *See* Carver, Raymond, collections
Wolff, Geoffrey, 55
Wolff, Tobias, 67n17, 85
women, representation of, xxii, 68, 70, 89, 98n4, 105
Woolf, Virgina, 56, 131, 143
World War I, xvi, 167–69
World War II, 52, 128–29

Zola, Emile, 134
Žižek, Slavoj, 77, 84, 86, 163

About the Author

Ayala Amir earned her Ph.D. at the Hebrew University of Jerusalem and taught at the Department of Comparative Literature there for many years. She is currently a lecturer in the Department of Comparative Literature at Bar Ilan University and teaching coordinator at the Open University, both in Israel. Dr. Amir has published articles on narrative study, modern and postmodern fiction, and the interconnections between literature and the visual arts.

Printed by Amazon Italia Logistica S.r.l.
Torrazza Piemonte (TO), Italy